Gendering Human Security in Afghanistan

This book employs the concept of human security to show what the term means from the perspective of women in Afghanistan.

It engages with a well-established debate in academic and policy-making contexts regarding the utility of human security as a framework for understanding and redressing conflict. The book argues that this concept allows the possibility of articulating the substantive experiences of violence and marginalisation experienced by people in local settings as well as their own struggles towards a secure and happy life. In this regard, it goes a long way to making sense of the complex dynamics of conflict which have confounded Western policy-makers in their ongoing state-building mission in Afghanistan. However, despite this inherent potential, the idea of human security still needs refinement. Crucially, it has benefitted from critical feminist and critical social theories which provide the conceptual and methodological depth necessary to apprehend what a progressive ethical programme of security looks like and how it can be furthered. Using this framework, the work provides a critical reconstruction of the effect of the US-led Western Intervention on women's experiences of (in)security in the three provincial contexts of Nangarhar, Bamyan and Kabul. This reconstruction is drawn from a wealth of historical and contemporary sociological research alongside original fieldwork undertaken in Delhi, India, during 2011 with women and men from the country's different communities.

This book will be of much interest to students of human security, state-building, gender politics, war and conflict studies and IR in general.

Ben Walter is Honorary Research Fellow in the School of Political Science and International Studies at the University of Queensland, Australia.

Series: Routledge Studies in Human Security
Series Editors: Mary Martin
London School of Economics
and
Taylor Owen
University of Oxford

The aim of this series is to provide a coherent body of academic and practitioner insight which is capable of stimulating further consideration of the concept of human security, its impact on security scholarship and on the development of new security practices.

The European Union and Human Security
External Interventions and Missions
Edited by Mary Martin and Mary Kaldor

National, European and Human Security
From Co-Existence to Convergence
Edited by Mary Martin, Mary Kaldor and Narcís Serra

State Responses to Human Security
At Home and Abroad
Edited by Courtney Hillebrecht, Tyler White and Patrice McMahon

Human Security, Changing States and Global Responses
Institutions and Practices
Edited by Sangmin Bae and Makoto Maruyama

Gendering Human Security in Afghanistan
In a Time of Western Intervention
Ben Walter

Gendering Human Security in Afghanistan

In a Time of Western Intervention

Ben Walter

LONDON AND NEW YORK

First published 2017
by Routledge
2 Park Square, Milton Park, Abingdon, Oxon OX14 4RN

and by Routledge
711 Third Avenue, New York, NY 10017

Routledge is an imprint of the Taylor & Francis Group, an informa business

© 2017 Ben Walter

The right of Ben Walter to be identified as author of this work has been asserted by him in accordance with sections 77 and 78 of the Copyright, Designs and Patents Act 1988.

All rights reserved. No part of this book may be reprinted or reproduced or utilised in any form or by any electronic, mechanical, or other means, now known or hereafter invented, including photocopying and recording, or in any information storage or retrieval system, without permission in writing from the publishers.

Trademark notice: Product or corporate names may be trademarks or registered trademarks, and are used only for identification and explanation without intent to infringe.

British Library Cataloguing in Publication Data
A catalogue record for this book is available from the British Library

Library of Congress Cataloging in Publication Data
A catalog record for this book has been requested

ISBN: 978-1-138-64064-1 (hbk)
ISBN: 978-1-315-63649-8 (ebk)

Typeset in Times New Roman
by Wearset Ltd, Boldon, Tyne and Wear

For my parents whose love and support made this book possible

Contents

Acknowledgements   viii

1 Introduction   1

2 Gendering human security   19

3 Community, tradition and gender in Afghanistan   48

4 Modernisation and fragmentation in Afghanistan   71

5 Nangarhar Province   91

6 Bamyan Province   111

7 Kabul Province   133

8 Conclusion   160

Glossary   170
Index   173

Acknowledgements

The completion of this book would not have been possible without the help of many supportive colleagues, friends and family members. Thus, in no particular order, I would like to extend heartfelt thanks to the following people. To my supervisors, Martin Weber and Andrew Phillips, whose engagement with, and support of, my project has been nothing less than extraordinary, I would like to say thank you for all the advice and encouragement you have given me from the time I started my thesis through to the publication of this book. I could not, in my wildest dreams, have wished for a better team to have helped me undertake this project.

I must also thank my good friends Shannon Brinncatt, Tim Aistrope and Lina Abirafeh for going above and beyond the call of duty to help me with their comments on draft chapters. Though these three busy scholars had a variety of their own projects to work on in 2016, each of them gave up their time to read multiple copies of my chapters and provide me with extensive feedback. In my theoretical discussion of Critical and Feminist Theory in Chapter 2, Shannon and Tim provided me with many helpful suggestions on clarifying and framing my argument. Lina Abirafeh, an accomplished feminist scholar and committed feminist activist, provided me with a series of constructive suggestions based on her years of experience in researching gender dynamics in Afghanistan.

I also need to acknowledge the help I received from the wonderful people I met in Delhi during my fieldwork research trip there in June of 2011. In particular, I must thank Said Reza Huseini, Ankita Jnu and Mansoor Ehsan, my friends at *Jawaharlal Nehru University* who enthusiastically helped me organise and conduct my focus group discussions with different groups of Afghans living in Delhi. On this matter, I must also thank the refugee women and men from Afghanistan who, during the focus group discussions, willingly took time out of their own lives to provide me with their informative understandings of Afghanistan's history of social change and gender dynamics. Furthermore, I am particularly indebted to John Mohammed Butt for his help in understanding the social history of Afghanistan through the competing discourses of Islam and Pashtunwali during our many detailed conversations.

The transformation of this book from a PhD thesis would not have been possible without the very adept translations of the focus group discussions (FGDs).

For this I must extend a very special thanks to the following people: Said Reza Husscin who translated the Hazara mixed sex and men's FGD; Mansoor Eshan who translated the Tajik mixed sex and men's FGD; Lima Hadi who translated the Pashtun women's FGD; Abdul Ahad Mohammadi who translated the Tajik women's FGD; and Masuma Hussaini who translated the Hazara women's FGD.

I also need to extend heartfelt thanks to my parents Kay and John Walter whose love and support for me over the years have given me the ability to keep pursuing my dreams. To my mother, Kay, and Aunt Jill I also owe a huge debt of gratitude for proofreading this manuscript countless numbers of times for clarity and copy errors. It is thanks to their earnest readings of the manuscript chapters that the book reads as well as it currently does.

I must also thank my wife's wonderful parents Bill and Donna Nackers for sharing their home with us and giving us a wonderful opportunity to pursue our dreams in academia. While we initially moved into their home to help her parents through a hard time in 2015, we ended up being helped far more by their kindness and generosity.

Finally, I must thank my wife, Kimberly Nackers, whose love and friendship have made it possible for me to deal with the many pressures involved in completing this project. I look forward to sharing the rest of my life with her.

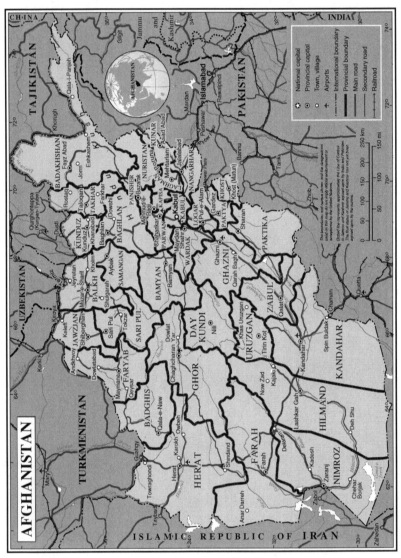

Map of Afghanistan's provinces

Source: United Nations profile map of Afghanistan (Map No. 3658 Rev. 7, June 2011).

1 Introduction

At its heart, this book attempts to tell a story about furthering security in Afghanistan in the time of Western Intervention that was occasioned by the overthrow of the Taliban in October, 2001. The story of security that I tell here refers to much more than just the abatement of armed violence wrought by warring factions. It is more thoroughly concerned with the pursuit of a holistic vision of security premised upon the well-being and happiness of people in their own communities.

Given the priority of human beings in this story, it was a straightforward decision for me to engage with the framework of human security. This concept prioritises the lives of concrete human subjects in counter-distinction to long-standing practices of national security aimed at securing the abstract bodies of states. In so doing, it makes security democratic by highlighting subjects' own perspective of security and, potentially, revolutionary in its challenge to dominant and institutionalised practices associated with national and international security.

Nevertheless, to make human security a viable vehicle for engagement in Afghanistan, it must present an account of security which is meaningful to human subjects themselves. For this reason, I build my account of what human security is through an exploration of the lives of women and their experiences of oppression and marginalisation in Afghanistan. Women's experiences of gender-based violence, whether physical, economic or emotional, provide a substantive account of security that speaks to the conflicts and hierarchies of power which jeopardise the well-being of society in Afghanistan more broadly. In so doing, the story of women speaks also to the lives of men and the insecurities and challenges they face within existing hierarchical gender structures.

Engaging in this reconstructive account of what human security means in Afghanistan from the perspective of women and men is not a simple task. To begin with, the expression of what security means in any given context ultimately involves an ethical claim which enjoins societal action to urgently redress harm. Thus, the possibility of arriving at a legitimate expression of security involves philosophical and sociological reflection about how ethics should be practised in global politics. At the same time, the heterogeneity of the social landscape of Afghanistan defies attempts to define or characterise it. People's social identities in Afghanistan exist at the intersection of gender, ethnicity, language, religion and socio-economic considerations. What makes this research even more difficult and ethically fraught is that women's lives in Afghanistan are all too often objectified and caricatured for the agenda of an external agent.

Women in Afghanistan beneath a Western gaze

Consider the image of a woman clad in a blue *burqa* (Arabic word for full body covering garment) in Afghanistan. Following the rise of the Taliban in 1996, and especially after their fall in 2001, this image became embedded in Western imaginations. As Charles Hirschkind and Saba Mahmood (2002: 339–341) observed, in the weeks and months after the September 11 attacks this image saturated Western media coverage of Afghanistan. It was routinely championed by a variety of prominent public figures, including male political leaders and first ladies (Weber, 2005: 371), feminists (Russo, 2006: 557–558) and talk-show hosts (Fluri, 2009: 245) as exemplary of everything at stake in the West's impending intervention into Afghanistan.

The very facelessness and voicelessness of this feminine figure invoked ideas of oppression, victimisation and backwardness: through no fault of her own, this woman was subjugated, brutalised and held back by violent and ignorant men as personified by the Taliban and other patriarchal authority figures (Moghadam, 2002: 245). Yet, at the same time, the existence of this woman's all-veiling *burqa* also presented the possibility that she could be unveiled. Thus, she existed in Western imaginations as a subject in transition from the personification of a barbaric and backward time to that of a modern liberated citizen of a democratic Western-liberated Afghanistan.

As many critical feminist scholars observed, this well-worn discursive framing of Afghan women helped Western governments legitimise the military intervention for their domestic audiences (Shepherd, 2006: 19–21). At the same time, these feminist scholars repeatedly raised concerns about the way in which this objectification of women in Afghanistan served to silence the voices of women and obfuscate their perspectives on the Western Intervention (Daulatzai, 2008: 420–421). Crucially, the framing of Afghanistan entailed in this image had even wider ramifications beyond merely being a rhetorical argument that legitimised war. This crude depiction of a burqa-clad victim was emblematic of the broader objectifying gaze Western politicians, policy-makers and academics used to perceive and, even more worryingly, problem-solve gender politics in Afghan society. Gender politics here refers to the discourses and practices within society which organise gender relations, gender identities and gender roles. In this regard, gender politics is concerned with the way in which power, position, choice, opportunities, access and rights are afforded to women and men in society.

Unfortunately, the narrowness of these conceptual lenses meant that the complexity of gender relations and gender politics in Afghanistan remained largely invisible to Western eyes even as their dynamics played out in full view. At the same time, the normative content attached to this vision of gender progress for women was highly problematic. According to this moral framework, women were cast as "victims" in need of "empowering" while men were characterised as patriarchal, if not misogynistic, figures who, as a sexual class, were holding back women's liberation. Much of the normative content which informed this analysis of Afghanistan was overtly Orientalist in its depiction of the Afghan subject as an alien "other". Here, Orientalism refers to the process in which Europeans characterised the lives of different societies as alien and "other" and incorporated this caricatured account of "Orientals" into their own worldview (Said, 1979: 72–73).

At the same time, the Western Intervention relied implicitly on the universalising and Eurocentric assumptions of Enlightenment-based philosophies like liberalism and modernisation theory. Based on these philosophical traditions, many politicians, academics and policy-makers maintained that sexual inequality between women and men in Afghanistan could be socially and technologically problem-solved through building a democratic government that enshrined women's rights and protections and gender-specific aid programmes that promoted women's empowerment.

The clumsiness of this attempt to socially transform gender relations in Afghanistan was not lost on the people of Afghanistan themselves. As Lina Abirafeh (2009: 55–57) observed from her own interviews with women and men in post-Taliban Kabul, there was a widespread anger at the way in which gender programming treated men and male viewpoints as patronising and an obstacle to women's empowerment. Moreover, such efforts to transform gender relations were not new in the Afghan context which had experienced similarly intrusive gender programming during the rule of the People's Democratic Party of Afghanistan and the Soviet Occupation during the 1980s. As in the past, the present intervention fed into a highly gendered social and political landscape which was already shaped by competing hyper-masculinist discourses of custom and religion. This coming together of foreign and local gendered discourses has served to make women's and men's lives a daily exercise in navigating a gendered battleground within which infringements are violently policed.

The research puzzle

The goal of this book is to revitalise the concept of human security by making it meaningful to women who, as a sexual class, represent some of the most subjugated and insecure subjects in Afghanistan. The way I go about this task is with recourse to the conceptual and methodological insights of feminist, critical and post-colonial theory. Conceptually, these theories help re-vision a lens of human security (hereafter HS) such that the experiences of marginalised women can be apprehended. Methodologically, these theories allow insight into the way in which progressive moral agendas, such as those associated with redressing inequitable gender relations, can be furthered.

Like feminist theory, HS emphasises the need to focus on the lives of concrete human subjects as opposed to artificial bodies, such as the territorial state, which assume precedence in national and international framings of security. However, as many feminists point out, despite its seeming overlap with feminist theory, the mainstream iteration of HS still suffers from problematic assumptions which stem from Enlightenment-based philosophy. Most importantly, the individual human subject who informs its analysis and prescription is for all intents and purposes a masculine agent. Thus, rather than providing an account of security which is sensitive to gender dynamics, the HS concept inevitably universalises the social, economic and political needs of an idealised masculine actor.

Despite these issues, a growing number of feminist practitioners have contributed to a constructive discussion on how HS can be re-visioned and re-purposed within feminist theory. This book seeks to both borrow from, and contribute to, this theoretical discussion with the intention of showing how a feminist HS framework could respond to pressing normative questions, such as those associated with redressing hierarchical gender relations in Afghanistan.

The insights I make use of within this feminist framework are drawn from a variety of critical literatures of global politics as I will articulate in Chapter 2. Obviously, feminist scholarship on the concept of HS plays a major role in the very instigation of this argument. At the same time, this framework benefits from the insights of post-colonial theory which shares the robust normative commitment of feminist theory and provides strong insights into understanding the political and cross-cultural differences entailed in post-colonial settings. Furthermore, the feminist politics advocated in this framework benefits greatly from recourse to the insights of critical feminist and social theory regarding the possibilities of apprehending and engaging with a moral debate.

The central message which emerges from these complementary, critical theoretical endeavours is that any attempt to articulate ethics must incorporate a very strong understanding of society itself. For, if it cannot articulate an ethic that is immanent to the societal relations of the world, it will remain a utopian project. Thus, the key to promoting a positive conception of security is through exploring the societal setting which forms the context in which people's lives are variously made secure or threatened. Within this setting, efforts to improve security involve challenging and transforming the hierarchical relationships of power which threaten people's lives and constrain their ability to go about their lives freely.

When I write this argument about Afghanistan, I write at a time of Western Intervention. The US military has now been engaged in America's longest running war in the history of its Republic, having spent 15 years fighting the Taliban and anti-government factions there. The US has held the greatest material influence on Afghanistan's post-Taliban history through its military and economic support. Nevertheless, it is important to note that a broader coalition made up of NATO and other supportive states, international organisations and humanitarian agencies have participated in what could be broadly dubbed a "Western Intervention".

It is this external intervention which provides the context within which I attempt to articulate what HS in society looks like from women's perspective.

I am keen to explore the disjuncture between a rhetorical promise to improve women's lives with the way in which this intervention has impacted women, and their communities, at a local level. In this exploration, I am not attempting to provide an explicitly policy-oriented account for problem-solving human insecurity. However, I am interested in showing the possibilities for ethical progress that are revealed by people's own struggles and challenges for change. Such instances reveal areas in which external agents could gainfully converge to discuss mechanisms for change; however, the actual form and content of such a dialogue-driven policy-making would need to unfold organically and reflectively.

My positionality as a researcher

Prior to elaborating on the specific methodological framework employed by this monograph to re-conceptualise HS, it is important to discuss how this research project came into being and what is my relationship to it as a researcher. This is all the more important given that I am a non-Afghan, white, male researcher, trying to understand women's lives and gender relations in Afghanistan. As suggested previously, Afghan women's subjectivities have perennially been misappropriated by external agents for their own ideological agendas historically and contemporaneously. The dangers of trying to "save" Afghan women or presume to speak for them has always been a pressing issue of concern to me as such exercises of power can occasion epistemic as well as concrete violence to these subjects.

It is a well-worn metaphor to liken the research process to a journey. Nevertheless, this framing neatly captures the many different paths I explored and the many moments of consciousness-raising and self-realisation I experienced on the way to finding a promising road of enquiry. In late 2008, after having completed my master's programme in International Relations (hereafter IR), focussing on mainstay courses like international security, foreign policy, arms control and IR theory, I entered a doctoral programme with a "hard-nosed" interest in understanding armed violence and security in Afghanistan. However, during my first-year review of the literature on conflict studies and empirical examinations of conflict in Afghanistan, I became increasingly dissatisfied with the story being told by this field in which conflict boiled down to the armed violence between government forces and insurgents or anti-government elements. In the context of Afghanistan, people's identities were summarily classified according to little-understood ethnic categories, such as Pashtun, Tajik and Hazara, and their political subjectivities were framed simplistically as either being for or against the US-supported government of Kabul. What particularly struck me reading this literature was the extent to which it was written by Western scholars and researchers for Western policy-makers to better "problem-solve" the ongoing foreign military interventions in which their governments were enmeshed.

My "light bulb" moment for resolving this dilemma came midway through 2009 when I took a moment to reflect more seriously on the people who most needed security in Afghanistan. I realised that the human beings in most need of security and well-being were Afghan women. This initial realisation was attended almost immediately by the observation that, for all the rhetorical concern expressed by Western leaders about women's lives in Afghanistan since 2001, there had been very little effort made to find out whether Afghan women felt their lives had improved after the intervention. Thus, in a rather happenstance fashion, I came to a realisation which had already been elaborated upon and unpacked at great length by critically-minded feminist scholars. As I found out through exploring this literature, these feminist scholars had shown how masculinised discourses helped facilitate a war in the name of "saving" Afghan women with the effect that Afghan women's lives and voices became instrumental objects. I felt that my own project could productively contribute to these established feminist critiques by initially exploring how women's lives had been affected by the intervention and, subsequently, by providing a deeper analysis of gender relations and gendered hierarchies of power contributing to women's, but also men's, human (in)security.

Despite this potentially interesting subject matter, I still felt ill-prepared to meet the conceptual and methodological challenges in undertaking a feminist-oriented research project on post-colonial subjects. How could I meaningfully comment on women's and men's lives in Afghanistan and claim to know their voices and aspirations from my secluded office desk at the University of Queensland in Brisbane? How could I be sure that my research would not facilitate further epistemic violence to Afghan women by appropriating their subjectivities to legitimise more destabilising interventions in the name of "saving" women in Afghanistan? Unsurprisingly, the answers to these questions did not avail themselves to me instantaneously. Instead, I began to read feminist literature relating to IR more carefully. Ann Tickner (1997: 611–613; 2005: 3–4) furnished me with an immensely important critique of the way gender inflected the meta-theoretical assumptions of IR. As Tickner (1988: 432) suggested, IR's ontology was filled with androgynous (but inherently masculine) individuals and state actors whose existence was posited as reflecting an objective and universal condition. Meanwhile, when engaging with the question of Afghan women's subjectivity, I found the scholarship of Chandra Mohanty (Mohanty, 2002: 409–503) extremely useful in understanding the post-colonial dimension of feminist theory. This work laid bare the heterogeneity of feminisms contained within the effacing label of the "Third World" as well as the danger in straight-forwardly assuming the existence of solidarities between Western and non-Western feminisms.

While familiarising myself with feminist literature in 2010, I was fortunate to obtain a copy of *Bartered Brides*. This informative anthropological text by Nancy Lindisfarne (then Tapper) explored the lives and gender systems of the Maduzai Durrani Pashtun tribes from Sar-e-pul in northern Afghanistan (Tapper, 1991). Not only did this work provide me with an intimate understanding of the traditional operation of gender through masculinised honour codes within Pashtun societies but it also gave insight into the complexities of social and political life within the kinship-based system of Pashtun tribes. After reading this work, I further discovered the extensive and critically reflexive anthropological literature on various peoples and regions within Afghanistan. Special mention should also be made here of Nancy Hatch Dupree whose extensive fieldwork and reporting on gender dynamics in Afghanistan prior to, and during, major war and upheaval provided me with major insights into women's and men's changing lives and relationships. This was particularly apparent in her eloquent and powerful coverage of the "family crisis" in Afghanistan as a consequence of decades of displacement and disruption.

Even though the empirical side of my research project into women's contemporary (in)security in Afghanistan was finally taking shape, I still lacked a comprehensive methodological explanation to account for my research process. At the end of 2010, during a mid-candidature review, I was very helpfully pressed on this matter by a feminist PhD peer at my alma mater to more fully explain how I could meaningfully access the voices of Afghan women and do so in a non-exploitative fashion.[1] My response to this query at the time was that I would be as humble and self-reflexive as possible in carrying out my research. This was not a flippant response designed to avoid a more serious discussion but reflected my own growing awareness that meaningful and ethical research required that the researcher engage in a constant process of self-reflection and circumspection about their own positionality.

This reflexive disposition towards my own research process was vitally helpful to me when I was unexpectedly given the opportunity to undertake fieldwork with Afghan participants in Delhi, India. Although I had reconciled myself that I was unlikely to be able to undertake fieldwork research for my doctoral thesis, a chance event in early 2011 changed my calculations entirely. While listening to AM radio on my routine car drive into the University of Queensland one day, I was lucky enough to hear a BBC world report by Nadene Ghouri (2011) on the remarkable life and accomplishments of John Mohammad Butt. Up until this point, I had been in a dilemma as to how I might arrange fieldwork research in Afghanistan considering the likely insurmountable ethical and logistical hurdles I would encounter in order to conduct research on a vulnerable group in a dangerous setting.

However, as I listened to the story of a British hippy who travelled to Afghanistan in 1969 and became accepted by the region's border tribes as a native Pashtun and later was revered as an Islamic scholar, it dawned on me that John Butt could offer me a wealth of insightful understanding from his own life experience as well as facilitating access to the many expatriate Afghans living in New Delhi, India, where he now resided. Upon hearing of my research project, John graciously agreed to my interview requests with him specifically and, after my arrival, helped to place me in touch with Said Reza Hussein, an enthusiastic and keenly intelligent university student, studying at Jawarhl Nehru University (JNU). Through Reza, I met several other kind and thoughtful students at JNU, including Dr Ankita Haldar and Mansoor Ehsan, who became my friends and collaborators in assisting my field research and understanding of Afghanistan. These participants' accounts were interpreted and triangulated with reference to a variety of historical anthropological scholarships[2] as well as a large range of contemporary sociological research[3] and feminist ethnographic literature on Afghanistan.[4] Though not without its challenges and difficulties, this research fieldwork proved immensely beneficial in my being able to learn first hand from different expatriate subjects about their understandings of the way gender relations had changed between women and men over time during Afghanistan's tumultuous history.

Gendering human security in Afghanistan

Prior to the formal articulation of human security (HS) in a 1994 United Nations Development Report, feminist theorists and activists were already engaging with some of its core themes through their efforts to "people" the discipline of IR (Pettman, 1996: 10–15). Here, feminist practitioners highlighted the inadequacy of realist and liberal models of IR whose statist ontologies remained abstract from the social and political relationships which made up human life (Peterson, 1992: 134; Enloe, 2014: 8–10). Given their shared focus on concrete humans, as well as their critique of the hierarchal forms of rule bound up in national security agendas, feminist practitioners were seemingly predisposed to embrace the HS concept. However, in the two decades following the enunciation of HS, this concept has attracted support and criticism from feminist scholars in equal measure. Natasha Marhia (2013: 20) best captured feminists' mixed response to the discourse on HS when she wrote that the existing literature was "decidedly ambivalent in its slippage between celebration and critique". As Marhia (2013: 20) noted, feminist proponents of HS argued that the concept could be repurposed to align with feminist approaches to politics and could advance feminist ethical agendas such as the transformation of gendered hierarchies of power. At the same time, she observed (Marhia, 2013: 20) that several other critically-minded feminist scholars had highlighted the problematic and gendered knowledge which underpins mainstream iterations of this concept.

Whether critical or sympathetic, feminist scholars' engagement with the concept and practice of HS begins with a deconstructive process referred to as "gendering" (Tickner, 2001: 2–3). Gender here exists as a socially constructed system of meaning which is typically premised upon a binary and hierarchical relationship between masculine and feminine characteristics (Pettman, 1996: 135–136). Masculine characteristics here, such as rationality, autonomy and objectivity, are valorised in distinction to feminine qualities such as emotionality, dependence and subjectivity. Feminist scholars note that gendered systems of meaning within dominant traditions of knowledge, like enlightenment philosophy, are implicated in creating a "common sense" (but entirely fictitious and arbitrary) world which is undergirded by unequal relations of power (Runyan and Peterson, 2013: 58–66). In addition to constructing women's and men's gender identities, this problematic binary system of meaning also orders the social, economic and political relations between them in ways that privilege the masculine over the feminine.

By applying this deconstructive approach, feminist scholars can highlight the biases and omissions of existing frameworks of knowledge while pointing to the transformative possibilities through which these frameworks and gender relations could become equitable and non-exploitative. In the case of HS, these scholars have shown that the androgynous individual who populates dominant conceptualisations of HS is, for all intents and purposes, a masculine subject. Moreover, they have emphasised that HS all too often facilitates the support of highly gendered campaigns like human development and traditional security.

In this book, I do not propose to fundamentally resolve this well-established and critically important feminist debate on HS one way or the other. I will not pretend to speculate on whether a gender-sensitive framework of HS could ever successfully transform harmful practices associated with maintaining exclusionary, gendered discourses like national security. My aims in this project are more modest in scope. What I will do is make a few key methodological suggestions pertaining to the task of re-visioning HS as a framework for mounting feminist, ethical critique. This task involves showing how it is possible for feminists to conduct meaningful research into changing gender relations and gender politics in complex contexts like Afghanistan. Also, and no less importantly, it requires elaboration of a framework which could sustain feminist ethical commitments to articulate the moral possibilities for gendered hierarchies of power to be challenged and, potentially, transformed. This methodological approach will then be utilised to provide a reconstruction of women's and men's changing lives and (in)security in Afghanistan.

My own suggestion for advancing a feminist framework is to highlight the necessity of understanding human beings' shared lives, coping strategies and struggles for change. The rationale for this approach is made with respect to the phenomenological methodology outlined in many arguments by Kimberly Hutchings on feminist ethics (Hutchings, 1992; Hutchings, 1999a; Hutchings, 1999b; Hutchings, 2000; Hutchings, 2013). Phenomenology, which literally translates as the science of experience, represents an approach to knowledge formation wherein a researcher acknowledges the inter-subjectively and socially constructed nature of reality. A researcher's consciousness is the product of their social relations and historical period even as their thoughts and actions contribute to the reconstruction of a wider social consciousness. As Hutchings (1999b: 108) astutely notes, this means that researchers must realise that ethical judgements are inseparable from the moral forms of life within which they are embedded. Moral judgements can only be intelligible to protagonists within a moral debate when the language and logic is familiar to them. If it is partially or completely unfamiliar then such judgements become challenging to understand. This disjuncture has been painfully on display in Afghanistan where Western efforts at "gender programming" face a variety of hurdles – not the least of which is that there is no word which conveys the meaning of "gender" in Persian/Dari or Pashtu (Abirafeh, 2009: 50–52). As Lina Abirafeh notes, through its English usage it became a Dari/Pashto word by default but without any meaning or context attached to this important term.

This insight had two important implications for my attempt to provide a gendered account of HS in Afghanistan. The first of these was to acknowledge that it was impossible, and undesirable, to find a neutral epistemological position from which a universal account of a feminine moral standpoint could be rendered. For instance, although gender empowerment programmes in Afghanistan are premised upon universal truths, these programmes inevitably represent the views of those harkening from a secular and Eurocentric background. Moreover, at its core, gender programming often treats Afghan women as unrealised "Western women" who must rise above their cultural backgrounds to become empowered. In this process, there is very little dialogue with actual Afghan women as to how they perceive themselves and what pathways they envisage for change.

Second, any normative claim of "what should be done" to redress exploitative gender relations in Afghanistan or in the West involves an exercise in power regardless of its truth value. For instance, it may very well be the case that many conservative masculine figures in Afghan society, such as mullahs and tribal elders, harbour anachronistic beliefs about women's roles in society but, labelling them as such and excluding such figures from discussions about gender programming, still represents a crude exercise in power with potentially calamitous consequences.

Acknowledging these points does not mean that ethical interventions to understand and redress HS fall victim to cultural relativism. Instead, it means that efforts to persuade others rest not on transcendent appeals to rationality but rather on putting into place the conditions wherein one's arguments will be understood as rational by participants and enable the relevant power structures to be assessed. The importance of understanding the conditions of ethical judgement within different moral contexts informs the empirical focus in this book on studying women's, and men's, struggles against gendered hierarchies of power in Afghanistan. Not only do these struggles reflect already existing possibilities for moral change within different contexts but they are carried out in ways which are imminently intelligible to participants.

To engage in this task, it is useful to identify the structures of power which are being struggled against. When I use the phrase "gendered hierarchy of power" I do so to refer to the structures and relationships which privilege masculine subjects over feminine subjects socially, economically and politically. In Afghanistan, as in the West, gendered hierarchies of power have been an omnipresent factor of social life throughout modern history. However, what is important to note is that, although often hierarchical, gender relations among women and men in Afghanistan differ greatly across communities. Although Western anthropologists broadly observed the presence of masculine honour codes in a variety of different communities, gender relations were not always straightforwardly ones of hierarchy. This difference is exhibited most notably in the traditional gender relations of nomadic Pashtun communities in contrast with their settled counterparts. The former communities exhibited far greater acknowledgement and valorisation of women's lives (as evidenced in celebrations accompanying the birth of daughters) than their settled kinfolk.

Introduction 11

The current post-traditional gendered hierarchies of power are particularly pernicious in the way in which women suffer from an array of gendered insecurities while at the same time they receive none of the societal obligations owed to them. These tensions and contradictions within the moral orders of Afghan communities do not go unnoticed. They play out in the harm they bring to women, and also to men, as well as their deleterious effect on the health of families and communities.

Importantly, these inadequacies of traditional, gendered justifications have lead to an untenable status-quo in the present but it has not gone unchallenged by women or men. Some of these challenges are reformist in nature. Their focus is to breathe new life into traditional, masculine honour systems by reforming or eliminating harmful practices such as that of *baad*, blood compensation marriage, among eastern Pashtun communities in Nangarhar Province. This practice involved a family giving one of their daughters in marriage to compensate for a murder committed by one of their members against the other household. Alongside this reformism, more fundamental challenges are levelled at the ethical justifications underpinning the dominant gendered honour system.

For instance, the tenets and message of Islam are often used by women, and men, to contest the legitimacy of the gendered constructions on which customary honour systems rest. Moreover, women in a variety of settings in Afghanistan are using traditional community-based dispute resolution forums, such as *shuras*, *jirgas* and *jalasas*, as an avenue to realise their rights and freedoms. In these acts women also gain a level of societal recognition of their agency and value as equal members of a community. As I will go on to show in three different provincial contexts in Afghanistan, these immanent struggles reveal possibilities for collaboration with external agents seeking to advance the cause of HS in a way which is meaningful for the human subjects themselves.

Chapter overview

This book aims to contribute to an ongoing feminist discussion on the potential for gendering HS. Its efforts in this regard are focused on showing the potential that a phenomenological methodology has for facilitating ethical engagement into complex, social settings which are characterised by hierarchical gender dynamics. The ensuing chapters are intended to advance this argument by showing how such a framework could provide a reconstruction of HS in Afghanistan which is meaningful to the most oppressed and vulnerable humans living there.

Chapter 2 lays the foundation for this argument by first situating HS within a long-running debate over the meaning and purpose of security as a discourse and a practice. This move helps show that, despite its potential value as a revolutionary paradigm, efforts to operationalise HS in a meaningful way are hampered by both conceptual and methodological issues. My suggestion for resolving these issues lies in turning to feminist and other critical theories of global politics. Here, a variety of critical scholars, including feminist and post-colonial theorists, offer complementary critiques which help to portray the perspective of the postcolonial female subject. Moreover, several feminist scholars have explicitly engaged with the question of re-visioning HS to focus on an ethic of care. Though the critical scholarship I review goes a long way to help conceptually revise HS, I think its methodology is an area that needs greater examination. By methodology here I am interested in understanding how it is possible to make accurate claims about what HS's ethics should be and how it should be advanced politically.

Chapter 3 will attempt to provide a strong reconstruction of gender relations and gender politics in what could be considered a "traditional" setting in Afghanistan prior to 1978. This chapter will delve into the fluid and multiple ways in which people construct their own social identity and that of "others" around them. This is done to give a qualified sense of what social life looked like in local settings for people variously according to socially-constructed, ethnic identities like "Afghan", "Tajik" and "Hazara". This examination reveals the politics and power associated with naming oneself and naming an "other" between, but also within, different communities. Following this deconstructive process, the chapter will provide a reconstruction of gender dynamics between women and men among "Pashuns", "Tajiks" and "Hazaras". Meanwhile, Chapter 4 will aim to show how social life and gender relations were changed by the decades-long conflict instigated following the 1978 Saur Revolution. This momentous event, in which the People's Democratic Party of Afghanistan seized power in a bloody coup, occasioned the Soviet invasion of Afghanistan and a catastrophic war that caused the death, injury and displacement of millions of Afghans. This chapter will close with an account of the effect that the contemporary US-led and internationally-supported state-building intervention in Afghanistan has had on gender dynamics.

In both Chapter 3 and Chapter 4, I will draw extensively on my primary fieldwork to provide insight into how women and men understood gender relations traditionally and how they believed them to change during Afghanistan's violent upheaval. At the same time, emphasis will be placed on the creative ways in which women and men have navigated and/or challenged the gendered hierarchies of power which constrain their lives. This empirical content is necessary for meeting the requirements of the phenomenological mode of research articulated previously. The presence of this synchronic and diachronic reconstruction of gender relations allows insight into the immanent possibilities for moral progress within the lives of different social groups in contemporary settings in Afghanistan. Importantly, these chapters' holistic reconstructions, which draw heavily on my own primary fieldwork, are particularly pertinent for assessing the plausibility of the secondary literatures which were predominantly utilised in building up the specific accounts of gender relations in the three case-study chapters which follow.

Chapter 5 examines the province of Nangarhar in Eastern Afghanistan. This province is important to consider because it has been cited by many Western researchers and policy-makers as a case in point of how state-building and development can proceed with beneficial results in Afghanistan. This process has involved the imposition of a broad counter-narcotics programme to stop opium-growing, alongside the wholesale implementation of neo-liberal agricultural programmes which are designed to bring modernisation and economic growth to the province. However, what emerges in this provincial context is the extent to which a US-led development mission fuelled the growth of a conflict-economy with a variety of adverse results for human beings in the province. Many pre-existing gendered hierarchies of power were exacerbated in ways which adversely affected women's and men's ability to gain meaningful forms of security and fulfilment in their lives. Despite this adversity, an investigation of different people's lives reveals a variety of ways in which women, as well as men, engage in everyday acts of resistance to challenge these hierarchies of power. In doing so, these human subjects reveal immanent possibilities for advancing meaningful forms of HS.

Chapter 6 explores Bamyan Province, which is predominately peopled by different groups of Hazaras who identify this region as their people's ancestral and spiritual homeland. In contrast to Nangarhar, Bamyan offers a case in point of where Western state-building takes place on a relatively smaller scale with an emphasis on the provision of micro-credit and community development council (CDC) projects alongside the construction of roads and basic infrastructure. These approaches are seen as offering a way to alleviate the burdens of poverty for many in a more marginal agricultural province through providing individuals and communities with the opportunity to increase their economic productivity either on or off the farm. While international aid has benefitted certain socio-economic groups in Bamyan, such as wealthier and more educated individuals, the increasing capitalisation of everyday life has produced greater insecurity for those people already living a marginal existence. Moreover, as in Nangarhar Province, this trend has exacerbated existing gendered hierarchies of power which constrain and jeopardise women's lives. Bamyan Province, and the Hazara peoples more broadly, offer a highly visible example of a social group engaged in transforming exploitative gender relations and gendered hierarchies of power.

Chapter 7 explores people's lives in the city and countryside of Kabul Province. This ancient Persian city, which would become the Pashtun capital of modern Afghanistan, stands as a confluence point for Afghanistan's ethnically and religiously mixed groups such as the Hazaras, Tajiks and Pashtuns, and other minorities like the Uzbeks and the Qizilbash. Western development in Kabul Province offers insight into the effect that the physical presence of this state-building project has on the city and province which has historically been the heart of Afghanistan. Perhaps the most dramatic effect has been the creation of a bubble economy in the city, based upon the wealth that has been created by the presence of the Western state-building mission and all that it entails: large development contracts for Western companies; well-paid foreign contractors; and a sharp divide between a smaller proportion of well-off Afghan families with access to services and formalised tenure in the city and the larger proportion of families living informally without access to basic services in varying degrees of hardship.

Notes on fieldwork

At the start, it is necessary for me to account for both the design of my primary research and the way in which it unfolded in the field. This is done in the interests of being as transparent as possible in the presentation of my research process and empirical findings. The approach I took was informed by the same phenomenological methodology outlined previously in relation to gendering HS. This meant that the focus of my research was to gain the perspectives and insights of women and men on the way in which society and gender relations had changed over time. Here, I was particularly interested in exploring participants' own accounts of the tensions and injustices inherent in gendered hierarchies of power as well as their accounts of resistance to these hierarchies.

The primary method I used to gain empirical insight into this phenomenon relied upon conducting semi-structured focus group discussions among two dozen women and men from three different ethno-linguistic groups from Afghanistan who had been living in Delhi, India, for several years. These discussions were self-contained within the three groups represented namely Pashtuns, Tajiks and Hazaras. Within the latter two groups (it was necessary to use a different approach for the Pashtuns as I will explain later), three separate discussion processes took place including: a mixed discussion between women and men; a women's group discussion; and a men's group discussion. The rationale for doing this was to allow women and men the chance to discuss gender issues collaboratively but also to do so separately in order to provide space for them to voice opinions or viewpoints which could otherwise have been self-censored or constrained by the gendered dynamics of power at play within a mixed-sex group.

This fieldwork research was facilitated with the help of the Young Men's Christian Association in Delhi which sought out prospective research subjects among expatriate Afghans and organised secure environments in which these discussions could be held. Given the sensitive nature of this research, ethical clearance for my project was gained within my own department as well as the Social and Behavioural Sciences ethics committee at the University of Queensland. This official ethical approval was conveyed verbally and in writing to each prospective research participant. Additionally, each participant was fully informed as to the nature and purpose of the research project in plain and accessible language. These discussions were all conducted in the native language of the participants with the help of university students from Afghanistan who were studying at Jawarhl Nehru University. These students were later instrumental in translating these conversations back into English.

The questions which drove the discussions in each group explored a variety of different social, political and economic topics; however, the pre-eminent theme of these conversations related to the changing nature over time of gender relations and gendered hierarchies of power within people's communities. In the first stage of the discussions, participants were asked questions about how particular social institutions and practices, such as marriage and child-rearing, took place in their grandparents' time prior to 1978. These discussions were aimed at providing a point of departure for understanding how gender relations existed during Afghanistan's twentieth-century period of modernisation and the way in which gendered hierarchies of power were variously navigated, subverted or challenged. With this baseline about traditional life in place, I next asked participants to reflect on the way in which gender relations and gender politics had changed in the tumultuous history of war and upheaval that followed this earlier time.

This fieldwork research yielded important insights into changing trends in gender relations among the different ethno-linguistic groups. These empirics are most useful in facilitating a broad reconstruction of the gender relations underpinning people's lives and moral horizons. As such, these focus group discussions will be used predominantly in Chapters 2 and 3 of this book. At the same time, it is necessary to point out that there were a number of unavoidable constraints on this research which limit its utility in reconstructing the three provincial case study profiles. Most obviously, the research participants did not necessarily hail from the provinces I was profiling or they had not lived in these areas for many years. Additionally, over half of the women and men who took part in these discussions came from wealthier, socio-economic positions, lived predominately in an urbanised environment and held formal education qualifications. This meant that their community group and world view did not necessarily align with the members of their broad identity group in Afghanistan whose lives took place in rural environments characterised by greater economic hardship. Finally, the Pashtun expatriate community in Delhi was far less open to this research project than were the Hazaras and the Tajiks. The reason given to me by the Pashtun worker from the YMCA who liaised with the local Pashtun community was that no families in this community wanted to take part in research of such a sensitive nature. This meant I could only arrange two small group discussions by coordinating with Pashtuns, who worked at the YMCA, and their partners. Nevertheless, this situation in and of itself provided a fascinating insight into the relative difference in gendered honour codes between groups and interesting results were obtained from the smaller discussions I held.

Notes

1 My thanks go to Elyse Fenton for her insightful comments and critiques of my research project which pushed me to take a more reflexive and critically self-aware stance as a scholar.
2 The 1960s and 1970s saw a large amount of excellent anthropological research conducted in Afghanistan which resulted in a variety of publications including: Tapper, Richard (1974). Nomadism in Modern Afghanistan: asset or anachronism. *Afghanistan in the 1970s*. E. L. Dupree and L. Albert. New York, Praeger Publishers: 126–143. Allan, Nigel (1974). The modernisation of rural Afghanistan: a case study. *Afghanistan in the 1970s*. E. L. Dupree and L. Albert. New York, Praeger Publishers: 113–125. Pedersen, Gorm (1994). *Afghan nomads in transition: a century of change among the Zala Khān Khåel*. London, Thames and Hudson. Tavakolian, Bahram (1984). "Women and Socioeconomic Change Among Sheikhanzai Nomads of Western Afghanistan".

The Middle East Journal 38 (3): 433–453. Shalinsky, Audrey (1989). "Women's Relationships in Traditional Northern Afghanistan". *Central Asian Survey* 8 (1): 117–129. Anderson, Jon W. (1978). "There Are No Khans Anymore: Economic Development and Social Change in Tribal Afghanistan". *The Middle East Journal* 32 (2): 167–183.

3 A large amount of this research has been conducted for the Afghanistan Research Evaluation Unit (AREU) some of whose notable publications are as follows: Wily, Liz (2003). Land Rights in Crisis: Restoring Tenure Security in Afghanistan. *Issues Paper Series*. Smith, Deborah (2009). *Community-based dispute resolution processes in Nangarhar Province*. Kabul, Afghanistan Research and Evaluation Unit. Wakefield, Shawna (2004). Gender and Local Level Decision Making: Findings from a Case Study in Panjao. *Case Studies Series*. Kabul, Afghanistan Research and Evaluation Unit. November. Hunte, Pamela (2009). Beyond Poverty Factors Influencing Decisions to Use Child Labour in Rural and Urban Afghanistan. *Synthesis Paper Series*. E. Winterbotham. Kabul, Afghanistan Research and Evaluation Unit.

4 For instance, see Daulatzai, Anila (2006). "Acknowledging Afghanistan". *Cultural Dynamics* 18 (3): 293–311. Daulatzai, Anila (2008a). "The Discursive Occupation of Afghanistan". *British Journal of Middle Eastern Studies* 35 (3): 419–435. Fluri, Jennifer (2008). "Feminist-nation Building in Afghanistan: An Examination of the Revolutionary Association of the Women of Afghanistan (RAWA)". *Feminist Review* 89 (1): 34–54. McBride, Keally and Annick T. R. Wibben (2012). "The Gendering of Counterinsurgency in Afghanistan". *Humanity: An International Journal of Human Rights, Humanitarianism, and Development* 3 (2): 199–215.

References

Abirafeh, Lina (2009). *Gender and international aid in Afghanistan: The politics and effects of intervention*. Jefferson, North Carolina, McFarland & Company, Inc., Publishers.

Allan, Nigel (1974). The modernization of rural Afghanistan: a case study. *Afghanistan in the 1970s*. E. L. Dupree and L. Albert. New York, Praeger Publishers: 113–125.

Anderson, Jon W. (1978). "There Are No Khans Anymore: Economic Development and Social Change in Tribal Afghanistan". *The Middle East Journal* 32 (2): 167–183.

Daulatzai, Anila (2006). "Acknowledging Afghanistan". *Cultural Dynamics* 18 (3): 293–311.

Daulatzai, Anila (2008). "The Discursive Occupation of Afghanistan". *British Journal of Middle Eastern Studies* 35 (3): 419–435.

Enloe, Cynthia (2014). *Bananas, beaches and bases: Making feminist sense of international politics*. Berkeley and Los Angeles, University of California Press.

Fluri, Jennifer (2008). "Feminist-nation Building in Afghanistan: An Examination of the Revolutionary Association of the Women of Afghanistan (RAWA)". *Feminist Review* 89 (1): 34–54.

Fluri, Jennifer (2009). "The Beautiful 'Other': A Critical Examination of 'Western' Representations of Afghan Feminine Corporeal Modernity". *Gender, Place & Culture* 16 (3): 241–257.

Ghouri, Nadene (2011). John Mohammed Butt: The hippie who became an imam. Deoband, India, BBC Radio 4.

Hirschkind, Charles and Saba Mahmood (2002). "Feminism, the Taliban, and Politics of Counter-Insurgency". *Anthropological Quarterly* 75 (2): 339–354.

Hunte, Pamela (2009). Beyond Poverty Factors Influencing Decisions to Use Child Labour in Rural and Urban Afghanistan. *Synthesis Paper Series*. E. Winterbotham. Kabul, Afghanistan Research and Evaluation Unit.

Hutchings, Kimberly (1992). "The Possibility of Judgement: Moralizing and Theorizing in International Relations". *Review of International Studies* 18 (01): 51–62.

Hutchings, Kimberly (1999a). Feminism, Universalism and the Ethics of International Politics. *Women, Culture, and International Relations*. Boulder, CO, Lynne Rienner Publishers: 17–37.

Hutchings, Kimberly (1999b). *International political theory: Rethinking ethics in a global era*. London, Sage.

Hutchings, Kimberly (2000). "Towards a Feminist International Ethics". *Review of International Studies* 26 (05): 111–130.

Hutchings, Kimberly (2013). Universalism in Feminist International Ethics: Gender and the Difficult Labour of Translation. *Dialogue, Politics and Gender*. J. Browne. Cambridge, Cambridge University Press: 81–106.

Marhia, Natasha (2013). "Some Humans are More Human than Others: Troubling the 'Human' in Human Security from a Critical Feminist Perspective". *Security Dialogue* 44 (1): 19–35.

McBride, Keally and Annick T. R. Wibben (2012). "The Gendering of Counterinsurgency in Afghanistan". *Humanity: An International Journal of Human Rights, Humanitarianism, and Development* 3 (2): 199–215.

Moghadam, Valentine M (2002). "Patriarchy, the Taleban, and Politics of Public Space in Afghanistan". *Women's Studies International Forum* 25 (1): 19–31.

Mohanty, Chandra Talpade (2002). "'Under Western Eyes' Revisited: Feminist Solidarity through Anticapitalist Struggles". *Journal of Women in Culture and Society* 28 (2): 499–532.

Pedersen, Gorm (1994). *Afghan nomads in transition: A century of change among the Zala Khān Khåel*. London, Thames and Hudson.

Peterson, V. Spike (1992). *Gendered states: Feminist (re)visions of international relations theory*. Boulder, CO, Lynne Rienner Publishers

Pettman, Jan Jindy (1996). *Worlding women: A feminist international politics*. New York, Routledge.

Runyan, Anne Sisson and V. Spike Peterson (2013). *Global gender issues in the new millennium*. Boulder, CO, Westview Press.

Russo, Ann (2006). "The Feminist Majority Foundation's Campaign to Stop Gender Apartheid". *International Feminist Journal of Politics* 8 (4): 557–580.

Said, Edward W. (1979). *Orientalism*. New York, Vintage Books.

Shalinsky, Audrey (1989). "Women's Relationships in Traditional Northern Afghanistan". *Central Asian Survey* 8 (1): 117–129.

Shepherd, Laura J. (2006). "Veiled References: Constructions of Gender in the Bush Administration Discourse on the Attacks on Afghanistan post-9/11". *International Feminist Journal of Politics* 8 (1): 19–41.

Smith, Deborah (2009). *Community-based dispute resolution processes in Nangarhar Province*. Kabul, Afghanistan Research and Evaluation Unit.

Tapper, Nancy (1991). *Bartered brides: Politics, gender and marriage in an Afghan tribal society*. Cambridge, Cambridge University Press.

Tapper, Richard (1974). Nomadism in modern Afghanistan: asset or anachronism. *Afghanistan in the 1970s*. E. L. Dupree and L. Albert. New York, Praeger Publishers 126–143.

Tavakolian, Bahram (1984). "Women and Socioeconomic Change among Sheikhanzai Nomads of Western Afghanistan". *Middle East Journal* 38 (3): 433–453.

Tickner, J. Ann (1997). "You Just Don't Understand: Troubled Engagements between Feminists and IR Theorists". *International Studies Quarterly* 41 (4): 611–632.

Tickner, J. Ann (1988). "Hans Morgenthau's Principles of Political Realism: A Feminist Reformulation". *Millennium: Journal of International Studies* 17 (3): 429–440.

Tickner, J. Ann (2001). *Gendering world politics: Issues and approaches in the post-Cold War era.* New York, Columbia University Press.

Tickner, J. Ann (2005). "What Is Your Research Program? Some Feminist Answers to International Relations Methodological Questions". *International Studies Quarterly* 49: 1–21.

Wakefield, Shawna (2004). Gender and Local Level Decision Making: Findings from a Case Study in Panjao. *Case Studies Series.* Kabul, Afghanistan Research and Evaluation Unit. November.

Weber, Cynthia (2005). "Not Without My Sister(s) Imagining a Moral America in Kandahar". *International Feminist Journal of Politics* 7 (3): 358–376.

Wily, Liz (2003). Land rights in crisis: restoring tenure security in Afghanistan. *Issue Paper Series.* C. Bennett, Kabul.

2 Gendering human security

This chapter argues that both "conventional" and "critical" accounts of security in the discipline of International Relations (hereafter IR) are inadequate for comprehending what this term means to people in Afghanistan. This is especially apparent with regard to the security challenges faced by Afghan women who represent the most vulnerable human subjects of this ongoing conflict. In the first case, conventional accounts of security equate this term with the freedom from violent threat to an individual or state by another actor. These accounts tend to be state-centric in their emphasis on the security of national governments as an 'a priori' condition for individual citizens to also be secure. Moreover, their equation of security with the absence of armed public violence speaks almost exclusively of a masculine subject's experiences of insecurity. Missing from this account are the different forms of gender-based violence, whether physical, economic or emotional, that women endure despite the absence of armed conflict.

While critical accounts of security go much further in articulating the forces of domination that threaten human beings, they fail to adequately articulate progressive ethical ideas that could transform these forces. To be sure, critical accounts of security provide rich and useful insights that are necessary for an initial apprehension of people's experiences of (in)security in Afghanistan. These accounts of security each adeptly highlight the "perspectival nature of knowledge" which plagues mainstream conceptualisations of security in IR. Moreover, these schools of thought share a commitment towards advancing progressive normative agendas in global politics. This is especially apparent in their critical exploration of gender, cultural and socio-economic issues which cumulatively layer to form a holistic account of the insecurity experienced by those marginalised by hierarchies of power.

Despite their strengths, these schools would still benefit from a more precise articulation of how progressive ethical ideas of security can be advanced in practice. I argue that this lacuna can be responded to by using the insights of these critical accounts of security to help re-vision human security as both a concept and a practice. The reason I engage with human security is that I believe this concept, in its very phrasing, offers a substantive account of security in terms of people themselves. Like critical accounts, it rejects conventional accounts of security in the discipline of IR which are centred on the abstract body of the state. However, unlike critical accounts of security, this project has a firm footing in the world of policy-making from whence it re-emerged in a 1994 United Nations Development Program (UNDP) report.

A variety of feminist scholars have already engaged explicitly with this project by evaluating the extent to which human security (hereafter HS) can be re-visioned using feminist theory. This work does much of the conceptual heavy lifting regarding the task of understanding how gender, as a system of meaning, serves to construct human beings themselves as well as the social relations they share. Although these accounts provide a great deal of nuance and understanding, I suggest they would benefit greatly in their reconstructive agenda by incorporating the perspectives and insights of critical feminist scholarship as well as critical social theorists. The scholarship of Kimberly Hutchings and Axel Honneth provides robust insights into how progressive arguments can be made in complicated, and often ugly, moral debates such as those concerned with increasing equity in gender relations in Afghanistan. Perhaps most importantly, Hutchings and Honneth admonish researchers and policy-makers to understand that arguments for ethical progress must be intelligible and relatable in the contexts in which they are made. They must, in short, come to terms with the immanent possibilities for moral change which already exist in societies.

It is for this very reason that I seek to engage with the existing struggles for moral change that are undertaken by different women and men in Afghanistan. The importance of these struggles is that they articulate critiques of inequitable social ideas and practices with a language and a logic that is shared by other parties to a moral debate. This methodological choice to focus on the moral arguments revealed by people's struggles against oppression offers feminists a way to articulate what HS should look like ethically and how it should be striven towards politically. Though the politics of making policy via such avenues could not be foreknown, they nevertheless offer a promising starting point for advancing progressive dynamics that help realise a meaningful form of security.

Conventional accounts of security

In the mainstream study of IR and its sub-fields, "security" is traditionally associated with the protection of state actors from the risk of inter-state conflict (Booth, 1994: 1–2). This conceptualisation of security is based on the Hobbesian assumption that human beings are selfish and dangerous individuals who possess absolute freedom to commit violence to each other in a state of nature (Hobbes, 2006: 101–102). This condition of anarchy is only ever escapable by human beings through the establishment of a sovereign state authority which can provide law and order to its citizens. However, at an international level, anarchy is unavoidable and consequently necessitates that states adopt self-help behaviour to ensure their survival against rival state actors (Waltz, 2010: 111). From this perspective, the concept of security is an entirely state-centric enterprise. States exist as both the primary actors in politics and referent objects to be secured; consequently, the military threats they face from rival states provide the content of a narrow, strategic interpretation of security.

This account of security held sway over the imaginations of academics and policy-makers alike throughout the Cold War as a way of explaining and managing the US and USSR's rivalry within a bi-polar international system. For neo-realists and strategic studies experts, predicting the future of this relationship was the paramount concern during this period. Based on their modelling of these states' behaviours as rational actors in an unchanging balance of power, these practitioners confidently predicted the Cold War would be an enduring feature of the international system for many decades into the future.

Then, in 1989, the Cold War ended without conflict through a series of peaceful revolutions and these models were shown to be completely abstracted from the contemporary social and political realities of the world. This momentous re-ordering of global politics was accompanied by a similar seismic shift in the academy of IR and its sub-field "*Strategic Studies*". Longstanding neo-realist arguments about the stability of the international anarchic system suddenly lost a great deal of their authority as that bi-polar system had changed through domestic political dissent. It seemed that states weren't the only, or most important, political actors and that political change could occur in unimaginable ways.

Following the failure of neo-realism's conceptual and literal architecture, space within IR opened to ongoing conversations about the meaning and purpose of security which had previously been marginalised by this academy. Scholars from critical schools of thought were now able to voice their objections to the version of security which had long been offered by IR (Lapid, 1989: 238). Chief among these was a fundamental criticism of neo-realism and strategic studies for constructing security as an exclusive domain of national governments and their standing armies. Critics noted that this paradigm was designed to ensure the survival of the state's government but was far less concerned about the plight of actual human beings living within a state's territorial boundaries (Tickner, 1995: 179–180).

As a result, these conventional accounts of security fare poorly when addressing what security means to different people in the local context of Afghanistan. The problem is that they offer a reductionist and state-centric depiction of global politics. Consequently, they lack any conceptual insight into comprehending complex, social contexts which are far removed from the "citadels of power" which uphold a liberal, international order. This makes them remarkably ill-equipped to respond to a puzzle about security which exists at the intersection of gender, religious, ethno-linguistic and socio-economic relations of power.

The conventionalism of the Copenhagen School

In the early 1990s, against the backdrop of massive changes in Europe's collective security arrangements, Barry Buzan collaborated with Ole Waever in a series of works which became known as the "Copenhagen School" (McSweeney, 1996: 81). The work of this school maintained Buzan's earlier approach of widening security to detail five sectors of risk but it also sought to deepen the meaning of security by acknowledging that actors other than the state, such as people and societies, were able to make claims about potential threats to their security (Wæver *et al.* 1993: 25).

This latter aspect was important because it meant that security and threat did not necessarily exist as external conditions to be studied by an analyst but instead was produced inter-subjectively by people. Moreover, unlike traditional security studies, the Copenhagen School raised "societal security" as a referent object to be secured in its own right alongside that of state security. In contrast to the latter, which focused on maintaining a government's sovereignty, societal security was taken to mean the strength and cohesion of a national identity. As the authors suggest: "societal security concerns the ability of a society to persist in its essential character" (Wæver *et al.* 1993: 24). Thus, while states were still the ultimate referent, societies' security should be increasingly used as a framework for understanding new and emerging "threats" like migration in Europe in the 1990s.

Some might consider it a categorisation error to list the Copenhagen School of Security with a conventional account of security considering their acknowledgement that the meaning of "security" is constructed by societies rather than existing as an objective reality. I make this suggestion because of the way in which this school ultimately privileges states and national societies as the primary actors and referent objects of security. In doing so, the school cannot help but track back to a loaded Western conception of security premised on the primacy of states and national societies.

This is illustrated powerfully by Lene Hansen (2000: 285–287) in an insightful feminist-inspired critique where she raises the Copenhagen School's silence on the gendered nature of what security means. The core question with which she challenges the Copenhagen School is how women's security issues could be understood if those women were not able to enunciate such issues without risk to their own lives. As she noted (Hansen, 2000: 286), the school's authors "make a self-confident claim to have tackled" the problem posed by ongoing widening and deepening of the concept of security.

The issue here was that the expansion of security's remit to deal with non-military threats and other referent objects to be secured could make the concept meaningless for academic and policy-making purposes; a critique which was also later levelled at the advocates of HS. The way in which Ole Waever tackled this issue was through "securitisation"; a process in which issues could be presented by actors to audiences as "security issues", that is an existential threat to a given referent object to be protected (Hansen, 2000: 288). Waever *et al.* (1993: 25) argued that, given this process, any new emerging definitions of security were dependent on their successful construction in discourse. Thus, securitisation could only be considered successful if a "securitising actor" could convince an audience about the "priority and urgency of an existential threat"; only then could it break free of rule-bound political processes.

It was this measure of "success" which would determine whether an issue could be considered a "security issue", that is an existential threat to a referent object's security. By highlighting the role of discourse, the Copenhagen School was gesturing to the fact that *security actors* were implicated in the discursive construction of the *referent objects to be secured* as well as the threats that jeopardised this object. This acknowledgement of discourse, and its role in the actors' construction of the world, was representative of a broader "discursive" turn within the field of security and IR. In this, there was a growing awareness that states and societies were implicated in constructing their own formulation of security.

Though the Copenhagen School's move here might appear to open up the concept of security, it provided a conceptually blinkered account of who could "speak security" as well as who and what could be considered "referent objects" of security. To begin with, the School only considered someone a security actor if they could successfully perform an act of securitisation which gained the acceptance of a collective audience (Buzan *et al.* 1998: 40–41). Consequently, the main securitising actors considered by this approach were taken to be "political leaders, bureaucracies, governments, lobbyists and pressure groups" (1998: 40–41). These actors were prioritised because their instantiation within dominant forms of institutionalised politics meant that they would be more successful in performing acts of securitisation which gained the acceptance of relevant audiences.

Obviously, such an interpretation subordinated the enunciation of a variety of threats posed to people globally on the presumption that their utterance would fail to convince larger collectives about the necessity of raising an issue to the realm of security. On this matter, the authors maintain that individuals and groups can only be considered as a "threatened object" (to be protected by security actors) if they possess a "collective identity" such as a national society. Moreover, because their definition of security was premised on the survival of a collective from existential threat, the only way an issue could be considered a security risk to this referent object was if it jeopardised its particularistic identity. In other words, the security of a society was determined by its ability to protect its "essential character" (Wæver *et al.* 1993: 23). As an example, national societies, such as the English, French and German, could have their "essential character" undermined or diluted by a growing presence of foreign migrants.

In this way, the school limited its conceptualisation of security to discursive moments in which securitisation crystallised an issue as a threat to the survival of a dominant state or social group with regard to their existence/identity. As Lene Hansen (2000: 288–290) suggested, this meant the authors were theoretically unable to account for the political practices which underlay the "successful" securitisation of issues. At the same time, their emphasis on preserving neatly defined identities precluded insight into the fact that the norms and rules of particular identities could be implicated in people's insecurity. To illustrate this point, Lene Hansen (2000: 286–287) introduced the school's blindness to the role of gender in ordering and threatening the lives of concrete human beings across societies. Hansen made this critique with reference to the risks of "honour killing" faced by women in Pakistan from within their societies if they were accused or suspected of infringing religious and customary sexual codes (2000: 291–293). In such a context, if a woman attempted to "securitise" this threat by making it a public concern, then the result would be swift punishment and or death. The political practices in these societal contexts meant that a strategy of "security as silence" was necessary in order for women to avoid the threat of gender-based violence (Hansen, 2000: 294–295).

Obviously, the fact that the threat of gender-based-violence could not be explicitly named did not mean that it did not exist. However, the Copenhagen School's approach of delineating referent objects to be secured meant they were remarkably ill-equipped to speak about gender as a collective issue of survival without the presence of a gender identity group (i.e. women) performing a successful "speech act" of this issue. Here, it is important to recall that the school could only bring gender into focus if it involved a threat against a "self-sustaining identity group" which was demarcated separately from other collective identities. Unfortunately, by virtue of the exclusivity inherent in gender identity it could not form the basis for a political community in the same way as other collective identities such as national, racial and religious. Moreover, as Hansen (2000: 299) observed, gender-based security threats were characterised by their inseparability from "national" and or "religious" forms of security. To make this point, she draws attention to the fact that the threat of Pakistani honour killings to women (and some men) is produced by the gendered norms of behaviour which are constructed within a dominant religious identity group. Because religion and gender are linked together in a particular way, the articulation of 'gender insecurity' is prevented "because it would be in opposition to the (constructed) foundational essence of the religious community" (Hansen, 2000: 299).

In addition to misunderstanding the politics of security, what became apparent was that the authors' ethical beliefs about security were fundamentally questionable on the grounds that they reflected a particular "European flavour" (Huysmans, 1998: 485). Most notably, the authors misunderstood that their articulations of security were thoroughly normative propositions which aim at realising a particular vision of the good. In other words, security cannot express a value-free statement of a fixed reality and is, instead, better conceived as a site of normative contestation over competing understandings of "the good". Thus, the authors were unable to reflect on their own normative preferences for "de-securitising issues" and returning them to the realm of "normal politics". As Matt McDonald (2008: 577) argued, this approach to dividing normal "politics" and "security" up into two opposed realms misunderstood the overlap between, and within, these terms. "Normal politics" could cultivate security practices which constituted threats, as was apparent in Hansen's account of honour killings in Pakistan. Meanwhile, questions of how societies should act to preserve security in specific instances could be characterised as "politically intense" or "even a form of 'hyper-politics'".

Critical accounts of security

The history of the twentieth century demonstrated powerfully that states were more often sources of insecurity to their own populations than guarantors of their safety and happiness. These issues animated a broader, critical appraisal of the IR Academy in what would become known as the "Third Great Debate" of the discipline in the early 1980s and continuing into the 1990s. Robert Keohane (1988: 379–382) captured the essence of this debate in his widely cited 1988 Presidential Address of the International Studies Association which contrasted rationalists (mainstream liberal scholars) with reflectivists (critical theorists).

Unlike conventional accounts of security, the reflexive theoretical traditions of Critical Theory, Feminist Theory, Post-Structuralism and Post-Colonialism, all shared a belief in the "perspectival nature of knowledge" and an overriding suspicion of the positivist meta-narratives found in security orthodoxy (Smith, 1999: 88–96). These traditions noted that conventional accounts of security are premised upon a fallacious binary logic in which a researcher is imagined to be able to separate themself from the object they are observing. This distancing allows researchers to claim impartiality and objectivity in making truth claims about the world. However, as critical scholars note, such a presupposition misunderstands the inter-subjective process in which "subjects" and "objects" are constructed and sustained. In other words, researchers are already, and always will be, a part of the world they are examining (Peterson, 1992b: 184–186). They are not separate from it. Indeed, they themselves, are produced by it.

In this vein, critical scholars (Ashley, 1989: 253–254) noted that realists' and strategists' description of an ineluctable condition of anarchy provided a self-serving political purpose by justifying the necessity of the state and its strategic practices. At the same time, most critical theorists in this field also shared an intellectual dissatisfaction with the story of security told by the Copenhagen School. Here, they again saw primarily Western and modernist-inspired security projects which aimed at explaining the world in terms of dominant and institutionally established forms of politics (Wilkinson, 2007: 7–8).

There are four broad trajectories of critical thought which engage with the question of what security means. Three of these critical theoretical branches of security studies are Critical Security Studies (Booth, 1994; Jones, 1995; Krause, 1998), Feminist Security Studies (Tickner, 2004; Enloe, 2014) and Post-structural Security Studies (Campbell, 1992). The fourth consists of an emerging body of scholarship which could be called "Postcolonial" or "Subaltern" security studies; moreover, the work of Post-Colonial Theory has always addressed issues of security (Hönke and Müller, 2012). Though the differences among these fields have often been played up, what becomes apparent on review is their shared commitment to advancing inclusive conceptions of security aimed at challenging hierarchies of power associated with the state and international order.

In this regard, the critical literatures which offer the most evident commitment to developing robust, normative agendas in global politics are Feminist

Security Studies and Postcolonial Security Studies. In this endeavour, these two emerging schools both go much further than Critical Security Studies and Post-Structural Security Studies. Moreover, they both fruitfully complement each other in ways which increase their normative potential. Feminist scholars inform researchers as to the way gender, as an omnipresent system of meaning, inflects all aspects of life. Meanwhile, Post-Colonial Theory helps to articulate differences in relationship to "subaltern" experiences of oppression. Taken together, these schools of thought go a long way to providing the tools necessary for apprehending social conflict in Afghanistan which exists at the intersection of gendered, religious, ethno-linguistic and socio-economic relations of power.

Critical Security Studies

Critical Security Studies (CSS) can be construed as a sub-discipline of Security Studies theory which shares a common epistemological commitment to highlight the perspectival nature of dominant forms of knowledge used by traditional IR theorists (Smith, 1999: 88–90). Notwithstanding this shared post-positivist starting point, there are two broad variants within CSS adopted by scholars. The first of these is the small "c" study of "critical security" which stems from Robert Cox's adage in 1981 that "theory is always for someone and some purpose" (Smith, 1999: 89). This framing of the remit of critical security was first clearly articulated by Keith Krause and Michael Williams in their preface to the 1997 co-edited book entitled *Critical Security Studies* (Krause and Williams, 1997). In their opening address, Krause and Williams argue in favour of developing an approach to studying security critically which is theoretically inclusive to a variety of post-positivist perspectives. On this matter, the authors note that applying the term "critical" to "security studies" involves interpreting the discipline rather than seeking to construct a "precise theoretical label" (Krause and Williams, 1997: 35–36).

As suggested by Steven Smith, the position taken by Krause and Williams here is self-consciously concerned with distinguishing itself from a second variant of capital "C" "Critical Security Studies" which has since become well known as the "Welsh" School (Smith, 1999: 89–90). This school's capitalisation of "Critical" reflects its homage to the philosophical heritage of the Frankfurt School of Critical Social Theory, which was exemplified in the works of Theodor Adorno and Max Horkeimer, as well as the critical scholarship of Antonio Gramsci (Smith, 1999: 89–90). Though it shares the post-structural commitment to deconstruction of Krause and William's articulation of "critical security", it more explicitly seeks to undertake the reconstructive work necessary to articulate an ethics of security (Booth, 1991: 321). Drawing their impetus from Gramsci and the Frankfurt School, these scholars were interested in articulating the forces of domination, such as global capitalism and national security, which constrained individuals' subjectivities and threatened their physical and emotional security (Jones, 1995: 305). From this critique, scholars of this tradition then incorporate a reconstructive agenda into their work by seeking to promote a global ethic based on human emancipation from the structures of exploitation and domination they have previously identified (Jones, 1995: 308–310).

It is in this reconstructive agenda that sympathetic critics of CSS find both its promise and its peril. On the one hand, a variety of different scholars support the progressive ambitions of these scholars in challenging inequitable hierarchies of power associated within a neo-liberal international system. At the same time, these critics note that while CSS practitioners like Booth acknowledge the politics inherent in claiming what security means, they fail to critically evaluate the plausibility of their own measures for achieving security ethics. Claudia Aradau makes this point when she suggests that, although Booth's commitment to emancipation is commendable, the content of this ethical prescription remains undefined and unaware of its own potential biases. On this matter, she (Aradau, 2004: 14–15) argues that "the question that arises is whether emancipation can be at nobody's expense". Similarly, she notes that Booth's concept of security as emancipation still confronts the dilemma of an exclusionary political logic based on applying a value universally. In so doing, it creates hierarchies of subjects who are treated as victims to be secured. Thus, while Booth's logic may very well recognise the hierarchies of power that dominate individual women in Afghanistan, his uncritical embrace of an ethic of empowerment means that he sidesteps the crucial contextual and political dynamics associated with such moral debates.

Feminist Security Studies

Feminist Security Studies could be considered to have coalesced in the 1980s and 1990s with noted feminists' incisive contributions to the mainstream discipline of the IR academy.[1] Long before their intervention into IR theory, feminist theory and feminist scholars (Peterson, 1992a; Pettman, 1996: viii, 8) had spoken of substantive issues of security by calling attention to the role which gender played in sustaining hierarchical forms of knowledge and practices. When engaging with the IR academy in the 1980s, feminists argued that the depiction of human beings and society by realist and rationalist forms of IR were premised upon deeply problematic gender assumptions about subjectivity and knowledge production.

Here, the central argument that feminists made in relation to the study and practice of international politics was that it was "axiomatically gendered" (Smith, 1999: 91). In other words, the binary process of knowledge formation which gave rise to the practice of "international" politics utilised gender in a hierarchical relationship between valorised masculine characteristics and denigrated feminine ones. Thus, realist and liberal IR arguments were premised upon elevating a particular construction of masculinity and masculine values to the realm of universality. For feminists, the effect of this masculinised conception of the world served to entrench structures of power, such as those associated with perpetuating the international liberal state order, and to marginalise and oppress women around the world (Hooper, 2012: 116).

Ann Tickner provided a very eloquent exposition of this fundamental problem in a 1988 journal article which reviewed Hans Morgenthau's construction of human nature. Tickner (1988: 432) argues that Hans Morgenthau reprises a Hobbesian ontology by constructing "political man" as being bestial, capable of incredible violence and possessing absolute freedom to act on his desires in a state of nature. Tickner (1988: 431) notes that, according to Morgenthau, this political realm, defined by logics of power and domination, can be rationally discerned to be an objective condition of human existence. Consequently, he suggests that it is both possible and prudent to develop a (realist) theory for policy-makers to understand the dynamics of the international politics in a "rational" and "unemotional" way, that is not influenced by moral values. Yet, to make these claims, Morgenthau unwittingly relies upon a partial and narrow construction of masculinity (i.e. men as powerful/ autonomous) to justify his belief in human beings' inability to trust each other. This particular account of masculine attributes, as well as masculinised men themselves, is elevated to represent an "objective" and "universal" account of humanity from which truths can be discerned using "rational" methods (Tickner, 1988: 432).

As Tickner (Tickner, 1988: 432–438) argues, there are two major problems with Morgenthau's account of human nature and international politics. First, his account of human nature is fundamentally flawed. Its preference for universalising a particular and aggressive kind of masculinity relies upon a thoroughly asocial account of human nature. On this matter, Tickner challenged Morgantheau's reading by asking how, if humans (i.e. men) were in a permanent state of mistrust and warfare, societies have persisted long enough to create political communities and states or even to reproduce in their own right? The silence of realist theory on these glaring omissions pointed to a second related and fundamental problem which was that Morgenthau and many other IR scholars advanced a theory which misunderstood the gendered nature of their claims to advance objective knowledge. Tickner (1988: 432) explains this proposition by highlighting Evelyn Fox Keller's feminist critique of the natural sciences that they, like IR theory, share "the assumption that the universe they study is directly accessible by concepts shaped not by language but only by the demands of logic and experiment".

This process, in which subjects separate themselves from the "other", is an integral aspect of masculine gender development towards the idealised masculine quality of autonomy. This is not a coincidence. As Tickner (1988: 432) notes of Keller's argument, other qualities associated with objectivity, such as rationalism, are inextricably linked to masculinity in such a way as to be synonymous with the public realm of scientific progress. As Keller argued, "the demarcation between public and private not only defines and defends the boundaries of the political but also helps form its content and style".

Post-Structural Security Studies and Post-Colonial Theory

Post-Structural Security Studies take their impetus from Foucauldian theory which emphasises the unavoidable relationship of truth and power (Dillon and Reid, 2001: 52). For post-structuralists, claims of knowledge involve an assertion of power as to what could be considered "truth" (Hansen, 1997: 374–376). Such claims are always made from a particular place and can never be considered to derive from a neutral and value-free position. As such, these scholars are sceptical of any theory or argument which seeks to provide a foundational account of security's meaning and purpose. Instead, post-structural security studies is interested in deconstructing the political and contingent nature of "regimes of truth" associated with the regulation of global politics, such as human nature and anarchy, in such a way as to challenge, and potentially overturn, this dominant understanding of things. Perhaps one of the best examples of this scholarship is offered by David Campbell in his text *Writing Security* which explores the reproduction of the United States through an exclusionary discourse of fear. In this work, Campbell (1992) offers an incisive critique of the exclusionary processes manifested in the social construction of US security as national security, that is it was a form of security premised upon the exclusion of dangerous "others".

Though post-structural critiques of IR and Security Studies provide excellent articulations of the structural disciplining forces in a neo-liberal world order, they tend to avoid articulating what security ethics should mean in practice. When turning to these tasks, it is important to highlight the scholarship of Post-Colonial theorists who used the insight of Post-Structuralism to develop robust, normative agendas. On this point, one must make note of the brilliant and accomplished scholarship of Edward Said whose critical work *Orientalism* helped to found Post-Colonial thought itself. In this work, Said (1979: 1–2) highlights the way in which the idea of "the Orient" was constructed by Americans and Europeans to categorise people from unfamiliar regions of the world. Said noted that the idea of "the Orient" and "the Oriental" existed in Western imaginations as an archive of meaning, which they could always draw upon to interpret "the other" (Said, 1979: 38–39). Thus, things and people from the Orient were able to be seen not as new and unknown quantities but rather familiar versions of a previously known thing. Said's concern with this construction of knowledge was that it was performative, that is it produced the effect that it named. In this manner, Said (1979: 71) argued that Orientalism was a "cultural repertoire" through which the Orient became "a theatrical stage affixed to Europe" whose "audience, manager and actors are for Europe, and only for Europe".

Feminist Security Studies and Post-Colonial Theory share conceptual insights about the role white, Western, masculine hierarchies have played in the construction of empire historically. At the same time, scholars from both these schools of thought work towards similar normative ends advocating the struggle against the discourses and practices that sustain the hegemony of Western liberal empire. There is perhaps no better example of this complementarity than in their ethical critique of the deployment of the "warrior myth" in Afghanistan. The warrior myth is the logic that justifies masculine violence to save a feminised object, for example, women and civilians. In the case of Afghanistan, a host of feminist writers have already critically reflected upon how this "warrior myth" was deployed as a justification for embarking upon the invasion and occupation of Afghanistan to oust the Taliban and liberate Afghan women.[2]

This rationale for the Western male warrior's action was, and still is, a major site of stabilisation between Orientalist and gendered tendencies inherent within modernisation-inspired thought. In other words, the construction of the barbaric, oriental male and the exotic, feminine other to be rescued serve to mutually reinforce the duplicitous, modernisation-inspired practices of state-building. This idea concerning the "warrior myth's" functioning in a post-colonial context has been previously elucidated by Gayatri Spivak (1994: 92) whose well-known saying, that this masculine imperative provides a rationale for "white men to save brown women from brown men", is still highly relevant. Using this logic, it can be argued that "third world women" need to be saved from the savage and barbaric practices of their traditional culture, thereby justifying the civilising mission of Western white men to bring these women out of their backward status into modernity. As Miriam Cooke (2002: 228) argues, when reflecting upon Spivak's rearticulation of the warrior myth:

> These women are to be rescued not because they *are* more "ours" than "theirs," but rather because they will have *become* more "ours" through the rescue mission.

The emergence of human security

Amid this ongoing academic debate over the meaning and purpose of security in the IR academy, the concept of Human Security (HS) was enunciated within a 1994 United Nations Development Project Report as a qualitatively different framing of security. Borne out of a series of discussions among communities of policy-makers, academics and NGO activists, the concept aimed to highlight that humans' well-being and freedom from threat was the irreducible goal of security. As Heloise Weber (2013: 29) suggests, while the substantive concerns of HS were not new (i.e. civil war, poverty, threats to human beings, etc.) this discourse was particularly successful with regard to reframing "what and who" was to be secured and "developed". In this regard, she suggests that it was instrumental in shifting the discourse within security and development studies away from state-centred and state-centric frames, towards that of the human being as the core referent of security and development (Weber, 2013a: 27). For instance, the concept advanced the international campaign to ban land-mines (Ottowa Treaty), it furthered calls for international responsibility regarding crimes against humanity (RtoP); and it has also been adopted in other global campaigns such as eradicating poverty and ensuring human rights (Martin Weber, 2013).

Though the last two decades have shown that HS persists in academic and policy discourse, orthodox and critical IR scholars have vociferously taken issue with its usefulness as a theoretic concept or as an institutionalised practice (Paris, 2001: 87–89; Chandler, 2008: 427–428). To begin with, many orthodox IR scholars, like Roland Paris (2001: 88), argue HS's extremely broad purview is overly inclusive, vague and lacking a clear definition with which to facilitate the actualisation of the concept in practice. At the same time, HS is accused of being unhelpfully polysomic through its apparent overlap with other UN campaigns such as the human developmental agenda and ongoing human rights campaigns (Owen, 2008: 113–127). Thus, for Owen Taylor, if HS cannot qualitatively distinguish itself from these pre-existing agendas, then it is of little use to policy-makers (Owen, 2008: 126–127). This point, and others like it, have provoked an ongoing debate among mainstream scholars, aimed at narrowing, defining and specifying what HS is, and what policy-making in its name entails (King and Murray, 2001: 591; Owen, 2004: 381).

These objectivist criticisms were often made in the name of rescuing HS from obscurity; however, in so doing, they were actually serving to stymie the radically progressive potential of the concept. What was misunderstood by those attacking the broadness of HS was that, for the concept to retain any relevance to human beings themselves, it had to be open to the manifoldly different ways in which HS can be understood (Hudson, 2005: 165–166; Newman, 2011: 15–17). As was demonstrated in the previous literature, constructions of security are not fixed but are inevitably produced through inter-subjective processes of deliberation between human subjects which specify referent objects to be secured and the threats which are posed to these referents. Fixed definitions of HS, such as the freedom of individuals from armed violence, closed off the possibility of seeing the variety of different human beings and the ways in which they were threatened.

As Susan McKay (McKay, 2004: 154) has suggested, even if major armed hostilities between opposing groups ended, this would not necessarily mean that women were "secure" from the threat of ongoing physical and sexual violence within their own homes and communities. Moreover, these definitional debates served to highlight the problematic way in which security itself was treated as a "capability" which humans either lacked or possessed (McSweeney, 1999: 3). In making such a move, writers like Amartya Sen and Martha Nussbaum, were constructing a particular kind of human life, premised on Euro-centric values of rationality and modernity, as that towards which other human beings would ultimately graduate (Marhia, 2013: 21–23). From this conceptualisation, human beings in the Global South would only become fully "Human" once they had thrown off the shackles imposed by their traditional cultures.

While HS has been repeatedly attacked for being too vague by mainstream scholars and policy-makers leery of abandoning national security paradigms, it has been subject to an even more sustained critique from a range of critical theorists (Christie, 2010: 185–186; Marhia, 2013: 19–20; Weber, 2013a: 27–29). These criticisms fall into two core argumentative points. First, critical scholars take issue with the narrowness of HS as a device for conceiving the "human" subject at an ontological level. This leads them to construct the human subject, and his/her path to security, in a universalistic process wherein individuals and societies follow the one and only path out of a backward/undeveloped state towards increasingly higher stages of development defined by increasing levels of modernisation, rationalisation and capitalisation (Wibben, 2010: 41). Second, these scholars suggest that the predominant ethical vision of HS is premised upon a liberal humanist tradition which argues for the universalisation of particular Western philosophical constructions of the good life (Marhia, 2013: 26). From these perspectives, the indelible legacy of Enlightenment philosophy is etched into HS in such a way that it can't apprehend actual human subjects nor can it understand and reflect on its universalising normative move. For these reasons, HS, for many of its critics, will always be complicit in reinforcing dominant and exclusionary paradigms like that of national security within a liberal capitalist order.

A variety of critical theorists have established HS's debt to the problematic streams of enlightenment philosophy previously discussed. Most notably, the human subject of HS is characterised in the following ways: as an autonomous individual with embodied rights (Chandler, 2013: 38); as an individual citizen of a sovereign state (Chandler, 2008: 428–429); and as an individual subject with "basic needs" whose fulfilment was necessary to promote human development (Shilliam, 2013: 96). In these propositions, HS draws upon Hobbesian and Lockean ontological frameworks to construct security, especially with regard to personal security and individual rights, as a by-product of a hierarchical political relationship between a citizen and a sovereign state. What is also apparent is the reappearance of Locke's tenet that individuals are possessive accumulators whose movement towards development and civilisation lies on a linear pathway of progress (Shilliam, 2013: 92–93). Thus, instead of providing a revolutionary concept for reshaping ingrained political orders, HS inevitably tacks back to a particular euro-centric conception of national security and human development. This critique gives impetus to Ken Booth's (2007: 324) conceptualisation of HS as a velvet glove covering an "iron fist of power" whose institutionalisation in different policy-making contexts has often served as a handmaiden to dominant, exclusivist conceptions of national security and disciplinary neo-liberal development by providing these hegemonic practices with a cosmetic veneer on what are otherwise unchanging programmes.

These critiques are well made and act as a cautionary warning to scholars and practitioners of HS that they may end up reinforcing the dominant views and practices they sought to change. Yet, in spite of this, the outright rejection of HS on the grounds that it is merely a restatement of a Western/liberal conceptualisation of individuals' security within a state framework may be overstated. It contains many elements which are antithetical to liberalism's ontological construction of "possessive individuals". For instance, all of the following issues expressed in HS call into question liberal framings of security: structural violence associated with the continuation of poverty; the collective challenge to all humans posed by climate change; and the commitment to uphold the cultural rights and indigenous rights of different communities globally. This reflexive awareness of the political and ethical dimensions of security means that HS can potentially articulate appropriate contextual understandings of different humans' well-being. In this regard, it can also be understood as an argument with a cosmopolitan ethos based on its radically democratic notion that human subjects are the foremost authorities on what their security entails. Thus, even if its mainstream policy-making expression has suggested otherwise, HS has the potential to be able to articulate a plausible and progressive account of security.

Caroline Thomas (2007: 107–110) arguably provides one of the most well-reasoned and thoughtful accounts of HS in her many publications on this subject. This is particularly evident in her unpacking of the "freedom from fear" and the "freedom from want" which are two routinely emphasised aspects of HS. For Thomas (2007: 110–111), the freedom from want (FFW) relates to meeting the broad material needs of human beings in regard to the need for shelter, food, health and a secure livelihood. Importantly, on this subject, she avoided the trap of merely paying lip service to "poverty" as in narrow orthodox accounts of HS. Instead, she drew attention to the ways in which poverty was exacerbated by the global capitalist system and the structural economic inequalities it sustained (Thomas, 2007: 120–123). She took a similarly critical view when providing an overview of what the freedom from fear (FFF) should be thought to entail. Usually, FFF, whether in policy-making documents or academic articles, was tied to the idea of the protection of the individual from physical armed violence (e.g. the foreign policy of Canada under Lloyd Axworthy). Thomas (2007: 109) pushed this subject much further than it was conventionally described by calling attention to the threats which jeopardise human beings' ability to gain recognition for the innate worthiness of their lives through participation in the community. The implication of this point was that "individuals'" attempts to feel secure about their own "identities" (i.e. their understandings of themselves) could be constrained and/or threatened. As she (2007: 109) noted, this implied a "radical account of politics as freedom from domination/exploitation, not simply the freedom to choose as in the liberal tradition".

The reason for invoking Thomas's sophisticated account of HS is that it shares the theoretical perspective of the critical schools of security previously mentioned. This is perhaps most evident in its identification of security as human fulfilment and freedom from oppression which resembles Booth's account of emancipation. Despite this similarity, the work of Thomas is distinguished by the explicitness of its appeal to engaging in concrete practices. In this regard, it offers an important contribution to a concept which already exists in policy-makers' imaginations and has life in different institutional settings.

Gendering human security with feminist theory

Feminists' work to "people" the study of IR was premised initially on a critique of the knowledge this study relied upon (Pettman, 1996: viii). In this endeavour, emphasis was placed on the discipline's ontology of masculinised actors (whether individuals or states) and the hierarchical, and gendered, binaries which underpin its epistemological and methodological claims to produce "secure knowledge". By critiquing this work, feminists opened space for alternative accounts of politics and ethics in IR and Security Studies. In their articulation of what such a project should look like, they critiqued the way in which dominant forms of knowledge (public/private, productive/reproductive, rational/emotional, civilisation/nature) subordinated and oppressed (non-white-Western-male-heterosexual) subjects. Feminists (Steans, 1998: 15–16) argued for a radical account of politics premised upon the inter-subjective lives and relations of people themselves and an ethical project of overturning relations of dominance.

Given these overlaps, it is perhaps unsurprising that a wide array of feminist scholarship positively embraced the concept of HS, following its formal enunciation and subsequent rise as a discourse in academic and policy-making contexts (notable scholars here include: Hoogensen and Rottem, 2004).

Though these scholars remain circumspect because of the danger that HS will be co-opted as a new technology in the service of unchanging, hegemonic expression, they nevertheless seek to re-vision and re-claim it as a vehicle for feminist politics (notable scholars here include: Hoogensen and Rottem, 2004; Hudson, 2005; Hoogensen and Stuvoy, 2006; Truong, 2009; Truong *et al.* 2006; Robinson, 2008, 2011). Their approach to this re-visioning process first relies upon questioning the use of "human" in orthodox accounts of HS as the term is revealed to denote little more than an abstracted androcentric (although undeniably masculine) individual. From this critique, these authors highlight the importance of context, relationality and inter-subjectivity when understanding how gender roles, identities and relations are produced and sustained in societies.

Heidi Hudson (2005: 158) explores African feminisms to make the case for a more "fluid" and "context-based" conceptualisation of gender, and gender politics, in HS. From this perspective, the conceptualisation of women's HS in Africa needed to be built from a non-Western and African form of feminism which understood the different ways in which gender inter-mingled with other social structures such as race, nationality and class (Hudson, 2005: 164). Any attempt here to treat gender in isolation of these other relational dynamics often led to a liberal/Western account which saw "brown women" as objects to be improved in the image of "white women" (Hudson, 2005: 169). Similarly, in their 2006 co-authored article, Hoogensen and Stuvøy (2006: 208) suggested a pathway forward for feminist theory to apprehend the transformative potential contained in the concept of HS, through focusing on women's resistance to gendered relations of domination. They argue that any account of HS must be premised on the inter-subjective social and political relations of given societies with an explicit focus on resistance to hierarchies of power (Hoogensen and Stuvøy, 2006: 221). This latter point was important because it provided a positive articulation of security (i.e. the freedom to become) rather than a negative form of security (i.e. the freedom from threat) (Hoogensen and Stuvøy, 2006: 221).

One of the most "critical" feminist accounts of HS was provided by Truong *et al.* (2006: xii) who argued that the referent object of security should "not just be an individual with rights and entitlements but also the social relations which mediate human life in ways that ensure its quality and flourishing". In this way, Truong was arguing for a thorough ethical and political account of the social relations which constructed and ordered human subjects. Such an account of HS reflected Truong's embrace of the feminist ethic of "care" as a guide for responding to epistemological questions of how HS can be accurately apprehended (Truong *et al.* 2006: xviii–xxii). This ethical account of care uses feminist theoretical and methodological insights to bring to the fore the ontological values and practices of care which sustain human life.

Truong (2009: 6) was interested in countering the dominant binary understanding of gender within orthodox HS discourse which was exemplified in their treatment of "care" as "female and private" and "security" as "male and masculine". For her, this problematic was exemplified in the division of social and political life into the two distinct compartments of "public" and "private" which she notes have been styled thus for administrative purposes (Truong, 2009: 6). Hence, politics and security were equated with the public realm while care and reproduction were held to exist in the subjective experiences of the private realm. However, orthodox HS practitioners lost sight of the inextricably interlinked nature of these domains. As Truong (2009: 6) noted, "care" was intimately implicated in the construction of the political subjects who deliberated and acted upon issues affecting their broader communities. At the same time, in the "private" sphere, caring-giving and care-receiving acts fulfil the emotional requirements of the very interpersonal relationships which "sustain the most basic goals in life", for instance, survival, development and basic functioning (Truong, 2009: 22). This relational account of gender and care was necessary in order to reconcile feminist epistemological concerns with HS as a framework.

In a similar fashion to Truong, Fiona Robinson (2008: 169) has drawn on the feminist ethic of care to provide a "comprehensive ontological and normative framework" for making HS relevant to human beings themselves. Coming from a critical feminist theoretical perspective, Robinson (Robinson, 2008: 171) is keen to highlight the way in which "dominant norms and discourses sustain existing power relations which lead to inequalities in the way in which societies determine how and on what basis care will be given and received". Robinson is particularly interested in bringing into focus the inequalities caused by the relations of domination inherent in a neo-liberal capitalist order which relies upon a narrow and masculinised conception of the subject as an economic actor (Robinson, 2008: 176–177).

This literal and figurative masculinised construction of the world ignores the labour of care and reproduction that is inherent in producing the global economy and, instead, maintains the fiction of humans existing as "autonomous" agents (Robinson, 2008: 170–172). In contrast, Robinson seeks to show the "self" or subject is produced relationally with others and that "morality" can only be understood in the context of these self-other relations. Thus, the dominant ontology of human beings as autonomous, isolated and self-reliant moral selves does not apprehend people's concrete experiences in different communities. Indeed, often, this perspective occludes from view the experiences of women who are more likely to define themselves in, and through, "their relations with children, other family members, including the elderly or chronically ill, friends or members of their communities" (Robinson, 2008: 170). The viewpoint of "political man" serves to not only distort the experiences of women but all people whose lives are ultimately based on interdependent relations of care.

These reformulations of HS with the feminist ethic of care highlight the inherently interlinked nature of politics and ethics in human relations. However, their normative preference for prioritising "care" as a form of moral life was critiqued on the grounds that it represented a potentially universalising move which elided the question of politics. What was apparent with Robinson's argument, as well as those of other care ethicists, was a tension between the idealisation of care as a virtue which could facilitate a more epistemologically secure, ethical perspective and her observance of "power relations", "complexity" and "context" (Robinson, 2008: 182–183). On the one hand, care ethicists insist upon the perceptiveness with which the ethical virtue of care frames social and political relations between people, yet, at the same time, they are plagued by the inherent politics which accompany any moral intervention in a specific context.

These points were articulated by Kimberly Hutchings (2000: 119–120) in a contribution which was sympathetic to the direction of Robinson's feminist project but remained circumspect regarding its emphasis on care as a singular and preferential form of theorising morality. Hutchings noted that Robinson was attempting to bridge the divide between Universalist justice-based ethics (e.g. formalised liberal frameworks such as the United Nations Human Rights Declaration) and difference-based accounts of morality (e.g. focusing on different communities' customary justice systems). In this effort, she suggests that Robinson ultimately falls short in this task because her particular "feminist standpoint" valorises the "virtue" of care from the outset without pausing to think about whether such a fixed account of a generalisable feminist perspective can be produced (Hutchings, 2000: 117). Moreover, there is very little attention to the gendered power and politics inherent in relations of care. For instance, in the context of Afghanistan, the relations of care, flowing from extended families and communities, were responsible for ensuring the well-being of women. Yet, at the same time, these relations of care were often inherently gendered in hierarchical ways which could sanction severe forms of violence and physical insecurity as was shown in Lene Hansen's example of Pakistani honour killings. The virtue of "care" did not necessarily represent an unambiguously progressive quality and it was certainly not removed from politics.

Fiona Robinson is aware of Hutchings' criticism and this underlying tension in her "critical ethical" perspective and her adoption of the virtue of "care" as a standpoint from which to gain insight into the character of moral relations. In her more recent publications on the ethic of care and the project of gendering HS, she has highlighted the dangers of attempting to find "epistemological security" (Robinson, 2011: 28). However, when enunciating this logic, Robinson doesn't quite manage to articulate how she can hold these two competing epistemological positions. Robinson (2011: 28) argues that she is "primarily concerned with making an ontological claim" with reference to Hutchings' argument that "ethical claims should be concerned with "the nature of the world we inhabit rather than a claim about what ought to be the case". Yet, her ability to follow through on this approach is undermined immediately by her insistence that the ethical character of this ontological level is defined by inter-subjective responsibilities which are fulfilled through "practices of care" (Robinson, 2011: 28). Though Robinson treats "relations of care" as an objective and progressive feature of ethical life, this, in many ways, is far from settled. Moreover, her ability to provide "political solutions" to the "problems of giving and receiving of care ... to ensure the flourishing of all persons" is likely to be hamstrung in practice because it lacks an account of the type of politics which are associated with engaging in an ethical debate (Robinson, 2011: 32–33).

This does not mean that feminist theorists engaging with HS using the ethic of care are pursuing an unrealisable goal vis-à-vis the quest to overturn gendered hierarchies of power which sustain exploitative relations in favour of more progressive ethical relations premised upon care. However, for such a project to be viable, it needs to follow the logic of its own "critical ethical" premises more closely. Thus, in Robinson's (2011: 28) own articulation, moral claims about the way the world "ought to be" as opposed to the way "it is" "cannot be judged or justified according to some external standpoint – rather, they are always context-dependent and always subject to revision and reconfirmation". The message here is that politics and ethics are always inextricably intertwined. For an account of the "ethic of care" to be plausible, it must be able to sketch the "moral grammars" of different contexts (i.e. the principles and languages used to construe the ethical good) and the way in which an "ethic of care" could make sense to the protagonists of moral debates in these contexts.

Feminist engagements with HS provide strong conceptual and methodological insights into re-visioning this project such that it can more appropriately apprehend how people's lives and well-being are affected by gendered hierarchies of power. However, the area where these accounts stand to benefit the most is through a more rigorous methodological explanation of how progressive forms of security could be furthered in practical contexts. Such work would initially involve detailing the logics of moral debates which allow protagonists to possess "moral authority" prior to articulating the intensely political logics which would allow external interventions to be seen as possessing moral necessity. For instance, how could critical feminists' emphasis on the virtue of "caring relations" become seen to embody a moral necessity in hierarchical and, often ugly, social contexts like Afghanistan.

Realising the normative dimension of human security

My own suggestion for resolving these tensions on the question of advancing human security in Afghanistan relies on the scholarship of Kimberly Hutchings

(1999a: 33–35; 2000: 121–122; 2013b: 24–25) and Axel Honneth (1996: 92; 2003: 173; 2014: 6–7). These scholars have both adeptly drawn on the philosophy of Hegel as resource for understanding how ethical critique could be made across boundaries of difference. Though these scholars draw on Hegel from the different critical positions of feminist theory and social theory, they both incisively show the value his philosophy holds in understanding ethical praxis in moral debates. In this regard, Hutchings (2013a: 31) and Honneth (2014: 127) argue in favour of reconstructing the logics or "moral grammars" of a conflict through a phenomenological mode of inquiry which highlights the immanent potential for moral progress within people's existing social relationships of recognition with each other.

As suggested by Hutchings (1999b: xiii–xiv), this means that the work of the ethical theorist first requires a strong *phenomenological dimension*. Practitioners must be able to understand and deconstruct their own identity and the identity of their dialogue partners to understand possibilities in which shared meanings over ethical progress could emerge between them. At the same time, Hutchings (2000: 122) notes that the work of the ethical theorist also possesses a strong *genealogical dimension*. This means that it is equally important to investigate how certain judgements are understood as embodying ethical necessity and the pattern of costs and benefits associated with this judgement. In this regard, Hutchings (2000: 122) observes that the feminist ethical theorist will be concerned with understanding the role of gender, in terms of identities, relations and roles, in constructing and maintaining patterns of benefits and costs to human subjects. Taken together these two tasks allow practitioners to potentially identify the possibilities for shared meaning to emerge in moral debates across linguistic and cultural boundaries.

The scholarship of Axel Honneth engages with the phenomenological potential of Hegel in a similar and complementary fashion to that of Kimberly Hutchings. In a recent work, Honneth's (2014: 6) argument in favour of engaging in a "normative reconstruction" shares much of the approach Hutchings takes in understanding the phenomenological and genealogical dimensions of ethical debate. Honneth (2014: 1) succinctly rearticulates Hegel's critique in relation to contemporary political philosophy which has "been decoupled from an analysis of society, instead becoming fixated on purely normative principles". As Honneth argues (Honneth, 2014: 3), a progressive theory of justice must be built on the immanent possibilities within existing societal institutions and practices. Like Hegel, Honneth (2014: 62) identifies justice with an individual's freedom to develop in their communities through mutual relations of respect and recognition. Such relations of recognition between people can be seen to undergird the material and ideational considerations which either permit or deny the types of lives to which people aspire as a pathway towards emotional fulfilment and happiness.

Honneth's account of "normative reconstruction" is highly relevant to the phenomenological and genealogical tasks of the ethical theorist outlined by Hutchings (Honneth, 2014: 57–58). In these tasks, Honneth provides a reminder of the care that needs to attend any decision of engaging in a debate over ethical life in society. As he (2014: 10) notes, in their effort to normatively reconstruct an ethical debate, researchers select "out of the diversity of social reality" the "institutions and practices that are truly capable of securing and realising general values". In engaging with this methodological task, Honneth (2014: 9) cautions against simply affirming existing instances of ethical life in society. In other words, researchers needed to be able to do more than merely point to the ethical claims among different people in society. They also had to be able to assay the legitimacy of such moral claims from the perspective of those who were constrained and threatened within society.

The insights of these scholars influence my own decisions in attempting to reconstruct social change and moral debate in Afghanistan. That is why I am interested in engaging with struggles for recognition that exist immanently in societies across Afghanistan. The importance of these struggles is that they articulate logics built on the invocation of broader, societal principles and they do so in a language and manner that is shared by other parties to a moral debate. Crucially, this methodological choice to focus on the immanent moral logics revealed by these struggles supplements feminist attempts to articulate what HS's ethics should look like and how best to strive towards these goals politically.

The feminist framework of HS which I build through the insights of Hutchings and Honneth goes a long way towards addressing the dilemma posed by my original research puzzle outlined in the previous chapter. Namely, how was it possible to make sense of what security meant for women who exist as the most vulnerable human beings in Afghanistan during a time of Western intervention. As I noted previously, this question exists at the intersection of gendered, religious, ethno-linguistic and socio-economic relations of power. Consequently, venturing moral critique into this complex debate, which is often characterised by hierarchical and ugly relations of power, is always an uncertain and hazardous exercise. Yet, by taking on board the phenomenological and genealogical recommendations of Hutchings and Honneth, it is possible to identify ways of plausibly articulating mechanisms of progressive change which are already immanent to societies themselves.

These twin insights suggest that the question of women's security must be approached with a strong understanding of the societal relationships of recognition which variously further or impede women's positive self-development. It is through these societal relationships that women, and indeed men, are variously made secure or insecure in their own lives. While ethical critique should always be made of relationships that deny and threaten people's ability to positively live their lives, care should always be taken to put into place the phenomenological conditions in which such an argument would be considered important.

A significant illustration of how such a progressive moral debate could be carried out in Afghanistan practically is offered by the radio soap opera "New Home, New Life" which began in 1993. This broadcast, which was avidly listened to by women and men across Afghanistan, told a story of a rural village peopled by recent refugees returning from conflict. In its stories of tragedy, adversity and love, the broadcast constructed a shared imaginary that ordinary Afghans could relate to. Moreover, the radio drama proved very adept in incisively critiquing gendered hierarchies of power by approaching such debates in an oblique rather than direct fashion.

When interviewing John Butt, one of the co-founders of this radio drama, on this issue, he offered the following story as an example of how such a process worked. He and his colleagues had an array of positive, negative and transitional characters who intertwined stories presenting moral arguments about Afghan society. One of these stories featured Jabhar Khan, a corrupt warlord and villainous character in the show who would not let his daughter-in-law Gulalai perform her work as a trained midwife. Because of this ban, one of Jabhar Khan's wives lost their newborn son to tetanus in the days following his birth. The moral of this story was that women should not be prevented from working because it is necessary for society to survive. As John suggested to me, this story, and others like it, were widely listened to by the Taliban and had an influence on softening their regressive beliefs about women's position in society.

> Once, the Taliban said to me in Kandarhar, "You know you have a Taliban representative in your soap opera don't you?" and I said "No, there's no Taliban representative."
>
> They said, "Yeah, there is."
>
> And I asked, "Who is it?"
>
> They said, "He's Jabhar Khan." And this Jabhar Khan is the man who hadn't allowed his wife to go and get vaccinated. He also didn't allow his daughter Gulalai to go to work.
>
> So, I said, "Why is he your representative?"
>
> And they said, "Because he isn't allowing his daughter-in-law to go to work and we're also not allowing women to go to work. So you're targeting us in fact through him."
>
> And you know they were laughing about it. They were laughing about it. So this shows that with soap opera you can do anything. But unfortunately, I had a lot of people there who didn't realise that soap opera, and this will come in my book *insha'allah* (if Allah wills it), you know the potential of soap opera to actually make a really big difference in society.

Social change in Afghanistan

In Afghanistan, social recognition between women and men has historically been circumscribed by masculinist honour codes within which men are positioned as the defenders of a household's honour which is indelibly inked into the bodies of *their* women (Tapper, 1981: 103–107). In this social system, "women" and "men" are not born as such but instead become sexed through their performance of socially recognised gender roles which are required to maintain a household's honour and reproduce the extended family network (Dupree, 2004: 311). The performances of these gender roles, which maintain a family's honour, are undertaken for the consideration and evaluation of a wider public audience of community members (Azarbaijani-Moghaddam, 2010). Though this social system was ultimately hierarchical in the way senior male family members were invested with authority over women and other family members, what is pertinent to note is that relations of respect and love bound women's and men's lives within the larger framework of the family which gave meaning and security to both of their lives (Dupree, 2004: 311). Moreover, social and financial ties of support and protection between men and women, as well as between wealthy and poorer households, were considered vital to the maintenance of families' and communities' physical and emotional well-being in society.

The onset of capitalisation in Afghanistan's rural agricultural settings exacerbated pre-existing hierarchical tendencies in this gendered honour system by weakening the social ties of obligation and reciprocity between men and women as well as those between wealthier and poorer families. The former was evidenced in the way in which marriage practices, whether bride-price, exchange or levirate, became stripped of the traditional obligations, not least of which was the obligation to ensure the emotional and physical well-being of the family's daughter, were altered due to changing external pressures (Dupree, 2004: 311). Meanwhile, as Anderson noted, the latter phenomenon was apparent in the transformation of Khans, from men with social obligations to their communities, into large landlords whose chief concern was their own family's profit and increased honour (Anderson, 1978: 169–171). The gendered honour system was further contorted with the onset of decades of total warfare starting in the 1980s and the disruption and displacement of established communities from their ancestral homes in Afghanistan to the uncertainty of life in Pakistan's refugee camps. These changed circumstances made it harder for families to practise the traditional lifestyles of their villages in the densely packed settings of the camps. Strict levels of *purdah* (the curtain) denied women mobility and the ability to interact socially outside the home; thereby, denying many women access to healthcare, education and their wider social networks (Dupree, 2004: 320–321). At the same time, the war and conflict gave rise to powerful Islamist Mujahedeen parties, who promulgated and publicly policed hyper-masculine understandings of customary honour codes which served to terrorise both men and women (Kandiyoti, 2009). The enforcement of honour, which had previously been the private prerogative of a family, became a very public affair which Mujahedeen commanders used as a political tool to control their captive audiences.

What was becoming evident was that these emerging relations of recognition, which underpinned this reformulated gender system, were untenable for sustaining women's security and happiness within family units. This was evidenced by the fact that women experienced all the horrible consequences of this new gender order while receiving none of the obligations and protections traditionally owed to them (Kandiyoti, 2009). Marriage practices have been stripped of their egalitarian quality and, instead, often facilitate the outright commodification of women's bodies. Violent sanctions are levelled at women for any perceived infringements of their household's honour. At the same time, the traditional ties of reciprocity designed to ensure women's physical and emotional well-being have dissipated. Moreover, quite perversely, the very actions which women take to improve their own lives, and mitigate the threats of forced-marriage and/or rape in a hyper-masculine setting, are denied social recognition and are violently punishable.

Though the Western Intervention in Afghanistan rhetorically held women aloft as victims whose lives would be uplifted in the process, women continue to face a variety of gender-based forms of violence (whether physical, economic or emotional). Moreover, in a variety of ways, this state-building intervention has exacerbated existing gendered hierarchies of power in society as is illustrated in the reconstruction I provide of the Western Intervention's influence on gender dynamics, especially regarding relationships of power, in three provincial settings in Afghanistan. Each of these provincial settings represent different instantiations of the Western Intervention. For instance, the size of the state-building and development intervention in Nangarhar Province dwarfed that of Bamyan.

Nevertheless, regardless of the scale of this intervention, perhaps one of the most consistent themes has been its promotion of a neo-liberal development agenda. Many critical journalists have observed that the privatised nature of development aid in Afghanistan has provided a bonanza for the "aid industry" first and foremost (Constable, 2007). At the same time, the promotion of this neo-liberal vision of Afghanistan has allowed unmitigated profiteering by powerful factions in Afghanistan due to the emerging bubble economy. Though a variety of wealthier, landed communities have benefitted from the Western Intervention, the poorer rural and urban masses of Afghanistan struggle to meet their daily survival needs. In this regard, the Western market-oriented development strategy in Afghanistan has tended to exacerbate individual and societal security by fuelling conflicts and reinforcing gendered hierarchies of power.

This is evidenced in Nangarhar where US-led counter-narcotics and counter-insurgency strategies informed development and state-building activities in the province. These policies increased violent dynamics of competition between different political factions for control over the emerging bubble economy while driving conflict within and between communities at a local level. Moreover, poor and remote farming communities suffered the most impact from this overarching strategy through the added economic burdens of meeting their household's basic needs without the security of upfront cash loans which are provided to farmers to grow opium.

Amid this conflagration of local and external hierarchies of power, women and men, creatively navigate within, and struggle against, these hierarchies of power with the intent of securing their own well-being and that of the community of which they are a part. As Axel Honneth (2014: 10) cautioned, it is important not to mistake the presence of ethical life for the actual mechanisms of change that will make life more ethical. Thus, when I cite the existence of struggles by women, but also men, against the gendered hierarchies of power which constrain and jeopardise their lives, I do so to illustrate the existing ways in which people challenge oppressive and hierarchical societal relations. These struggles should not be romanticised. Indeed, many contemporary changes that challenge traditional hierarchical customs are most likely wrought out of sheer necessity to enable people's bare survival. Nevertheless, these struggles allow a feminist HS framework to articulate an important access point for engaging in ethical change. Though the politics of making policy via such avenues could not be foreknown, they nevertheless offer a promising starting point for advancing progressive dynamics that help realise a meaningful form of security.

Conclusion

This chapter has aimed to demonstrate that conventional conceptions of security, as iterated in the International Discipline, are ill-suited to the task of understanding what the term means in the complex social world of Afghanistan. This is especially true in relation to understanding what security means from the perspective of women who, as a gender class, tend to be the most subjugated and marginalised members of society holistically. Unfortunately, it is this conventional account of security which has framed policy-making perspectives associated with the broader US-led Western Intervention in Afghanistan. The problematic result of this has been that powerful Western policy-makers within this coalition have been unable to apprehend the complex social world in which they are immersed and which is influenced by their actions.

Nevertheless, what this chapter has also aimed to show is that it is possible to build a critical account of what HS means for women and also for men. My own suggestion here is that scholars should explore the societal relationships of power which permit or deny recognition of the life desired and aspired to by a person. This insight, which has been articulated most significantly by Kimberly Hutchings and Axel Honneth, provides the impetus for me to focus on marginalised people's struggles against hierarchical societal relationships of recognition. In addition to highlighting the moral injustices themselves, people's struggles are undertaken using a language and a logic that is intelligible to society more broadly. As I will go on to show in three different provincial contexts of Afghanistan, these immanent struggles reveal possibilities for collaboration with external agents seeking to advance the cause of HS in a way which is meaningful for the human subjects themselves.

Notes

1 Noted contributors to this emerging dialogue included the following scholars: Tickner, J. Ann (1988). "Hans Morgenthau's Principles of Political Realism: A Feminist Reformulation". *Millennium: Journal of International Studies* 17 (3): 429–440. Enloe, Cynthia (2014). *Bananas, beaches and bases: Making feminist sense of international politics*. Berkeley and Los Angeles, University of California Press. Cohn, Carol (1987). "Sex and Death in the Rational World of Defense Intellectuals". *Signs* 12 (4): 687–718.
2 For instance, see Tickner, J. Ann (2002). "Feminist Perspectives on 9/11". *International Studies Perspectives*. Youngs, Gillian (2006). "Feminist International Relations in the Age of the War on Terror: Ideologies, Religions and Conflict". *International Feminist*

Journal of Politics 8: 1. Razack, Sherene (2005). "Geopolitics, Culture Clash, and Gender After September 11". *Social Justice* 32: 4. Young, Iris (2003). "The Logic of Masculinist Protection: Reflections on the Current Security State". *Signs* 29: 1. Hunt, Krista (2002). "The Strategic Co-optation of Women's Rights". *International Feminist Journal of Politics* 4: 1.

References

Anderson, Jon W. (1978). "There Are No Khans Anymore: Economic Development and Social Change in Tribal Afghanistan". *The Middle East Journal* 32 (2): 167–183.

Aradau, Claudia (2004). "Security and the Democratic Scene: Desecuritization and Emancipation". *Journal of International Relations and Development* 7 (4): 388–413.

Ashley, Richard K. (1989). "Untying the Sovereign State: A Double Reading of the Anarchy Problematique". *Millennium* 17: 227–286.

Azarbaijani-Moghaddam, Sippi (2010). A Study of Gender Equity through the National Solidarity Programme's Community Development Councils. Kabul, Danish Committee for Aif to Afghan Refugees (DACAAR).

Booth, Ken (1991). "Security and Emancipation". *Review of International Studies* 17 (04): 313–326.

Booth, Ken (1994). Security and Self: Reflections of a Fallen Realist. *Strategies in Conflict: Critical Approaches to Security Studies*. York University, Toronto.

Booth, Ken (2007). *Theory of world security*. Cambridge, Cambridge University Press.

Buzan, Barry, Ole Wæver and Jaap De Wilde (1998). *Security: a new framework for analysis*. Boulder, CO, Lynne Rienner Publishers.

Campbell, David (1992). *Writing security: United States foreign policy and the politics of identity*. Minneapolis, University of Minnesota Press.

Chandler, David (2008). "Human Security: The Dog That Didn't Bark". *Security Dialogue* 39 (4): 427–438.

Chandler, David (2013). Rethinking the subject of human security. *Globalization, Difference, and Human Security*. M. K. Pasha. Oxon, Routledge.

Christie, Ryerson (2010). "Critical Voices and Human Security: To Endure, To Engage or To Critique?" *Security Dialogue* 41 (169): 169–190.

Cohn, Carol (1987). "Sex and Death in the Rational World of Defense Intellectuals". *Signs* 12 (4): 687–718.

Constable, Pamela (2007). "A Wake-Up Call in Afghanistan". *Journal of Democracy* 18 (2): 84–98.

Cooke, Miriam (2002). "Islamic Feminism before and after September 11th". *Duke Journal of Gender Law and Policy* 9 (227): 227–235.

Dillon, Michael and Julian Reid (2001). "Global Liberal Governance: Biopolitics, Security and War". *Millennium – Journal of International Studies* 30 (1): 41–66.

Dupree, Nancy Hatch (2004). "The Family During Crisis in Afghanistan". *Journal of Comparative Family Studies* 35 (2): 311.

Enloe, Cynthia (2014). *Bananas, beaches and bases: Making feminist sense of international politics*. Berkeley and Los Angeles, University of California Press.

Hansen, Lene (1997). "A Case for Seduction? Evaluating the Poststructuralist Conceptualization of Security". *Cooperation and Conflict* 32 (4): 369–397.

Hansen, Lene (2000). "The Little Mermaid's Silent Security Dilemma and the Absence of Gender in the Copenhagen School". *Millennium – Journal of International Studies* 29 (2): 285–306.

Hobbes, Thomas (2006). *Leviathan*. London, Continuum International Publishing Group.
Hönke, Jana and Markus-Michael Müller (2012). "Governing (in) Security in a Postcolonial World: Transnational Entanglements and the Worldliness of 'Local' Practice". *Security Dialogue* 43 (5): 383–401.
Honneth, Axel (1996). *The struggle for recognition: The moral grammar of social conflicts*. Cambridge, The MIT Press.
Honneth, Axel (2014). *Freedom's right: The social foundations of democratic life*. New York, Columbia University Press.
Hoogensen, Gunhild and Svein Vigeland Rottem (2004). "Gender Identity and the Subject of Security". *Security Dialogue* 35 (2): 155–171.
Hoogensen, Gunhild and Kirsti Stuvøy (2006). "Gender, Resistance and Human Security". *Security Dialogue* 37 (2): 207–228.
Hooper, Charlotte (2012). *Manly states: Masculinities, international relations, and gender politics*. New York, Columbia University Press.
Hudson, Heidi (2005). "'Doing' Security As Though Humans Matter: A Feminist Perspective on Gender and the Politics of Human Security". *Security Dialogue* 36 (2): 155–174.
Hutchings, Kimberly (1999a). Feminism, universalism and the ethics of international politics. *Women, culture, and international relations*. Boulder, CO, Lynne Rienner Publishers: 17–37.
Hutchings, Kimberly (1999b). *International political theory: Rethinking ethics in a global era*. London, Sage.
Hutchings, Kimberly (2000). "Towards a Feminist International Ethics". *Review of International Studies* 26 (05): 111–130.
Hutchings, Kimberly (2013a). A place of greater safety? Securing judgement in international ethics. *The vulnerable subject: Beyond rationalism in international relations*. A. R. Beattie and K. Schick. Hampshire, Palgrave Macmillan.
Hutchings, Kimberly (2013b). Universalism in feminist international ethics: Gender and the difficult labour of translation. *Dialogue, politics and gender*. J. Browne. Cambridge, Cambridge University Press: 81–106.
Huysmans, Jef (1998). "Revisiting Copenhagen: or, on the Creative Development of a Security Studies Agenda in Europe". *European Journal of International Relations* 4 (4): 479–505.
Jones, Richard Wyn (1995). "'Message in a Bottle'? Theory and Praxis in Critical Security Studies". *Contemporary Security Policy* 16 (3): 299–319.
Kandiyoti, Deniz (2009). "The lures and perils of gender activism in Afghanistan". *The Anthony Hyman Memorial Lecture*. School of Oriental and Africa Studies, University of London.
Keohane, Robert O. (1988). "International Institutions: Two Approaches". *International Studies Quarterly* 32 (4): 379–396.
King, Gary and Christopher J. L. Murray (2001). "Rethinking Human Security". *Political Science Quarterly* 116 (4): 585–610.
Krause, Keith (1998). "Critical Theory and Security Studies. The Research Programme of Critical Security Studies". *Cooperation and Conflict* 33 (3): 298–333.
Krause, Keith and Michael Charles Williams (1997). *Critical security studies: Concepts and cases*. Cambridge, Cambridge University Press.
Lapid, Yosef (1989). "The Third Debate: On the Prospects of International Theory in a Post-positivist Era". *International Studies Quarterly* 33 (3): 235–254.
Marhia, Natasha (2013). "Some Humans are More Human than Others: Troubling the 'Human' in Human Security from a Critical Feminist Perspective". *Security Dialogue* 44 (1): 19–35.

McDonald, Matt (2008). "Securitization and the Construction of Security". *European Journal of International Relations* 14 (4): 563–587.
McKay, Susan (2004). Women, human security, and peace-building: A feminist analysis. *Conflict and human security: A search for new approaches of peace-building*. H. Shinoda and H.-W. Jeong, Institute for Peace Science Hiroshima University (IPSHU). 19: 152–170.
McSweeney, Bill (1996). "Identity and Security: Buzan and the Copenhagen School". *Review of International Studies* 22 (01): 81–93.
McSweeney, Bill (1999). *Security, identity and interests: a sociology of international relations*. Cambridge, Cambridge University Press.
Newman, Edward (2011). "A Human Security Peace-building Agenda". *Third World Quarterly* 32 (10): 1737–1756.
Owen, Taylor (2004). "Human Security–Conflict, Critique and Consensus: Colloquium Remarks and a Proposal for a Threshold-based Definition". *Security Dialogue* 35 (3): 373–387.
Owen, Taylor (2008). "The Uncertain Future of Human Security in the UN". *International Social Science Journal* 59 (s1): 113–127.
Paris, Roland (2001). "Human Security: Paradigm Shift or Hot Air?" *International Security* 26 (2): 87–102.
Peterson, V. Spike (1992a). *Gendered states: Feminist (re) visions of international relations theory*. Boulder, CO, Lynne Rienner.
Peterson, V. Spike (1992b). "Transgressing Boundaries: Theories of Knowledge, Gender and International Relations". *Millennium – Journal of International Studies* 21 (2): 183–206.
Pettman, Jan Jindy (1996). *Worlding women: a feminist international politics*. New York, Routledge.
Robinson, Fiona (2008). "The Importance of Care in the Theory and Practice of Human Security". *Journal of International Political Theory* 4 (2): 167–188.
Robinson, Fiona (2011). *The Ethics of Care: A Feminist Approach to Human Security*. Philadelphia, Temple University Press.
Said, Edward W. (1979). *Orientalism*. New York, Vintage Books.
Shilliam, Robbie (2013). Developmentalism, human security, indigenous rights. *Globalization, difference, and human security*. Oxon, Routledge.
Smith, Steve (1999). "The Increasing Insecurity of Security Studies: Conceptualizing Security in the Last Twenty Years". *Contemporary Security Policy* 20 (3): 72–101.
Spivak, Gayatri Chakravorty (1994). Can the subaltern speak? *Colonial discourse and post-colonial theory*. P. Williams and L. Chrisman. New York, Columbia University Press.
Steans, Jill (1998). *Gender and international relations: an introduction*. New Brunswick, Rutgers University Press.
Tapper, Nancy (1981). "Direct Exchange and Brideprice: Alternative Forms in a Complex Marriage System". *Man* 16 (3): 387–407.
Thomas, Caroline (2007). Globalization and human security. *Globalization, development and human security*. A. McGrew and N. K. Poku. Cambridge, Polity Press.
Tickner, J. Ann (1988). "Hans Morgenthau's Principles of Political Realism: A Feminist Reformulation". *Millennium: Journal of International Studies* 17 (3): 429–440.
Tickner, J. Ann (1995). Re-visioning security. *International relations theory today*. K. B. S. Smith. University Park, The Pennsylvania State University Press: 175–197.
Tickner, J. Ann (2004). "Feminist Responses to International Security Studies". *Peace Review* 16 (1): 43–48.

Truong, Thanh-Dam (2009). "Feminist knowledge and human security". *ISS Working Paper Series/General Series* 481: 1–28.

Truong, Thanh-Dam, Saskia Wieringa and Amrita Chhachhi (2006). *Engendering human security: Feminist perspectives*, London, Zed Books.

Wæver, Ole, Barry Buzan, Morten Kelstrup and Pierre Lemaitre, (eds) (1993). *Identity migration and the new security agenda in Europe*. New York, St Martin's Press.

Waltz, Kenneth N. (2010). *Theory of international politics*. Long Grove, IL, Waveland Press.

Weber, Heloise (2013). Global politics of human security. *Globalization, difference, and human security*. M. K. Pasha. Oxon, Routledge: 27.

Weber, Martin (2013). The fantastic world of human security through global governance. *Globalization, difference, and human security*. M. K. Pasha. Oxon, Routledge: 129.

Wibben, Annick T. R. (2010). *Feminist security studies: A narrative approach*, Oxon, Routledge.

Wilkinson, Claire (2007). "The Copenhagen School on Tour in Kyrgyzstan: Is Securitization Theory Useable Outside Europe?" *Security Dialogue* 38 (1): 5–25.

3 Community, tradition and gender in Afghanistan

To outline the potential for positively advancing a feminist ethical vision of human security in contemporary Afghanistan, it is first necessary to ground the country's historically evolving gender identities and gender relations. This reconstructive work is necessary to satisfy the phenomenological and genealogical tasks required of ethical practitioners when attempting to advance moral critique and avenues for practical change. As previously mentioned by Hutchings (2000: 122), phenomenology requires practitioners to understand that the "nature and conditions of ethical judgement are inseparable from the moral forms of life within which they are embedded". This means that, for moral judgements to carry authority, they must be intelligible to all the different actors engaging in a debate. At the same time, practitioners must undertake a genealogical investigation of the way in which certain moral judgements come to be understood as embodying ethical necessity. On this matter, feminist ethicists are particularly focused on exploring the role that gender plays in constructing the hierarchies of power which discipline human subjects (Hutchings, 2000: 122).

In this and the following chapter of the book, I will attempt to fulfil these two essential tasks by reconstructing the evolution of gender identities and gender relations in Afghanistan. In particular, I seek to highlight women's, and men's, historical efforts to navigate and resist gendered hierarchies of power in Afghanistan. This will provide insight into the ways in which moral critique could be appropriately mounted in relation to advancing more progressive gender relations in Afghanistan's contemporary setting of an ongoing intervention by the international community. In this first contextual chapter (Chapter 3), I will illustrate the richness and complexity of Afghan society by providing a synoptic overview of the way in which gender operated in "traditional" social contexts prior to major societal upheaval in 1979. Meanwhile, the ensuing contextual chapter (Chapter 4) will provide a diachronic overview to show how gender relations in people's social contexts have changed over time. I will focus on the impact that successive periods of state-building and violent conflict have had on the lives and social relations of women and men and their communities over time in Afghanistan.

Owing to the extremely heterogeneous nature of society in Afghanistan, providing such a phenomenological and genealogical reconstruction of gender identity and gender politics is not a straight-forward proposition. Afghanistan is comprised of several large, ethno-linguistic groupings, such as the Hazaras, Tajiks, Uzbeks and Pashtuns, as well as several other distinctive minority groups such as the Aimaq, Nuristani, Baloch, Hindus and Sikhs. Although Afghan society could be understood solely with reference to these ethno-linguistic groups, they do not necessarily form the only, or most cogent, form of identification for women and men in their communities. As Richard Tapper argues, all too often objectivist practitioners misconstrue social identities like "Kurd" or "Kuchi" as genetically fixed entities rather than the result of ongoing political and cultural processes. On this point Tapper (2008: 101) wryly observes:

> Unfortunately, the expectation of some academics and administrators that every human being should have a single, fixed, unchanging, objectively determinable ethnic identity will always be frustrated by those cussed creatures human beings themselves.

In order to redress this conceptual myopia, Tapper suggests that researchers should understand identities, whether ethnic, linguistic, sectarian or other, as "flexible, negotiable, multiple and always situational". Thus, he notes, with reference to Jenkins (Jenkins, 1997: 47), that, while there are "primary identities" to which people may lay claim, these identities should not be considered "primordial".

In order to engage in this task of reconstructing people's primary identities, I follow Tapper's suggestion (Tapper, 2008: 102–104) to explore the power and meaning which is bound up in processes of naming; specifically, the processes by which individuals and communities ascribe names for themselves (autonyms) and for others (exonyms). This exploration provides an initial disaggregation of Afghanistan's broader "ethnic" categories like Pashtun, Tajik, Uzbek and Hazara by revealing the cultural and political processes underpinning such labels. Following on from this initial disaggregation, I will add specificity to this account of subjects' identities by referencing the term "*qawm*".[1] This term, which anthropologists have long used in their discussions of Afghanistan, denotes the "primary" social solidarity groups with which people identify themselves. The benefit of using *qawm* is that this word helps to account for Afghanistan's social polysemy through an acknowledgement of the multiple shifting forms of community with which a subject may self-identify.

To add to this discussion of social identity, I will next seek to reconstruct gender roles and gender relations in Afghanistan's different ethno-linguistic communities. I will do this by exploring the way in which gender relations operated among *qawm*s at the local level of Afghanistan in two broadly different societal modes: sedentary and nomadic *qawm* communities. Here, I will be interested in grounding the following details: the gendered identities and gendered roles of women and men within the household and the community; the political economy between different households in a *qawm*; and the ways in which women were able to variously manipulate or resist gendered hierarchies of power within their households and communities. To finalise this reconstruction of identity and gender relations among different subjects, I will explore the similarities and differences between broader "*qawm*" identities based on affiliation to the country's larger ethno-linguistic groups with regard to the Pashtun, Tajik, Hazara, and so forth.

The politics of identity in Afghanistan

A useful starting point for differentiating the groups within Afghanistan is to take the commonly accepted ethno-linguistic groupings and disambiguate their meaning through historical reference to autonyms and exonyms (Tapper, 2008: 99). A large amount of power is tied up in processes of naming oneself and naming others which, in the context of Afghanistan, provides a good understanding of its complicated and conflicted history. These political practices of naming were all explicitly emphasised by women and men from the three different expatriate communities with whom I organised my Focus Groups Discussions (FGD) in Delhi. It is instructive to note that the word "Afghan" is Persian and translates literally as "Pashtun" (while "Afghanistan" translates as "the land of the Pashtuns") (Tapper, 2008: 103). In the country's pre-national history, these terms were used by Persian-speaking non-Pashtun groups to describe a particular people who inhabited a particular space to the south of the Hindu Kush. At the very beginning of the mixed conversation in the Tajik FGD, three of the participants offered these observations:

FATIMAH: I've heard many times myself, Pashtuns say, "it is Afghanistan, it means house of Afghans" so Afghanistan belong to Afghans only. It is not Tajikistan, neither Uzbekistan. They are always saying this, that it is Afghans' land, and the leadership of Afghanistan belong to Afghans only, and may remain so.

OMID: Sometimes the Pashtuns say that you Tajik people should live in Tajikistan, it (Afghanistan) the land of Pashtuns and belongs to the Pashtuns.

GHADIR: Afghanistan's earlier name was Khurasan but the country was named "Afghanistan" during Ahamad Shah Kingdom in 1747. So, it is a fake name imposed on this country.

In a similar vein, the work of anthropologists like Nancy Lindisfarne (then Tapper) (1991: 39) and Richard Tapper (1984: 239), showed that the Durrani Pashtuns (one of two supra tribal confederations of the Pashtuns), who were at the centre of the state-building process in Afghanistan, claimed "Afghan" as an autonym for themselves and denied it for non-Durrani Pashtuns and all non-Pashtun peoples. In the context of northern Afghanistan, these anthropologists argued that, for this group, all non-Durrani Pashtuns and Sunni Persian speakers, for example, Ghilzai (another broad Pashtun tribal confederation), Tajiks and Aimaq, were dubbed as *Farsiwan*; interestingly, non-Pashtuns, including Sunni Persian speakers (Tajiks, Aymaks, Arabs, etc.) as well as Uzbeks and other Sunni Turkic-speakers, but not the Shia Hazara, could be given the broad designation of "Uzbek". However, it was the *Farsiwan* (Persian speaker) whom the Durrani considered the greatest threat to their social purity despite the ostensible similarities between the two groups including shared religion, ethnicity and language. The exonym of "*Farsiwan*" actually implied these non-Durrani Pashtuns probably spoke Persian inside their homes and were, as such, Pashtun imposters (Tapper, 1991: 39).

Meanwhile, the many different nomadic Pashtun tribes were most likely to refer to themselves by reference to their sub-tribal *qawm*s or the term *maldar*, a Persian word for herd-owner (Tapper, 2008: 98); these nomads' autonyms would undoubtedly have been shared by many of the more settled Pashtun tribes, including settled pastoralists. However, what was most apparent in the east of Afghanistan was the urbanised Afghans' usage of the term Kuchi, a Persian word for those who travel, as an exonym to label nomadic Pashtun groups. As Tapper (2008: 103) suggests, its usage in this way was pejorative in much the same way that the word "Gypsy" has been used in Europe as an exonym for people who call themselves Roma. In the last few decades, the term "Kuchi" has gained considerable traction as an exonym for Pashtun nomadic groups across Afghanistan, though it typically has not resonated with these people themselves. Since the fall of the Taliban, this word has come to have powerful political value, as is expressed in the reservation of seats for the "Kuchi" in parliament; however, this has not necessarily produced positive outcomes for marginalised "Kuchi" themselves (Samuel Hall, 2010: 1–44).

This complexity in naming oneself and naming others is also present in the use of autonyms and exonyms by non-Pashtun groups. For instance, though the majority of people in Afghanistan speak Persian, the Pashtun term *Farsiwan*, which literally translates as Persian speaker, is acknowledged by very few groups as an autonym and it is used by different groups in entirely different ways. As was noted for Pashtuns, and Durrani Pashtuns, this term was highly pejorative even though its usage as an exonym had very little consistency, that is Pashtuns could be labelled *Farsiwan* as could Sunni Persian speakers of other groups. In a similar sweeping move, self-designated "Uzbeks" used the term *Farsiwan* as a label for virtually everybody else in Afghanistan including Tajiks, Aymaqs, Hazaras and Pashtuns (Tapper, 2008). Meanwhile, the translation of the word "Tajik", which stemmed from Ancient Parsi (Persian), essentially meant a stranger.[2] This word for stranger was incorporated by Turkic speakers to refer to Persian speakers as "Tajiks" or "non-Turks". "Tajiks" themselves were more likely to frame their identity in terms of their location or kinship group. This is expressed among the various sub-groups of the "Aimaq" (Wily, 2004: 7), who are Persian-speaking Sunni Muslims, tribally organised and said to be descended from Turkic tribes and whose lifestyles revolve around a semi-nomadic existence in the west of Afghanistan; the Aimaq are also known by the exonym as "Sunni Hazaras" (Wily, 2004: 7). However, since the rise of the Panjshiri Tajik nationalist movement under the leadership of Ahmed Shah Massoud during the Mujahedeen war, the term "Tajik" has increasingly been used by some Sunni Persian-speakers as an autonym. Finally, it is important to unpack the term Hazara in this milieu. Hazara is a Persian term, literally translating to a "thousand", which is used by Hazara people themselves as an autonym. This term is also used as an exonym by other groups to describe Hazaras but its usage in this way often carries the weight of a great amount of historical prejudice, particularly in the case of Pashtuns – but also for other groups. This prejudice, in the case of Pashtuns, is perhaps demonstrated most notably by Hafizullah Emadi (1997: 371) quoting various derogatory terms that could be used in public to insult Hazaras:

> They were subjected to all kinds of public humiliation and taunted by derogatory terms such as *Hazara-e-mushkur* (mice-eating Hazaras), *bini puchuq* (flat-nose*)*, *khar-e-barkash* (load-carrying donkey), etc.

This initial disambiguation of broad identity groups reveals that practices of identifying oneself and others with a particular community are always ambiguous and imbued with politics. In the same vein, when drilling down to the local context, what becomes apparent is the extent to which the same ambiguity and power infuse communal relations of recognition. One way to attempt to access such social complexity in people's core relationships of belonging at a local level is through the idea of *qawm*. While the idea of *qawm* is often used to denote concrete and autochthonous groupings, a better comprehension of *qawm* sees it as a flexible and shifting imagination by subjects of their social solidarity groupings.[3] These can be based on kinship, religious beliefs, socio-economic classes, professional ties, for example, around an *arbab* (village interlocutor with the state) or a *mirab* (village water distributor) as well as a particular geographic place like a valley (Roy, 1990: 25–26). Moreover, depending on the conversation they are having, subjects can variously cite belonging to several different types of *qawm*, as Alessandro Monsutti (2009: 10) notes in the Hazara region of Jaghuri:

> In Jaghuri, if asked about his *qawm*, a man can answer without ambiguity by naming his lineage, his village, his district of origin or by declaring himself Hazara. Such polysemy is not due to conceptual vagueness but expresses the fact that the relevant identity depends on the context and the supposed knowledge that people facing each other attribute to one another.

In addition to addressing the flexible and inter-subjective basis of people's communal identity claims, *qawm* also allows insight into the politics and power wrapped up in community membership in local every day contexts. For instance, in Afghanistan, while a person may reside in a particular village, the question of whether or not they belong to the village's community is often related to their household's relative status and wealth – particularly in relation to possession of land and other resources. Shawna Wakefield (2004: 7–9) of the AREU noted this in the village of Obtoo, Bamyan province, where there were marked differences among participants' responses in describing their local community even though they commented on the fact that they were all Hazaras. These differences related to whether participants were landed, landless or "Sayyeds".[4] Thus, landless men felt they were not part of the community or community decision-making and one landed man, who had lived in the village for five years, said that he was not part of the community because he was a recent arrival. "Sayyeds" were considered a different group but were held in positive reverence due to their spiritual lineage. Landed community leaders, perhaps to extract aid from the Western foreigners, argued that everyone living in Obtoo was part of the community (Wakefield, 2004: 7–8). Similarly, in the Durrani Pashtun context of Kandahar, Nancy Lindisfarne, then Tapper (1981: 401), noted that particularly destitute and impoverished households could lose membership in their *qawm*s as a result of having lost their wealth and household honour. However, she contrasted this with the *qawm* dynamics of the Maduzai sub-tribe of the Durrani Pashtuns in the ethnically mixed region of Sar-e-Pul in Afghan Turkestan, where this community was more likely to act to guarantee the basic security of its weakest members in order to retain the strength of their group against the many other groups in the region (Tapper, 1981: 401).

Gender dynamics in Afghanistan

Life in Afghanistan, as everywhere else in the world, is gendered. Ideas of masculinity and femininity arising from belief systems such as custom and religion influence how gender identities are construed by society. The fact that life is gendered does not automatically mean that all gender relations between women and men are typified by patriarchal hierarchy. This point has been highlighted consistently by anthropologists and sociologists who have explored gender relations within different communities across Afghanistan.[5] What can be surmised from their research is that there are two broad systems of gendered knowledge which inform people's understanding of ideal social relations and their comportment as honourable members of their communities.

The first system of meaning derives from the Islamic belief systems adhered to by most of Afghanistan's different communities. This belief system presents honour in a universal sense as the struggle which all human beings must undertake in order to emulate the reason and justice found in the divine teachings of the *Qur'an* and the traditions of the Prophet (*hadith*) (Anderson, 1985: 205). As different authors have shown, the religious themes of Islam permeated the local cultures of Afghanistan as is apparent in the adoption of a variety of Arabic and Islamic terms. *'Aql* (reason) and *Naf* (desire) are two such terms which gave people their sense of selfhood in relation to the wider communities into which they were born (Anderson, 1985: 205). Taken together, these terms were understood as comprising a dialectical struggle by all people to exercise reason over their passions in striving to lead honourable lives.

The adoption of these terms into everyday language was itself gendered in its tendency to treat *'Aql*/reason as a masculine characteristic and *Naf*/desire as a feminine characteristic; however, the explicitness of hierarchy within this gendered binary was tempered by the broader acknowledgement of the universal possession of both these qualities by women and men (Anderson, 1985: 205). Both women and men had a duty to struggle to exercise reason and maintain honourable conduct in order to control their passions in the emotionally charged context of people's lives as social beings in the mortal world. For instance, in communities across Afghanistan, *'aql* (sensibility) and *nafsh* (passion) are recognised as capacities present in all humans and they inflect most social relationships, including marriage and interpersonal relations. As Jon Anderson (1985: 205) notes, among Pashtuns, *joma'a* (society), which specifically means "the gathering", represents both the context and the goal of human beings' ongoing process of learning to develop "ordered capacities and orderly presence". He expands on the implications of these qualities among different women and men in their communities, noting:

> Persons differ in these respects in many ways and at different times, ideally "growing" in 'aql until they present a calm repose of elderly dignity disengaged from the mundane and momentary; so the mature have more, or more developed 'aql than the immature or unsocialised, the religious more than the irreligious, men generally more than women, each by virtue of their wider engagement in society, but also the older more than the younger irrespective of gender, in each case because of opportunity to develop a social capacity inherent to all humans.

This conception of human reason and honourable conduct is obviously gendered in its association of the masculine with the public sphere. Nevertheless, an egalitarian ethic also pervades this system of knowledge through its emphasis on the universal potential for all human beings to develop into reasoning and ethical actors. While Anderson writes here specifically about Pashtun communities, the fundamental premises of Islamic belief were present in Afghanistan's many different Islamic communities including the Shia Ismaili and Shia Imami Hazaras as well as the Sunni Hanafi Uzbeks and Tajiks.

Alongside Islamic thought, there was a second customary belief system centred upon masculine honour codes according to which men were positioned as the protectors of a community's honour which was seen as residing in women's bodies (Tapper, 1991: 106–108). In this way, customary belief systems presented a more hierarchical depiction of gender roles and gender relations. One of the most well-known and enduring examples of such honour codes is *Pashtunwali* which literally translates to the way of the Pashtuns. Its fundamental principles relate to ensuring a household's ability to control its resources and protect its honourable name through control of its womenfolk (Boesen, 1983: 107). In contrast to the universal, religiously-inspired sense of honour, "honourable life", according to custom, related to the esteem with which one was perceived by one's peers in the course of one's worldly life (Tapper, 1991: 15). This concept of honourable life, and its everyday practice, was often linked to the suppression of women's autonomy, as could be seen in the reduction of their bodies to commercial objects of exchange by men in the transaction of marriage. What is important to note is that, although men possessed power in their households over women and also had greater opportunity and influence in the community at large, in many ways men's lives were constrained just as much as women's by this honour code.

There were often times when men, especially those whose lives were bound into the most masculinised honour systems like those of the Pashtuns, expressed a clear dissatisfaction and rejection of the forces which constrained their own actions even though they were unable to change this status quo (Tapper, 1991: 215–216; Caron, 2011: 180–181). For instance, men, like women, had no say in their marriage and, while they possessed the ability to marry a second time for "love", this option was usually the preserve of rich and powerful men who could afford to pay the high costs of bride-prices (Tapper, 1991: 121). Moreover, and of more fundamental importance, this gendered notion of honour delineated a particular type of conduct to which men must always aspire. Honourable conduct here related men's duty to ensure the control of their women's honour. Women were very well aware of what honour meant for men and the household name; moreover, they were equally well aware that the disjuncture between the ways in which honour was variously acted out for the consideration of the wider community, and the messier practices of women and men in reality, often involved contravention of the supposedly incontrovertible. This was demonstrated in women's practices of engaging in, or just threatening to engage in, extra-marital affairs (Olesen, 1982: 122–123; Tapper, 1991: 232–233).

As was stated earlier, despite the masculinist emphases of such honour codes, the mere presence of customary senses of honour, observed by Afghanistan's many different communities, did not necessitate that a community's gender relations were always characterised by patriarchy. On this matter, it is instructive to note that, although social groups differ in Afghanistan according to ethnicity, language, religion and culture, it is possible to disaggregate gender relations according to two different *qawm* settings. The first type of *qawm* is typified by sedentary farming and settled forms of pastoralism and is apparent in every major, ethno-linguistic group in Afghanistan. Within this grouping, the formation of *qawm* communities relies upon a hierarchically gendered masculine honour code which valorises the masculine subject as a producer and defender of community, while positioning the feminine subject as a reproducer of both the household and the community and whose body signifies that which must be protected (Boesen, 1983: 112–113; Shalinsky, 1989a: 118; Tapper, 1991: 15–16). What this means in an ideal community is that *qawm*s are composed of nuclear and extended-family households in which decision-making power regarding a household's labour is vested in the patriarch over his wives and children. In contrast, the second type of *qawm* is configured around a pastorally-based mode of production, which relates exclusively to the many different nomadic Pashtun tribes who are increasingly labelled with the imprecise term "Kuchi", as well as the nomadic *qawm*s of the "Aymaqs" (Tapper, 2008: 97, 103). Though *qawm*s involving nomadic forms of household production are typified by a similarly gendered logic of patriarchy in which men hold ultimate responsibility for defence of the household and the community, what is different to sedentary communities is the recognition of the mutual importance of women and men in securing a household and a community's prosperity (Tavakolian, 1984: 438–440). Thus, in nuclear and extended families in these *qawm*s, decision-making authority, in both the household and in the community, is democratically vested in men and women rather than a single patriarchal figure (Tavakolian, 1984: 440–441).

Gender dynamics among the Pashtuns, Tajiks and Hazaras

Thus far I have attempted to provide insight into the politics of identity in Afghanistan as well as a broad insight into the way in which two gendered belief systems influence gender relations. In what follows, I will provide a more detailed view of the way these belief systems influence the gender relations and gender politics of three major ethno-linguistic groupings in Afghanistan, specifically the Pashtuns, Tajiks and the Hazaras. This overview aims to provide a "bird's eye" coverage of the different social contexts and gender relations of these communities across Afghanistan. By undertaking this reconstructive act, I am able to outline the antecedents of contemporary gender dynamics of power in Afghanistan within, and between, different communities. I am also going to show some of the ways in which women, the most oppressed subjects of gendered hierarchies of power, were able to variously navigate, subvert or challenge such societal structures. These struggles are important because they reveal an already existing challenge to inequitable social relations. In this way, it offers a plausible example of the way in which the phenomenological and genealogical requirements of an ethical debate could be satisfied. To undertake this reconstructive exercise, I draw on an extensive array of anthropological and historical sources as well as focus group discussions (FGDs) which I conducted with women and men from these groupings.

The Pashtuns

The segmentary Pashtun tribes, who have historically represented about half of Afghanistan's population, are broadly structured into two supra-tribal confederations known as the Durrani and the Ghilzai (Rubin, 2002: 26). Of these two, the Durrani have historically formed a demographic majority in Afghanistan (primarily in the south and east) while the Ghilzai, though still a significant minority with large tribal populations in the east of the country and in the mountainous borderlands of Pakistan, were far more prevalent in the tribal areas of Pakistan (Rubin, 2002: 26). Originally, the vast majority of Pashtun tribes were nomadic; however, over time, some of these tribes, under the direction of central ruling authorities, spread to the north and west of the country where they have pursued more sedentary agricultural and pastoral lifestyles in previously non-Pashtun parts of the country. Though nomadism persisted throughout the twentieth century, the number of permanent nomadic communities has shrunk in Afghanistan and Pakistan.

As Vartan Gregorian (1969: 30) has shown, what becomes apparent from an historical overview of the Pashtuns is that the "state" of Afghanistan was created by elite Durrani Pashtun rulers who came from the two sub-tribes of the Barakazai and Popalzai and, more specifically, the Muhammadzai and Sadozai clans of these respective sub-tribes. With respect to these two clans, he explained that, with only brief interruptions, they occupied the throne of Afghanistan for the preceding two centuries (Gregorian, 1969: 30). These Durrani clans' ascent to power over both their Ghilzai competitors and other communities was no doubt assisted by their geographical location on, and control over, the vast tracts of land suited to agricultural and pastoral activities which stretched from Kandahar to Herat (Gregorian, 1969: 30). Though the state that began to emerge over time in Afghanistan was organised most obviously for the benefit of these two clans and their kinsfolk, by prevailing over opposing tribes and increasing their control over the state they inevitably benefitted all Durrani and Ghilzai Pashtuns, whose tribes would be enlisted in support of furthering the royal Durrani power-holders. This involved their participation in major campaigns such as the colonisation of the traditionally Turkic regions of Afghanistan's north and the Persian regions of the west and their participation in military campaigns against the Hazara (Lee, 1996: 477). What should be noted is that this rise to power by certain Durrani clans, especially during Abdur Rahman Kahn's establishment of complete rule over Afghanistan (1880–1901), was accompanied by the catastrophic violence of a war comparable to the contemporary revolutionary and civil wars in Afghanistan (Lee, 1996: 600–601).

When examining gendered dynamics in Pashtun society, it is worth restating that they varied a great deal depending on whether the group was settled or nomadic. In the case of the former, communities were highly stratified and production and reproduction was strictly segregated into specific gender roles in which the patriarch had absolute control over a household's resources and his wards, that is women and children (Tavakolian, 1984: 434). Although women's labour was vital to a household's productive economy, as well as its reproduction, women had little independence due to the masculinised community and household. For settled communities, much of this stratification was due to the overriding importance of a highly masculinised honour code in which the ideal attainment of the honourable life, which is highlighted by the tenets of *Pashtunwali*, related to a household's ability to increase its standing relative to others, through the ability of its patriarch to control its resources, including its women, to reproduce the household unit (Kakar, 2003). Gaining honour in this sense was often directly related to a male head's ability to acquire resources and power, to make bride price payments and to ensure the birth of sons who would provide labour and defence against others (Tapper, 1981: 401).

In a Focus Group Discussion (FGD) which I organised in New Delhi, July 2011, three Pashtun women discussed a series of questions I had posed. These women shared the experience of having grown up in Afghanistan during the

Soviet and Mujahedeen war of the 1980s – a time of conflict and displacement. Though they were from relatively wealthy families, they all came from more stratified, rural farming communities. Farishta and Kashmala were originally from the eastern provinces of Kapisa and Laghman, which abutted Kabul Province. Meanwhile, Pashmina originally came from the northern province of Kunduz. In their FGD, these women all had strong memories of the way in which life and gender relations were characterised within their communities during their grandparents' lives. In this recollection, they highlighted the subjugation of women within a masculinist customary system of honour. They noted that women were treated as the wards of the household patriarch and had little autonomy or agency over their choices in life such as in education and marriage. Kashmala, originally from Laghman, had herself been married at a young age and had five daughters and one son. She remarked that:

> In the past, in the rural areas, when our grandfathers were getting married, women had no role in their marriage. They did not have any rights.

Farishta, who was from Kapisa province, to the north-west of Laghman, agreed with this sentiment saying:

> In the period of our grandparents, when girls were getting married they were too young and they didn't even know about what responsibilities they have as a daughter-in-law in their new homes. And when a girl was married till the last day of her life, nobody, including her mother and father, could know about the problems that she had with ... any member of her father in-law's family.

More broadly, these three women observed that different households within a village or community were engaged in competition with each other in order to gain honour. In their descriptions of these gender relations and the context of a competitive masculinised society, they reaffirmed the work of noted anthropologists of the 1960s and 1970s. This was especially apparent in relation to the question of the honour accorded to the rich and landed families who could pay large bride prices for daughters.

In contrast, nomadic Pashtun communities were characterised by a far greater egalitarianism between women and men. Even though these groups shared their settled tribespeople's religious and customary forms of belief, they did not adopt their rigid formulation of a gender hierarchy of men over women. To a large extent, this egalitarianism was most likely driven by the communal and interdependent nature of life for nomadic groups. Unlike in more settled Pashtun communities, women were vital to the productive economy of a household, as well as its reproduction. In addition to the reproductive work which women did vis-à-vis raising children, cooking, fetching water and maintaining a household, they were also responsible for generating productive wealth from a household's herd (Tavakolian, 1984: 434). Although it was men's responsibility to drive the herd and, when the time came, go to the village bazaars to sell livestock products for cash or goods, it was the women's work which determined the quantity and quality of these tradable commodities. This was particularly evident in the case of a household's dairy production, where the amount and quality of saleable surplus products was created more by women's labour than the size of the herd since the women organised the milking, cheese-making and tending to animals (Tavakolian, 1984: 434). This continuing legacy of women's importance in nomadic Pashtun tribes was observed in 1992 by sociologists who conducted fieldwork with these tribes around Quetta in Pakistan (Davis et al. 1995). From their research, they noted that women were regarded as unparalleled managers of the health of a family's herd as well as of its productivity – a point readily attested to by their menfolk (Davis et al. 1995: 490).

Moreover, in contradistinction to their settled counterparts, cross-cutting networks of both women's and men's patrilineal kinship groups were vital for a household's survival, and thus rivalries between households, based exclusively around men's patrilineal kinfolk and control of resources, did not materialise. At the same time, differences between gender roles within the family and within the wider community of both settled and nomadic Pashtuns are evidenced in many ways. Perhaps most importantly, it should be noted that, for nomadic Pashtun communities, the birth of girls as well as boys was treated with equal joy, owing to the vital importance of both women's and men's labour in fulfilling a household's productive potential. In contrast, among settled Pashtun communities, the birth of a son was met with celebration while the birth of a girl was treated with silence, because only men could increase a household's productive wealth and since girls were destined to become the property of another household (Boesen, 1983: 113–115). On the other hand, following marriage in nomadic communities, women still remained connected to their patrilineal families and, of particular importance, their family's resources. Thus, even though women were not formally given shares of their family's inheritance, as per Islamic law, their brothers were socially-obligated to provide them with resources equivalent to their shares later in life, which would include the bride-price that a groom's family originally paid to his wife's family. These resources would be under the control of the woman herself (Tavakolian, 1984: 446).

Over the course of the twentieth century, what became apparent was that, as nomadic communities increasingly adopted settled farming lifestyles, their gender relations became more hierarchical. Nevertheless, the formation and maintenance of these hierarchical gender relations based on masculine honour did not go unchallenged by the women who were most affected by them. As different anthropologists observed at the time, women were able to variously navigate, subvert or challenge these gendered formulations of power. When I organised an FGD, this was observed in a variety of ways by the Pashtun women who took part. In their recollection of women's positions within their families and communities, the respondents reiterated a longstanding criticism of the privilege and power conferred on men over women by this masculinist system. One of the most usual means with which women were able to gather and collectively articulate resistance was with *Landays* – a famous form of Pashtun poetry. For instance, Farishta noted that her grandmother used a *Landay* for describing the pain and difficulties she had in her life. Meanwhile, Kashmala recalled, with some sadness, a *Landay* her mother hummed:

> You'll be regretful at the moment
> When you see my body being put in the grave
> Whenever I remember this *Landay*, then I feel like crying and I really feel sad when I remember how hard life was for my mother, grandma and other women in those times.

Landays were also used by women to subvert and challenge hierarchical gender structures in familial and communal life (Tapper, 1991: 21–23, 208). For instance, consider the following *Landay* observed by Boesen (1983: 120):

> I love! I love! I do not hide it. I do not deny it.
> Even if they cut out my beauty-spots with their sharp Daggers.
> Come and sit beside me, my beloved!
> If shyness prevents you from taking me in your arms,
> I shall take you in mine.
> Just place your hand on my hand
> For long I shall think of how we placed our hands on each other.
> My beloved! Come and sit beside me for a moment.
> Life is like the dusk of a winter's evening.
> It passes so quickly.
> My loved fled from the battle.
> Now I regret the kiss I gave him yesterday.
> My Beloved! Jump into my bed, don't be afraid!
> If it breaks, the Little Awful One will repair it!

In addition to articulating their own desires and visions in imaginative verse, these forms of expression concerning the pursuit of happiness through romantic or illicit love could be acted upon by women themselves (Olesen, 1982: 122–123). These actions reflected women's intimate understanding of the masculine honour system's operation which bound men's lives to upholding idealised masculine qualities in the same way it forced women into following subservient positions within the household. Women could use this understanding to navigate and subvert the gendered hierarchies of power which disciplined their lives. However, what is perhaps most important to highlight regarding *Landays*, as well as *matluna* (spoken proverbs), is that women used these forms of discourse to reject the premises of the hierarchies which disciplined their lives. Though they might outwardly appear to be adopting a certain form of appropriate womanhood, when alone, women nevertheless spoke with each other about their visions of themselves and society which fundamentally rejected masculinised control of their lives. While this protest never amounted to an overt challenge of patriarchy, it nevertheless remained a persistent expression for women's feelings of anger and unrealised expectations about their place in society.

The Tajiks

The ancestors of those who have become known as "Tajiks" in Afghanistan were most likely some of the oldest settled inhabitants of the region. Their predecessors date back 3000 years to the rule of the Achaemenid Empire (Gregorian, 1969: 13). The blanket term of "Tajik", though, does little to describe the differentiated character of these nontribal Persian-speaking groups in Afghanistan. As members of the Tajik Focus Group Discussion (FGD) helpfully pointed out to me the term "Tajik" is something of a misnomer and can't in any way be taken to refer to a primary group identity. Ghadir, a middle-aged man from Badakhshan, who was a poet and writer, helpfully unpacked the etymology of this term:

> Basically, according to ancient Persian and in "Ashkani Pahlawi" (language from the middle Persian Period) Tajik was used to describe a stranger. It's the same as the Arabs referring to a non-Arab as Ajam. Similarly, Persians were calling the Arabs Tazi (Non-Persian), hereby, in this context Tajik means "Stranger".
>
> Meanwhile the word Tajik has been imported from Ancient Parsi into the Turkic Language, and the Turks were using the word 'Tajik' with the same meaning as Stranger, and Turks were using Tajik for Persians (Non Turkic Speakers).
>
> Turks, Arabs and Tajiks were always living close to each other. They have had close relations and lots of wars and struggles through their past history. Hereby, Tajik was an identity. It means to be neither Arab nor Turk. Nonetheless, after the establishment of Safawi Iran the term (Tajik) has been limited to the Persian Speakers out of Iran territory.

Similarly, the Persian-speaking inhabitants of Afghanistan, who were termed "Tajiks", did not form an overarching solidarity group and were, instead, more likely to self-identify themselves by their extended kinship groups as well as by their geographic location (Dorronsoro, 2013: 12–13). For the most part, these communities are practitioners of Sunni Hanafi Islam, but the self-designated Wakhi, variously known as "Mountain Tajiks" or "Pamir Tajiks", from the Wakhan corridor of Badakshan Province, are associated with Shia Ismaili Islam (Shahrani, 1984: 145). Consequently, when trying to pin down idealised traditional lifestyles of different Tajik communities, claims about these people will always be prefaced by the need for specificity. In my own case, the way in which I will endeavour to achieve this sensitivity to understanding those falling within the identity of "Tajik" is by explicating the dynamics of a few different local contexts such as the north-eastern valleys of Parwan, Panjshir and Andarab, and Afghan Turkestan.

In the first instance, Tajiks in the north-eastern mountains and valleys of the Hindu Kush in Afghanistan, which includes the regions surrounding Kabul such as Parwan, Andarab, Panjshir, Kapisa and Baghlan, are descended from the original Persian-speaking inhabitants who settled in Afghanistan in the sixth century BC (Gregorian, 1969: 13). Though these particular groups of Tajiks have never held an overarching political affiliation, they have shared ways of life across local communities; livelihoods centred on pastoralism and agriculture and beliefs based around Islam and traditional customs. In addition, the Tajiks of north-eastern Afghanistan have never been tribally organised, in the same sense as the local and supra-tribal solidarities of the Pashtuns, although many of their traditional ways of life share similarities with the Pashtuns. For instance, in local *qawm* groups, families' livelihoods took on a competitive hue in their quest for worldly honour as defined by the control of a household's resources and the reproduction of its male lineage (Uberoi, 1964). Though these Tajiks identified themselves thoroughly with the Hanafi School of Islam, many of their practices, as is also true for the Pashtuns, deviated from, or clashed outright with, the tenets of Islam. This is evidenced by the Tajiks' engagement in the practice of bride price marriages, forbidden by Islam, as well as the avoidance of Islamic inheritance laws for women, and a non-compliance with the spirit of Islam which supported women's equality with men before the eyes of God (Uberoi, 1964).

In contradistinction, Tajik communities, living endogamously in the north of the country in what is called Afghan Turkestan, as observed by Olesen (1982) in Tashqurghan, or mixed with Uzbeks in Fãrghanachi communities as observed by Shalinsky (1989b: 139), are often far more influenced by the spirit and tenets of Hanafi Islam. For instance, in the province of Tashqurghan, while bride-price payments represented a norm in society, women could and did inherit and could act upon their rightful shares (Shalinsky, 1989b: 135). Meanwhile, as Shalinksy (1989b: 134) argued with respect to the Fãrghanachi, which is a term used to describe the Uzbeks and Tajiks who fled to northern Afghanistan in the 1930s because of Soviet persecution, idealised ways of being adhered closely to the letter of the law of Islam, especially on the matter of women's rights. Thus, women had to consent to their marriages, had the option to divorce and were entitled to their share of an inheritance. Shalinksy argues that the reason for these more progressive ways between women and men in this community is because of their socio-cultural position in Afghanistan as landless traders and merchants whose legitimacy as an identity group derives from this adherence to the letter of Islamic law in contrast with other groups in Afghanistan (Shalinsky, 1989b: 134–135).

To some extent, these differences entailed within the moniker "Tajik" were expressed in the Delhi FGD with women and men from this broad identity group. Three women and two men were from Kabul but two men were from the divergent cultural contexts of Sarepul and Badakhshan provinces. All of the participants in this group were articulate and thoughtful in their responses when speaking about the roles of sex, gender and society over the course of

Afghanistan's history. Though these participants denied a communal association between people based on the term "Tajik", they all viewed their Persian history with pride. As many repeatedly mentioned in response to my questions, Tajiks have historically been associated with greater levels of urbanisation and education than other ethno-linguistic groups in Afghanistan. This vision of a linear scale of modernisation characterised the way they contrasted social differences, including gender relations, among urbanised, educated Tajiks with other ethno-linguistic communities in rural settings. One middle-aged man called Massoud, originally from Sarepul, captured this shared sentiment in a response to a question as to how life differed for Tajik families living in cities and the countryside prior to 1978:

> The gaps between the city inhabitants and the countryside created a wall of pessimism between villagers and cities inhabitants, who were benefitting from much better facilities. Undoubtedly, women's lives in the cities and countrysides are different too. Since the opportunities that the women have had in the cities, such as: education, work and other opportunities as equally as men, but this didn't exist for the women in the countrysides. The Tajik are more educated and more liberal than other ethnic groups, and mostly they are living in the cities.

Similarly, when a question was put to the group a moment later as to the historical difference between marriage practices in the city and the countryside historically, Omid, who had lived and worked in Kabul, responded:

> There were differences, and still it continues. In the cities the families have been asking the girl's view about the man whom she is supposed to get married with. But at the countryside parents have been deciding without giving a chance for the girl to express her idea, or consent about marriage. However, in the city, the girl's family are not asking for money, called "Walwar" or "Toyan". However, the girl's family asks for large amounts of money from the groom in the countryside.

Nevertheless, many of the participants who praised Tajiks' civilisational modernity also acknowledged the presence of more customary ideas about gender relations within the family, which were apparent in both urban and rural contexts. When I asked the group whether the birth of a girl and the birth of a boy were celebrated with equal happiness, two male discussants highlighted the primacy such beliefs have been accorded among urban and rural contexts in Afghanistan:

GHADIR: The boys are responsible for earning money and maintaining the family expenses in Afghanistan. However, it might be different in some other countries like: Europe and Australia, where, both men and women could do work outside and have the same opportunity in society, but in Afghanistan it is different. So, due to social culture which has given less space and opportunities for a girl to work outside and maintain the family expenses, families pay less attention to them though ... If a boy is born in a family, the family bursts crackers and holds a party for several nights, but in the case of a girl, the family has sorrow and considers it as a shame for family honour.

DONESH: The problem is mostly due to the social impacts and social customs. Undoubtedly, these nonsense customs dominated even educated people like engineers and doctors, who behave the same as the uneducated regarding the girl and boy issue in their families. It is very common, if a mother gives birth to a baby girl, the family feels shy due to the girl's birth. And many of these families who have three or four girls and no son, they are trying to continue to have more babies, till they get one son.

The Hazaras

Next it is time to turn to the Shia Imami and Shia Ismaili Hazaras of Afghanistan.[6] They speak a dialect of Persian called Hazaragi, have a distinct sense of peoplehood on ethnic and sectarian grounds and represent a large minority of Afghanistan's population. Descended from Mongolian and Turkic tribes, the Hazara have historically occupied central Afghanistan on the raised Hazarajat plateau, which is formed by the central provinces of Bamyan, Ghanzi, Maidan Wardak, Uruzgan and Ghor, as well as Afghan Turkestan (Dorronsoro, 2013: 44). During the expansion of the Safavid Empire into Afghanistan during the sixteenth century, the Hazaras became adherents of Imami (twelver) Shia Islam, with some practising Ismaili (sevener) Islam (Canfield, 1973: 515). Moreover, within the Hazara ethno-linguistic group, there is also a separate, and venerated, group of people called *Sayyed* Hazaras who can trace their lineage back to the Prophet Muhammad's daughter Fatima (Mousavi, 1997: 210). The non-Sayyed Hazaras, like the Pashtuns, had tribal identities based on lineages which were linked, at least in popular belief, to Genghis Khan and his descendants.

Up until the end of the nineteenth century, the Hazara communities were tribally based. However, as will be shown, this changed dramatically during the rule of Abdur Rahman Kahn from 1880 to 1901, a period characterised by bloody campaigns against the people of the Hazarajat. This period marked the end of autonomous rule by Hazaras' own *Mirs* (tribal leaders) and saw the outright enslavement of many Hazaras by conquering Pashtun tribal leaders (Mousavi, 1997: 120–123). While the modernising and reformist King Amanullah formally outlawed slavery in 1919, Hazaras, in many ways, remained slaves to the ruling Pashtun classes of Kabul and Kandahar as household servants and lowly paid labourers (Mousavi, 1997: 160–161). Moreover, from the period of the conquest and occupation of the Hazarajat onwards, there were large migrations of Hazaras to Iran and to Quetta in Pakistan, forming a significant diaspora in these countries (Wily, 2004: 8–10). As a result, when looking at Hazaras' traditional ways of being, one must consider the extent to which the evolving state run by Durrani Pashtuns was refashioning their lives and social systems inside and outside the Hazarajat. Outside the Hazarajat, Hazaras lived and worked in urban cities, such as Kabul, occupying the lowest socio-economic position in society. Inside the Hazarajat, wealthier Hazara community leaders were co-opted as middle-men to extract excessive rents from the rural Hazara peasantry while a host of policies aimed at advancing a distinctly Pashtun state took effect with the goal of erasing the Hazara cultural identity (Emadi, 1997: 368; Wily, 2004: 30–34).

The focus group discussions, which I held with Hazara women and men in Delhi in 2011, offered a profile of the heterogeneity contained within this broad ethno-linguistic community. Over the course of two days, a dozen people, including four women and eight men, engaged in a thoughtful and deeply personal conversation about their own experiences as Hazaras in Afghanistan. The participants in this discussion came from Kabul and many provinces in the Central Hazarajat, including Ghazni, Wardak, Bamyan, Baghlan and Kandahar. In undertaking these discussions, I was very fortunate to have Said Reza Hussein as a translator and leader of the group's discussion. He added further detail and context when translating my questions in addition to highlighting interesting themes which emerged during the course of the conversation. This was illustrated in one salient instance when I asked the group whether women ever ran away from abusive spouses and in-laws to their family's home. It was a question that I had posed in all of my FGDs, based on previous anthropologists' observations of these practices. This practice of running back to one's family home demonstrated a possible way that women could exercise agency to navigate, if not resolve, an abusive relationship. All of the participants agreed that such practices did occur albeit rarely because families were concerned with upholding their honour within a patriarchal society. Reza creatively pushed this issue further by asking whether a woman could go to her father's house and ask for a divorce.

REZA: Let's assume that a girl escaped to her father's house and remained for some weeks and insisted on remaining due to fear from her husband as she might be exposed to domestic violence in her husband's house. Do you remember any case that related to our discussion in which a girl came to her father's house and her father defended her and even asked her to get a divorce?

AHMAD NASIR: [seems very serious when he answers]: Yes. It happened.

DELARAM AND MARJAN: Yes, it happened but most of the times the families would try to resolve this problem by negotiation and convincing the girl to return to her husband's house.

ABDUL GHULAM: I would say yes. It happened and some people even divorced.

REZA: So, we can reach this conclusion that the result of this escaping was either interference by elders of the two families to resolve the problem or advising for divorce.

EVERYBODY: Yes, but getting a divorce is not a common practice. We only know a few cases.

Reza developed this very interesting topic of conversation, which was also animating the participants, by asking in which regions divorce had been practised as well as the logistics of such an undertaking with regard to which official or religious authority would annul the marriage. Ahmad Nasir, an older gentleman from Bamyan, responded to these questions by drawing on his own life experiences in the rural province.

> Yes, it happened in many places such as Bamyan where I am coming from. It all depended on the girl's family. If her father said that he didn't want to send his daughter back to her husband's house, then it would be very difficult to convince him. Here the girl herself didn't have much right to discuss the situation and state her own decision. In many cases, we have seen, the husband's family would bring some elders and a Mullah and a Sayed to find out a solution and return the bride but it did not work and they eventually had to go away with a negative result.

What was interesting about the discussion in which Ahmad Nasir and his fellow participants were engaged in was their open acknowledgement of a variety of practices which directly challenged the customary senses of honour which undergird Hazara communities as well as many other groups in Afghanistan. In this respect, the group engaged with, and elaborated on, issues regarding women's rights which had previously been observed by Robert Canfield in his fieldwork in Bamyan province during the 1960s.

It should also be noted here that the tradition of women holding positions of power over larger communities, usually as a result of coming from powerful lineages, has persisted and colours many Hazaras' living memories (Manalan and Smith, 2009: 12). Moreover, even though Hazara women and men occupy gendered roles in society, what became apparent was the extent to which women could subvert and manipulate this gendered system. As was the case among Pashtun women, these forms of resistance are most palpable in the form of Hazara poetry, including *dobaitis* (couplets of two rhyming verses) and *chahârbayti* (four verses of matching rhyme and rhythm), which are accompanied by musical instruments, as well as two-verse lullabies (Doubleday, 2011: 6). This is notably demonstrated in the following forms of poetry which are respectively sourced from Sayed Mousavi (1997: 85) and Hiromi Sakata (1987: 92):

Dobaiti

> My Love, do not make any noise, I am in the middle of cooking
> Kiss me discreetly, so that my husband may not see
> The light of my life climbs up and down the valley
> I cannot bear to see him go under the heat of the mid-day sun
> The old man could be my grandfather
> The young man, the light of my life.

Lullaby

> Baby's father went hunting
> He went to the Marghozar Mountains
> The door latch is straw
> The rooster stands at the door
> Come by the tobacco field path
> Come to the bed on the platform
> Lalui lalui mother's father.

Thus, as among Pashtun women, poetry and musical verse are of immense importance in the lives of Hazara women. Moreover, as Mousavi (1997: 84–86) and Sakata (1987: 92) noted, in addition to being preservers of musical tradition, women were active innovators in ways that were of vital importance for musical production, more broadly, in society. In a similar way to *landay*s, these poems could also contain an element which spoke not only of idealised lives of women but also indicated subversive forms of everyday agency that were utilised by women to resist the gendered hierarchies of power in order to improve their lives. However, in contrast to many other settled communities in Afghanistan, what was apparent among Hazara women was the greater recognition of women's individual agency, such as on the issue of elopement marriages and women's communal agency. As I suggested previously, this communal aspect related to women's ability to foster stronger relationships within their *qawm* network.

Conclusion

What this chapter has aimed to do is provide an understanding of the traditional social contexts in which different women's and men's lives were embedded in Afghanistan prior to 1978. As was made clear, the invocation of "traditional" here was not used to suggest that ways of being were not already changing as in fact they always were. Instead, "traditional" here was used to establish some of the enduring qualities of different settled and nomadic communities vis-à-vis their gender relations and modes of production and reproduction. Though the social context of Afghanistan writ large has always been defined by heterogeneity and fluctuation, what I endeavoured to show was the extent to which plausible claims could be made about differences between communities. This required spending the necessary time in attempting to understand and to map the way in which different people described their own *qawm*s or communities. Furthermore, with recourse to the straightforward approach of understanding *qawm* communities by virtue of exonyms and autonyms, I intended to plausibly suggest the differences between and within larger ethno-linguistic groupings such as the Pashtuns, Tajiks, Hazaras and so on. This enabled me lastly to suggest how families' and communities' lives existed traditionally in Afghanistan, with a particular focus on the ways in which women from different ethno-linguistic groups were able resist the gendered relations of domination that undergirded the social contexts of their lives.

Notes

1 A good working conceptualisation of *qawm* in this regard is offered by Roy Olivier who notes that such solidarity groupings are numerous and flexibly interchangeable. See Roy, Olivier (1989). "Afghanistan: Back to Tribalism or on to Lebanon?" *Third World Quarterly* 11 (4): 70–82.

2 Basically, according to ancient Persian and in "Ashkani Pahlawi" Tajik was used for stranger, such as: the Arabs refer to non-Arabs as Ajam. Similarly, the Persians called the Arabs Tazi (Non-Persian), hereby, in this context Tajik means "Stranger". Meanwhile the word Tajik has been imported from Ancient Parsi into Turkic Language, and the Turks were using the word "Tajik" with the same meaning as Stranger, and Turks were using "Tajik" for Persians (Non-Turkic Speakers).

Tajik male focus group participant from Badakshan Province, Afghanistan

3 For an excellent representation and analysis of the term *qawm* see: Bleuer, Christian (2007). "Afghanistan and the Qawm: An Important Yet Unknown Concept". *Ghosts of Alexander: Conflict and Society in Central Asia* https://easterncampaign.com/2007/05/06/afghanistan-and-the-qawm-an-important-yet-unknown-concept/ Accessed 15 July, 2016.

4 Sayyeds are different People who, whether they are Hazara, Tajik, Arab or Pashtun, trace their lineage back to the Prophet Mohammed and live within the various ethno-linguistic groups of Afghanistan. See Anderson, Jon (1985). "Sentimental Ambivalence and the Exegesis of 'Self' in Afghanistan". *Anthropological Quarterly* 58 (4): 203–211.

"How Afghans define their relation to Islam". In *Revolutions and Rebellions in Afghanistan: Anthropological Perspectives*, (eds) Nazif Shahrani and Robert Canfield. Berkeley, University of California, 274.

5 Indeed, before revolutionary war took hold of Afghanistan in 1979, a range of female anthropologists observed this in their fieldwork among Afghanistan's different communities. For instance, in the context of Tajiks in Afghan Turkestan see Olesen, Asta (1982). "Marriage Norms and Practices in a Rural Community in North Afghanistan". *Folk* 24: 112–141. In the context of Uzbeks in Kunduz, see Shalinsky, Audrey C. (1989b). "Talking about Marriage: Fate and Choice in the Social Discourse of Traditional Northern Afghanistan". *Anthropos* 84 (1/3): 133–140. When examining Pashtun contexts see Tapper, Nancy (1991). *Bartered brides: Politics, gender and marriage in an Afghan tribal society*. Cambridge, Cambridge University Press. Also, see Boesen, Inger (1983). Conflicts of solidarity in Pakhtun women's lives. *Women in Islamic societies: Social attitudes and historical perspective*. B. Utas. London, Curzon Press, 104–127. Finally, for insight on Hazara contexts see Sakata, Hiromi Lorraine (1987). Hazara women in Afghanistan: Innovators and preservers of a musical tradition. *Women and music in cross-cultural perspective*. E. Koskoff. Urbana and Chicago, University of Illinois Press, 85–95.

6 In Afghanistan there are two prominent Shia sects of Islam including Imami (also referred to as twelver) and Ismaili (sevener). Though both Shia sects of Islam use the term "Imam" to trace the descent of Ali, the son-in-law of the prophet Muhammad, they differ on who the rightful heirs are to the imamate. The Imamis follow a line that ended with the twelfth who disappeared and whose reappearance they await as it will herald the end of days. Meanwhile, the Ismailis follow a line of Imams that diverged from the Imamis at the Seventh Imam (hence the colloquial name 'seveners') but continues to the present day in the person of Agha Khan who also heads up a major humanitarian agency the Agha Khan Development Fund (AKDF also known as AKDN). See Canfield, Robert 1984. "Islamic coalitions in Bamiyan". In *Revolutions and rebellions in Afghanistan: Anthropological perspectives*, (eds) M. Nazif Shahrani and Robert L. Canfield. Berkeley: Institute of International Studies, 220–221.

References

Anderson, Jon (1985). "Sentimental Ambivalence and the Exegesis of 'Self' in Afghanistan". *Anthropological Quarterly* 58 (4): 203–211.

Bleuer, Christian (2007). "Afghanistan and the *Qawm*: An Important Yet Unknown Concept". *Ghosts of Alexander: Conflict and Society in Central Asia* https://easterncampaign.com/2007/05/06/afghanistan-and-the-qawm-an-important-yet-unknown-concept/ Accessed 15 July 2016.

Boesen, Inger (1983). Conflicts of Solidarity in Pakhtun Women's Lives. *Women in Islamic societies: Social Attitudes and Historical Perspective*. B. Utas. London, Curzon Press: pp. 104–127.

Canfield, Robert L. (1973). "The Ecology of Rural Ethnic Groups and the Spatial Dimensions of Power". *American Anthropologist* 75 (5): 1511–1528.

Caron, James (2011). "Reading the Power of Printed Orality in Afghanistan: Popular Pashto Literature as Historical Evidence and Public Intervention". *Journal of Social History* 45 (1): 172–194.

Davis, Diana K., Karimullah Quraishi, David Sherman, Albert Sollodt and Chip Stem (1995). "Ethnoveterinary Medicine in Afghanistan: An Overview of Indigenous Animal Health Care among Pashtun Koochi Nomads". *Journal of Arid Environments* 31 (4): 483–500.

Dorronsoro, Gilles (2013). *Revolution unending: Afghanistan, 1979 to the present*, New York, Columbia University Press.

Doubleday, Veronica (2011). "Gendered Voices and Creative Expression in the Singing of Chaharbeiti Poetry in Afghanistan". *Ethnomusicology Forum* 20 (1): 3–31.

Emadi, Hafizullah (1997). "The Hazaras and their Role in the Process of Political Transformation in Afghanistan". *Central Asian Survey* 16 (3): 363–387.

Gregorian, Vartan (1969). *The emergence of modern Afghanistan: Politics of reform and modernization, 1880–1946*. Stanford, Stanford University Press.

Hall, Samuel (2010). A Study of the Kuchi Population in the Kabul New City Area. *Report commissioned by the Japanese International Cooperation Agency*. Kabul, JICA

Hutchings, Kimberly (2000). "Towards a Feminist International Ethics". *Review of International Studies* 26 (05): 111–130.

Jenkins, Richard (1997). *Rethinking ethnicity: Arguments and explorations*. London, Sage.

Kakar, Palwasha (2003). Tribal Law of Pashtunwali and Women's Legislative Authority. *Afghan Legal History Project*. Boston, Harvard Law School.

Lee, Jonathan L. (1996). *The" ancient supremacy": Bukhara, Afghanistan and the battle for Balkh, 1731–1901*. Leiden, E. J. Brill.

Manalan, Shelley and Deborah J. Smith (2009). Community-Based Dispute Resolution Processes in Bamyan Province. *Case Study Series*. V. Quinlan. Kabul, Afghanistan Research and Evaluation Unit.

Monsutti, Alessandro (2009). Local Power and Transnational Resources: An Anthropological Perspective on Rural Rehabilitation in Afghanistan. *Central Asia Initiative Working Paper No. 2*. Los Angeles, University of California, Los Angeles (UCLA) Asia Institute: 1–38.

Mousavi, Sayed Askar (1997). *The Hazaras of Afghanistan: an historical, cultural, economic and political history*. New York, Routledge.

Olesen, Asta (1982). "Marriage Norms and Practices in a Rural Community in North Afghanistan". *Folk* 24: 112–141.

Roy, Olivier (1989). "Afghanistan: Back to Tribalism or on to Lebanon?" *Third World Quarterly* 11 (4): 70–82.

Roy, Olivier (1990). *Islam and resistance in Afghanistan*. Cambridge, Cambridge University Press.

Rubin, Barnett R. (2002). *The fragmentation of Afghanistan: State formation and collapse in the international system*. New Haven, Yale University Press.

Sakata, Hiromi Lorraine (1987). Hazara women in Afghanistan: Innovators and preservers of a musical tradition. *Women and music in cross-cultural perspective*. E. Koskoff. Urbana and Chicago, University of Illinois Press: 85–95.

Hall, Samuel (2010). A Study of the Kuchi Population in the Kabul New City Area. *Report commissioned by the Japanese International Cooperation Agency*. Kabul, JICA.

Shahrani, M. Nazif (1984). Causes and context of responses to the Saur revolution in Badakhshan. *Revolutions and rebellions in Afghanistan: Anthropological perspectives*. N. Shahrani and R. L. Canfield. Berkeley, California, Institute of International Studies.

Shalinsky, Audrey C. (1989a). "Women's Relationships in Traditional Northern Afghanistan". *Central Asian Survey* 8 (1): 117–129.

Shalinsky, Audrey C. (1989b). "Talking About Marriage: Fate and Choice in the Social Discourse of Traditional Northern Afghanistan". *Anthropos* 84 (1/3): 133–140.

Tapper, Nancy (1981). "Direct Exchange and Brideprice: Alternative Forms in a Complex Marriage System". *Man* 16 (3): 387–407.

Tapper, Nancy (1991). *Bartered brides: Politics, gender and marriage in an Afghan tribal society*. Cambridge, Cambridge University Press.

Tapper, Richard (1984). Ethnicity and class: dimensions of intergroup conflict in north-central Afghanistan. *Revolutions and rebellions in Afghanistan: Anthropological perspectives*. N. Shahrani and R. L. Canfield. Berkeley, California, Institute of International Studies: 211–229.

Tapper, Richard (2008). "Who Are the Kuchi? Nomad Self-Identities in Afghanistan". *The Journal of the Royal Anthropological Institute* 14 (1): 97–116.

Tavakolian, Bahram (1984). "Women and Socioeconomic Change among Sheikhanzai Nomads of Western Afghanistan". *Middle East Journal* 38 (3): 433–453.

Uberoi, J. P. Singh (1964). *Social Organization of the Tajiks of Andarab Valley, Afghanistan*, Australian National University.

Wakefield, Shawna (2004). Gender and Local Level Decision Making: Findings from a Case Study in Panjao. *Case Studies Series*. Kabul, Afghanistan Research and Evaluation Unit. November.

Wily, Liz Alden (2004). Land Relations in Bamyan Province. Findings from a 15 Village Case Study. *Case Studies Series*. Kabul, Afghanistan Research and Evaluation Unit.

4 Modernisation and fragmentation in Afghanistan

In the previous chapter I provided what I termed a *synoptic* overview of women's and men's lives within different communities in Afghanistan. This reconstructive exercise drew attention to the politics within practices of naming oneself and another with respect to ethnic, sectarian, linguistic and *qawm* differences among people. At the same time, it also provided insight into the religious and customary beliefs which informed a person's sense of themselves in relation to the social world at large. Although these beliefs were gendered, it did not necessarily mean that gender relations were hierarchical nor that all gender politics were ever unchanging. These two points were consistently emphasised to me by the women and men participating in the Focus Group Discussions (FGDs). In these discussions, both women and men pointed to the existence of a variety of practices wherein masculine social hierarchies of power were navigated, subverted or overtly challenged by women and men. The insights that these participants shared with me corresponded directly with the important anthropological work conducted in Afghanistan in the twentieth century by contemporary feminist researchers.

In this chapter, I aim to provide a *diachronic* overview of social change in Afghanistan among different communities over the course of time from the foundation of the state of Afghanistan to the contemporary period of US and NATO-led state-building. When undertaking this reconstruction, I will be particularly interested in focusing on processes involved in consolidating, modernising and, ultimately, violently contesting the state in Afghanistan. This chapter seeks to provide insight into the way in which social dynamics among communities changed during this tumultuous history. In particular, I am interested in showing how gender relations and gender politics were affected during these periods of change. This synoptic and diachronic reconstruction of social life in Afghanistan provides much of the important initial work necessary to engage with contemporary moral debates and related violent conflicts as I attempt a feminist-inspired account of human security.

As I have suggested previously, by referencing the work of Kimberly Hutchings (Hutchings, 2000: 122; Hutchings, 2013: 25) and Axel Honneth (Honneth, 2014: 6), the tasks of the ethical practitioner rely on a phenomenological and genealogical process. The phenomenological process refers to understanding the conditions necessary for moral claims to be intelligible between people. Honneth (2014: 127) likens this process to the development of a moral grammar which allows different protagonists to make their claims intelligible to each other. Meanwhile, the genealogical process refers to understanding how certain moral judgements, which might serve to exclude and oppress people, come to possess authority. As Hutchings (2000: 122) suggests, feminists are particularly concerned with the genealogical process because it introduces the question of gender and gendered forms of knowledge which may be used to uphold masculinist structures of power, in economics, politics and society, which disproportionately oppress women. The reconstruction of this historical dialectic of social change in Afghanistan provides an awareness of how the US and NATO intervention in Afghanistan fed into the country's evolving social and political dynamics.

I will construct this account of social change in Afghanistan by first exploring the state's violent historical formation at the close of the nineteenth century. In the second section, I will explore the twentieth-century modernisation and contestation of the state by different armed factions following the revolution of 1978 and Soviet invasion of 1979. It is hard to do justice to the enormity of the social upheaval and violence that was unleashed during the decades of war and conflict which followed these events. However, I will attempt to show how different dynamics of conflict affected people's well-being and changed existing gender hierarchies of power from 1979 to 2001. In the final section of this chapter, I will show how the US and NATO state-building mission fed into Afghanistan's pre-existing social and political dynamics following the military defeat of the Taliban at the end of 2001. My argument here has benefitted from the feminist scholarship and original research of Lina Abirafeh (2009) and Julie Billaud (2015) on Afghanistan. These scholars provide an insightful account of the disconnection of the gendered policies of the US and Nato mission with actual lives of both women and men.

The consolidation and modernisation of a Pashtun state in the twentieth century

Afghanistan history, from 1835 to 1901, saw the rise of successive centralised Durrani Pashtun rulers in early periods contesting, but later cooperating with, the British Empire, which gave cartographical and political meaning to the name "Afghanistan" (Rubin, 2002: 47–52). The co-production of "Afghanistan" was a project financed by the British Empire and carried out by ruling Durrani Pashtun tribes to create a buffer state between British India and the Russian Empire, in what is often referred to as the "Great Game" (Lee, 1996: xiv). This became particularly apparent with the rise of Abdul Rahman Khan in 1892, whose conquest over Pashtun and non-Pashtun groups alike and extension of a central authority's coercive control over the territory of Afghanistan was tacitly recognised, funded and armed by the British Empire who dubbed him the "Iron Emir" (Lee, 1996: 599). To a large extent this violent and exclusionary process of state-formation produced enduring enmities among different ethno-linguistic groups. This point has been made in a variety of literatures and was reiterated by Ghadir, a middle-aged man, during a FGD I convened with women and men from Tajik communities in Delhi:

> The problem of ethnic rivalries and hostilities has existed for a very long time. Abdul Rahman's massacre of the Hazaras and Tajiks in Badakhsan should be pointed out. For instance, in our province (Badakhshan) the name of "Afghan" or "Ogho" means hazard and danger. It is due to the brutal massacre of people based on their ethnic line by the central government of Afghanistan which has been dominated by Pashtuns for three hundred years.

Ghadir was originally from Badakhshan. He came from a settled Tajik community whose family held prominence with different central governments. Through his own and his family's experiences, Ghadir relayed the way in which non-Pashtuns in Badakhshan specifically, and Afghanistan more broadly, were subjugated by Pashtun rulers. For instance, he observed that:

> My grandfather was the regent during Amanullah Khan's time, when Amanullah Khan was traveling outside the country, my grandfather was acting on behalf of king Amanullah Khan. But when Nadir Khan came to power, he sentenced my grandfather for eight years of prison. Then, after three months, Nadir Shah gave an order to shoot him. My grandfather's son, who was a general with a high education in the military, ceased to hold his military title.

In addition to the violent subjugation and even enslavement of non-Pashtun groups, which included the Hazaras as well as Uzbeks and Tajiks in Afghan Turkestan, Abdul Rahman Khan's rule also involved a major programme of resettling nomadic Pashtun tribes, both voluntarily and forcibly, in non-traditional Pashtun lands to the north and west of the Hindu Kush (Tapper, 1973: 55–60; Lee, 1996: 477–479). This programme continued from 1901 to 1919 under the rule of Emir Habibullah Khan, the eldest son of Abdul Rahman Khan, whose central state's coercive capabilities were also financed and supported by the British (Gregorian, 1969: 206–207). After Habibullah's death in 1919 and up until 1929, his eldest son, Amanullah Khan, ruled the country. King Amanullah, who was inspired by Mustafa Kemal Attaturk and the "Young Turks", undertook a dramatic programme of modernisation and liberalisation in an attempt to make Afghanistan an independent and self-reliant, modern country (Gregorian, 1969: 214). As Barnett Rubin (2002: 54–57) notes, this programme relied on three key areas: tax reform, land reform and investment in transport, in addition to a variety of legal reforms, which included the abolishment of Hazara slavery and the establishment of a secular constitution which promoted equal rights for women and men.

Amanullah's attempts to modernise the country in this rapid, dramatic fashion soon brought him into open conflict with a number of tribes and other political actors. His policies of increased direct taxation of agriculture and livestock brought him directly into conflict with powerful, landed khans, whose support had always been vital for the maintenance of a central authority in Kabul, while his moves to secularise the functioning of the state and sever the traditional role of the *Ulema* (religious scholars) provided another source of conflict (Rubin, 2002: 56–57). In 1929, Tajik farming communities north of Kabul revolted and, under the leadership of Bacha-Yi-Saqoa brought Amanullah's rule to an end. The tribal authorities of Kandahar, Khost and Nangarhar were also in open revolt (Rubin, 2002: 57–58). Interestingly, but perhaps unsurprisingly, by the end of his rule, Amanullah had far greater support among the Hazaras, to whom he had granted national citizenship and religious rights, than he did among the Durrani Khans in Kandahar – the traditional backers of Pashtun rulers in Kabul.

Bacha-Yi-Saqoa's reign was short lived, he was overthrown by powerful Durrani tribes, known as the Musahibin, led by Nadir Shah (Rubin, 2002: 58). After hanging Bacha-Yi-Saqoa and establishing his own rule in 1929, Nadir Shah continued the long-standing tradition of Durrani Pashtun leaders by forming a central government based on Pashtun Nationalism – a tradition that was followed, subsequently, by his son, Zahir Shah, and nephew, Daoud Khan. This policy of Pashtunisation, which, in no small way, had been shaped by British recognition and support of the Pashtuns as "natural rulers", carried distinct tones of scientific racism. As Nick Cullather (2002: 8) noted, this imperialist sentiment was expressed by Rudyard Kipling in his book *The Man Who Would Be King*. In it, the title character explains to the Afghans: "You're white people, sons of Alexander, and not like common, black Mohammedans."

Similarly, according to Antonio Giustozzi, German emissaries to Afghanistan in the 1930s, invested considerable energy in propagating racial theories concerning the "Aryan" origins of the Pashtuns and, to a lesser extent, some of the Tajiks (Giustozzi, 2008: 35). The immediate effect of this policy for Nadir Shah, as had been the case for Abdul Rahman Khan, was to rally various Durrani and non-Durrani Pashtuns to brutally subjugate all of the challengers to his rule, including the Kohistani Tajiks, the Hazaras and the Shinwari Pashtuns (Dupree, 1980: 461; Cullather, 2002: 8–9). This, in turn, allowed for the continued colonisation of non-Pashtun lands by Pashtun nomads and peasants as had happened during the rule of Abdul Rahman Khan in the 1890s, when Pashtun nomads were sent to settle and cultivate the newly depopulated environment north of the Hindu Kush in the traditional lands of the Uzbeks and Tajiks in areas that are now called Jauzjan, Sari Pulm Faryab and Kunduz (Bleuer, 2007: 11–12). One of the effects of this Pashtunisation, which from the outset was linked with very direct and bloody violence, was that, over time, it came to do epistemic harm to the non-Pashtuns of Afghanistan, essentially labelling them as backward peoples who had to be organised by the more advanced Pashtuns, the bringers of the modern "nation" state (Emadi, 1997: 160–165). This cultural imperialism would later become institutionalised within all aspects of the "central government", as noted by Cullather (2002: 28) with reference to Prime Minister Daoud Khan's rule from 1953 to 1963:

Daoud's regime made no effort to disguise its chauvinism. Controlling positions in government, the army, the police and the educational system were held by Pashtuns to such a degree that the appellation Afghan commonly referred only to Pashtuns and not to the minorities who collectively comprised the majority.

Initially, at the beginning of Zahir Shah's rule in 1933, any attempts by the Kabul monarchy to improve or modernise the Pashtun countryside were strongly resisted by the rural tribes. Moreover, for almost all of these autonomous tribal Pashtun groups, an encounter with the central government was usually an unpleasant affair (Cullather, 2002: 518). However, throughout the 1930s, with European assistance especially from Germany, the King began a tightly controlled process of economic modernisation which saw the construction of textile, carpet and furniture industries; these were run by ruling elites under royal licence (Cullather, 2002: 519). Additionally, new tax codes and state trading firms began to bring previously untaxed sectors, such as stock raising and trading, within the reach of Kabul's assessors and accountants.

With the end of World War Two, modernisation of the Pashtun nation took off with support from the Great Powers, the US and the USSR, replacing the previous British, French and German roles (Cullather, 2002: 513). In an experiment planned by Durrani ruling elites in conjunction with the outside powers, Afghanistan was to become a test case for the limitless benefits of US and Soviet-led modernisation; both shared a belief in the modernisation and capitalisation of agriculture. The component parts of this national development focused on the development of large signature projects, such as roads and airports, dams and their irrigation networks designed for agriculture, as well as the provision of credit and loans for fertiliser, seed and agricultural equipment (Emadi, 1996: 206–207). The prime targets of these modernising efforts were the mobile communities of Pashtun nomads, whose autonomy and violent resistance to the state had proved an ongoing source of instability, as well as the Pashtun landless peasants and rural poor more generally (Cullather, 2002: 525).

It was thought that the potential of these groups to rise up against their landlords and the government itself could be resolved through the process of turning them into productive and loyal modern farmers who would consolidate the state in the countryside (Cullather, 2002: 525). Afghanistan's mission of 'getting to Denmark' (Fukuyama, 2014: 21–22) provided much initial excitement and optimism among its local and foreign planners. However, inevitably, as happened in many other areas of the "developing" world, this programme produced social dislocation, environmental degradation and increasing class exploitation between wealthy landed elites and the rural poor who were ostensibly to be the beneficiaries of the entire project. This point is highlighted by Hafizullah Emadi (Emadi, 1996: 207) who noted that, while the modernising efforts of the US and USSR led to a "semi-modernisation" in some parts of the country, in others it resulted in the commercialisation of agriculture, the proletarianisation of the peasantry and the concentration of land in the hands of the landed and propertied class within the state apparatus who could benefit most from access to credit and modern forms of agriculture.

The violent contestation of the "State" in Afghanistan from 1978 to 2001

It is very hard to capture, with any true justice, the scale of the violence unleashed on ordinary people during the three decades of violence which followed the "Saur" or February coup of 1978 and the subsequent invasion by the USSR in late 1979. During this period until the fall of the Taliban in 2001, over one million Afghans lost their lives, due to the direct and indirect effects of conflict and war (Lacina and Uriarte, 2009: 10–14). This conflict led to the displacement of half of Afghanistan's population both internally and, more importantly, externally with the outflow of roughly six million refugees from Afghanistan by 1990 (Schöch, 2008: 50). Understandably, these decades completely changed the political dynamics of power. Perhaps most notably, they resulted in the transformation of the traditional patron-client relations of power between ruling Durrani Pashtun tribes and wealthy land-owning khans in the far-reaching rural provinces that had previously facilitated the "State" of Afghanistan (Roy, 1989: 73–76). In place of this traditional power structure, new forms of political organisation and patronage emerged, based around various Islamist Resistance Groups or Mujahedeen with varying levels of access to foreign funding from Iran, Pakistan, Saudi Arabia and the US.

One of the best interpretations of the violent contestation of the Afghan State from 1978 to 1996 is offered by Barnet Rubin in his book *The Fragmentation of Afghanistan*. In this work, Rubin provides a concise account of the way in which an elite class, with the help of foreign funding from the US and USSR, were able to build up powerful armed forces that could rule Afghanistan independently of the country's tribes (Rubin, 2002: 20). At the same time, this modernisation process sowed the germ of revolution in the minds of a newly-educated class of youth. As he noted, (2002, 75–77) this younger generation would come to fight in all the major factions of the impending revolution and war, including: the socialist party, the nationalist Islamist party and the Fundamentalist Mujahedeen. In fact, all of the political leaders of these factions attended and graduated from Kabul's universities prior to 1979, including: Ahmed Shah Massoud, Burhaddin Rabbani, Taraki, Najibullah and Hekmatayar. Not surprisingly, the ideological visions of these young men were fundamentally incompatible and would lead to ongoing conflict between various factions for supremacy to rule Afghanistan. Thus, from the time of the Saur coup of 1978 up until the present, Afghanistan's history has been marked by militarised conflict and social upheaval.

Between 1979 and 1989, the majority of the fighting and aerial bombardment occurred in the countryside of Afghanistan, with the exception of Herat in 1979 (Rubin, 2002: 122). Mirroring the contemporary US and NATO mission in Afghanistan, most of the major conflict occurred in the south and east of the country among the traditional tribal lands of the Pashtuns. During the course of this war, from 1979 to 1990, some three million people, the majority being Shia Muslims or Persian speakers, fled to Iran, while another three million people, the majority of whom were Pashtuns, fled to the refugee camps in Pakistan's North West Frontier Province (NWFP) and Quetta (Schöch, 2008: 50). Notably, there was virtually no major conflict between communist forces and Mujahedeen groups in the central region of the Hazarajat or north of the Hindu Kush in Afghanistan's historically Tajik- and Uzbek-dominated regions (Rubin, 2002: 234–239). In fact, in the Hazarajat region, Herat and Afghan Turkestan, local politics led to violence being primarily directed more generally towards Pashtun administrators, wealthy, landed khans and Pashtun settlers.

The departure of Soviet military forces in 1989 and the administration of the People's Democratic Party of Afghanistan leader, Najibullah, led to a reduction in the scale of conflict between the major Mujahedeen parties; however, opposing factions eventually defeated the PDPA forces and their arrival in Kabul in 1992 led to a sharp rise in internecine violence within and between different ethno-linguistic communities. Within these communities, violence was directed towards intellectuals and urban Afghans who had had any ties to the communist regime. At the same time, the commanders and cadres of these Mujahedeen parties were unleashing some of the most horrific ethno-sectarian violence, including rape, murder and torture, against soldiers and civilians alike from opposing groups (Gossman, 2005). Deep historical enmities, the trappings of legitimacy through holy war and a deeply gendered conception of honour fuelled the rise of hyper-masculinised ways of fighting war. In these situations, the territory over which different groups were fighting was as much inscribed on the bodies of non-combatant women, men and children as on the strategic geographical terrain of cities, villages and valleys.

The rise of this hyper-masculine violence, which disciplined women and men alike, was caused by the breakdown of, rather than the fulfilment of, more traditional and patriarchal gender relations around the country. The true character of this hierarchical and violent gendered social setting was conveyed to me in depth by women and men in the Tajik FGD. Through their own personal experiences and those experiences of their families, the participants conveyed the enormity of the violence and chaos to which they had borne witness. Towards the end of the first day's discussion, the group had been considering a series of questions which I had posed about the Mujahedeen civil war, centred in Kabul. Donesh, like many other members of the FGD, had lived through the violence inflicted by the Mujahedeen parties in Kabul during this time. In describing the gendered nature of this violence, which terrorised women and men alike, he expressed a sentiment echoed in subsequent FGDs:

> The Mujahedeen are calling themselves Muslim but in reality they're drinking every night and raping innocent girls. These Mujahedeen were selling and purchasing girls with money. The Mujahedeen committed a thousand kinds of different crimes against humanity. We cannot explain all of it in one or two days. This is what we've seen with our own eyes. It did not only

happen in one part of Kabul City, but people all around the city and country experienced this horrible situation and saw all these crimes with their own eyes.

In making this point, Donesh referred to my line of questioning about whether Mujahedeen fighters committed the same horrific violence against members of their own community as they did to others. Similarly, I wanted to know how the participants, who were from predominantly urban backgrounds, characterised their lives during the war in relation to rural communities. Donesh continued by emphasising the general deplorability of all Mujahedeen groups' un-Islamic and dishonourable behaviour:

> You've already asked about partiality and impartiality, but for the Mujahedeen being impartial and innocent did not make any difference. They were attacking everybody. It was like setting fire in a jungle and burning every type of tree, both the dried and the green ones. They were like a fire, which entered the city and burned everything.

The way in which this emerging hyper-masculine construction of gender disciplined men, and not just women, was demonstrated by Omid, a middle-aged woman who had lived in Kabul with her husband, children and family during the Mujahedeen violence of 1993 to 1996. Her account illustrates the way in which men too faced forms of gendered insecurity when they failed to meet the idealised role of masculine warrior.

> During the war among Mujahedeen groups in Kabul, we were moving our property from one part of the city to another. I remember that while we left our house, due to a horrible fight among Mujahedeen, a middle-aged man in our neighborhood preferred to stay in his house to take care of his property, though his family had left the neighborhood already.
>
> The Mujahedeen entered his house one day and asked him if he belonged to any Mujahedeen groups. He replied to them that he was an ordinary man and belonged to no party or group of Mujahedeen. Then these armed Mujahedeen started beating him badly and said to him that ordinary civilians should be beaten as well, since ordinary people are only watching the Mujahedeen without taking part in the battle.

What these acts of violence revealed was the underlying gendered nature of ethnic identities. These identities were exclusionary in their separation of members and non-members into different groups. At the same time, they were hierarchical in the way in which they positioned men/subjects as the defenders of the community's honour which was indelibly inked on the bodies of its women/objects. This was illustrated when Fatimah recounted a story of the systematic way in which the Hazara Mujahedeen used linguistic differences to determine whether someone was a Pashtun or not. Fatimah, like Omid, was originally from Kabul and had lived in different parts of the city during the Mujahedeen civil war from 1993 to 1996.

> My brother was crossing Deh Mazang (Traffic Circle) for Darul Aman (Palace in Kabul) but on the way he was stopped and imprisoned by Hazaras from Hezbi Wahdat. The Hazaras had check points. They were checking people, who were crossing their region by bicycle and buses. They were asking the passengers to pronounce some words, which were difficult for Pashtuns to pronounce correctly. For example, they used the word "Qorot" (dried yoghurt), since Pashtuns pronounce Qorot as Korot. Through these tricks and facial features they could distinguish Pashtuns from others. And then they killed the Pashtuns.
>
> As I said before, my brother had been asked by Hazaras to pronouce Qorot. Since we are Tajik, my brother pronounced it correctly as Qorot. But the Hazaras could not believe he was not Pashtun, since my brother's face features and his big eyebrows make him look like the Pashtuns. My brother was telling the Hazaras' armed men that he is not Pashtun, he is Tajik. But they rejected him, and thought he was lying. My brother was kept by the Hazara armed men belonging to Hezbi Wahdat for twenty days. My brother later told us, that he saw many horrible and shocking events. The Hazara armed men cut many women's parts, who were mostly Tajik women. They also put nails into the head of the two Pashtun men who were their prisoners.
>
> My brother said that, after twenty days, a Hazara man came and saw me, he recognised me, since we've known each other from a long time back. He took me with him and told the other Hazaras that my brother is a driver and a Tajik not a Pashtun. Then, they released my brother from prison. So, if that Hazara man had not seen my brother, they might have killed my brother too because they thought he was Pashtun.

This complete abrogation of accepted societal customs of honorable conduct and universal religious imperatives was one of the major causes fueling the rise of the Taliban in Kandahar. From this province, the Taliban, with strong support from the government of Pakistan, would go on to conquer almost all of Afghanistan by the end of 1998. The rise and rule of the Taliban was in many ways a return of a Pashtun-friendly regime. Taliban forces violently persecuted the populations of Uzbek, Tajik and Hazara who, as part of the Northern Alliance, had been fighting them. Taliban law courts also oversaw the return, to the Pashtun, of lands to the north and west of the Hindu Kush and allowed the nomadic Pashtun tribes to return to the Hazarajat. Though the rule of the Taliban has become synonymous in the West with a war on women's rights, it has to be remembered that their period of rule, especially in the Pashtun tribal home lands to the south and the east, presents a far more complicated picture. Many women, at the time, suggested that the Taliban had at least brought stability and a reduction in crime due to their harsh and swift interpretation of Sharia law (Smith,

2009: 26). The Taliban held de facto power across all of Afghanistan, with the exception of Ahmed Shah Massoud's Tajik force in the Panjshir Valley. However, the leaders of nearly all of Afghanistan's other major armed factions, such as Burhaddin Rabbani, Rashid Dostum, Abdul Rasul Sayyaf, Gulbuddin Hekmatayar, Jalalludin Haqqani, Ismail Khan and Mohammed Fahim remained poised and ready to re-stake their claims to power in Afghanistan if given the chance. Following the events of 9/11, the US aligned themselves with the Northern Alliance, composed of Massoud's Panjshiri Tajiks, and other Mujahedeen commanders like Ismail Khan. This strategic alignment was not questioned at the time but it had unfortunate consequences because the overthrow of the Taliban and their subsequent treatment as a terrorist organisation, rather than as a political faction, produced the existing and ongoing rivalry between the Taliban and the current Afghan government.[1]

Gender, development and security: the contemporary project of US and NATO state-building in Afghanistan

This section will aim to show the way in which the US and NATO state-building intervention fed into the existing dynamics of power among different armed factions for control of Afghanistan. At the same time, I wish to explore how this intervention also fed into existing societal dynamics regarding gender relations and gender politics. I am particularly interested in understanding the role that gender has played discursively in legitimising the intervention as well as its practical expression in the international aid programme. Though this military intervention comprised a multi-national cast of state and organisational actors including non-NATO countries like Japan and organisations like the World Bank, it can, for the most part, be characterised as a US-led NATO mission. The US has had the greatest influence as it has largely bankrolled this holistic endeavour. The US has been the largest troop contributor to the conflict in Afghanistan and has spent some $556 billion[2] of the estimated total of $800 billion,[3] spent on all international military and aid spending from 2001 to 2010. Moreover, the overwhelming share of US and Western spending has been militaristic in nature, having been spent on the development of Afghan Security Forces, with only some $40 billion having been spent on humanitarian and development aid.[4]

The return of the US and modernisation theory to Afghanistan

When seeking to ground the initial founding of the current Afghan State, it is useful to return to two important meetings which took place in Germany between the 29 November and 2 December, 2001. The first of these was the Bonn Process which led to a grand political bargain being struck between three key parties, namely expatriate Afghan intellectuals, Durrani Pashtun tribal aristocrats associated with Zahir Shah and Hamid Karzai and, finally, the Northern Alliance warlords and other militant factions who would hold ultimate power in the future state (Giustozzi, 2004: 2–4). The second meeting brought together the leaders of Afghan "civil society", most notably wealthy and influential businessmen, in the first "Afghan Civil Society Meeting" in Bad Honnef, Germany (Giustozzi, 2006: 221). Their purpose was to discuss the role of private investors in the coming reconstruction of Afghanistan.

These two meetings established the factionalised and self-serving nature of the role of political elites within the central government while cementing the "business-friendly" character of the impending reconstruction of Afghanistan for a select few wealthy local and expatriate Afghans in league with these powerful elites (Giustozzi, 2006: 226). This new Afghan elite in many ways knew the Western discourse of state-building and human rights better than US and NATO policy-makers and were happy to rhetorically support a liberal human rights-based discourse, as is evidenced in their rhetorical commitment to the Afghan Constitution, knowing full well that this sideshow had little bearing on the way in which they would empower themselves in the state-building process.

Indeed, these powerful men, together with their broader *qawm* networks, understood very well how to position themselves to obtain the full benefit of the impending Western state-building programme. A heavy US military presence and an international aid bonanza would fuel the increase in rents that could be extracted from the rapidly growing bubble economy of the region. They profited from the illicit economy (Goodhand, 2008: 411–412), such as opium smuggling, as well as the "licit economy" (Lister and Pain, 2004: 3), in which their high level of power and vertical integration at the top of the market food chain in Afghanistan facilitated their ability to win aid contracts, such as in construction, and, at the same time, to extract massive amounts of project funding through graft (Waldman, 2008: 3).

In the rural countryside of Afghanistan, the US pursued a strategy of modernisation inspired by their previous actions during the Vietnam War in which development aid was tied directly to counter-insurgency aims in order to "Win Hearts and Minds" (Goodhand and Sedra, 2010: 2). This policy simultaneously led to foreign armies being providers of aid as well as aid agencies becoming part of this militarised framework, as can be seen in the organisation of army Provincial Reconstruction Teams (PRTs) (Olson, 2006: 13–14). I will explicate the self-serving nature of Western state-building through their ownership of the Afghan Development Compact process as well as the way in which donors' money was spent in what could be called the "corporate outsourcing" of development in Afghanistan (Waldman, 2008: 3). In many ways, this led to a boom time for the workers and managers of the international aid and private security industries, who have reaped large windfalls in consultancy salaries and huge profits from multi-million dollar contracts (Waldman, 2008: 1). This contextualisation of what Western state-building has involved in Afghanistan, allows me to explore the effect of this project on Afghanistan's factional competition for power in an evolving conflict economy.

The overall militarisation of state-building in Afghanistan is immediately apparent in the following figures which highlight the disparity between money spent on reconstruction and that spent on fighting. Between 2001 and 2010, $57 billion in aid was disbursed in Afghanistan by the international community against $90 billion pledged and, of the figure actually spent, $29 billion went to funding the Afghan National Army (ANA) and the Afghan National Police (ANP) (Rivas, 2011: 1–2). Moreover, as Matt Waldman (2008: 1) has demonstrated, at least 40 per cent of this $57 billion in aid went back to foreign contractors in logistical costs, operating salaries and corporate profits, leaving only $17 billion in aid spent directly on the Afghan people. In stark contrast, the United States alone has spent $523 billion militarily through the Department of Defence (Belasco, 2011: 17). Not surprisingly, the most obvious signs of Western development in Afghanistan have involved the construction of large military bases, such as the central US Army and Air force Base in Bagram, as well as regional military bases, in addition to large road works, most notably the Kabul to Kandahar Road, that are required in order to facilitate the coalition's fight against the Taliban, and other insurgents, in the southern, south western and eastern Pashtun provinces of the country bordering Pakistan (Lister and Pain, 2004: 4).

What is also important to note about the transition from the Afghan Compact of 2006 through to the Afghanistan National Development Strategy (ANDS) in 2008 is the growing emphasis on linking a particular type of security, namely counter-insurgency and counter-narcotics, to development (Government, 2008: 5–6). Thus, the development aid contributed by major donors was aimed simultaneously at securing counter-insurgency objectives and at increasing economic development of the countryside using developmentalist and neo-liberal economic approaches (Pain and Shah, 2009: 45–46). This ongoing militarisation of aid was further entrenched by the Provincial Reconstruction Team (PRT) framework, which was universally implemented by the International Security Assistance Force (ISAF) in October 2006, whereby donors and NGOs (Non-Governmental Organisation) worked in close conjunction with a military PRT team (Williams, 2011: 68–69). Though humanitarian and reconstruction aid is theoretically meant to be provided in a neutral fashion, the model of the PRTs, which was implemented across Afghanistan, has moved NGOs towards supporting directly, or indirectly, this militarisation of aid, meaning that much of the development is being done in order to bribe communities away from the Taliban through "quick impact projects" (QIPs) with the overarching strategy of "winning hearts and minds" (WHAM) (Goodhand and Sedra, 2010: 2; Williams, 2011: 69).

The effect of the US and NATO intervention on gender dynamics

As I suggested previously when introducing this book, women have occupied a position of primacy in the West's state-building campaign in Afghanistan as objects in need of liberating. Despite this rhetorical concern, women's health and well-being have continued to fare poorly. Moreover, women face a variety of gender-based forms of violence, including physical and sexual violence (Raj *et al.* 2011). Gender-based violence in Afghanistan also causes economic and emotional insecurity as is demonstrated in the continuing commodification of women in marriage, their later subordination within their households (Abbasi-Shavazi *et al.* 2012) and the struggles of widowed households living in poverty (Schütte, 2014). These indicators highlight the prevalent and severe gender-based violence experienced by women.

The decision of the US in 2001 to empower and legitimise the warlords, who, among other atrocities, had sanctioned the killing and rape of women, revealed the true priorities of the US in Afghanistan at the time. They were intent on fighting the Taliban and Al-Qaeda – not on ensuring justice and reconciliation for women and men who had suffered through the crimes and violence of the Mujahedeen's civil war. Nevertheless, it is important to understand the concrete agency which has been applied within this intervention to improve women's lives and transform gender relations. In this respect, I am helped by the scholarship of Lina Abirafeh and Jill Billaud, two feminist researchers who have pursued similar research questions and have published books based on original fieldwork undertaken in Kabul, Afghanistan.

Lina Abirafeh's 2009 book, entitled *Gender and International Aid in Afghanistan: The Politics and Effects of Intervention*, explores the aid intervention in Afghanistan as a political exercise from the highest to lowest levels in practice. Abirafeh (2009) seeks to understand the impact of gender-focused aid on people's well-being, from democracy building to economic programmes targeting all women. Throughout the work, she (Abirafeh, 2009: 9–11) observes the disjuncture between the rhetorical gendered discourse associated with empowering women and the actual condition of women in post-Taliban Afghanistan. At the same time, Abirafeh pays special attention to the disjuncture between the goals of gender programming and the implementation of these programmes. She (Abirafeh, 2009: 16–18) notes that the Western gender intervention has been informed by United Nations Security Council Resolution (UNSCR) 1325 and the Convention on the Elimination of all forms of Violence Against Women (CEDAW). However, she observes that there has been a large disconnect between the progressive principles entailed in these global agreements and the actual implementation of the programme.

As an example, Abirafeh, highlights the "constitutional democracy" which was co-produced by the US and NATO in collaboration with the Northern Alliance (Abirafeh, 2009: 17). She notes that, on paper, the constitution adopted by the *Loya Jirga* or Grand Assembly in January 2004 was very progressive, particularly with regard to Article 7 which requires Afghanistan to observe the *Universal Declaration of Human Rights* and all its covenants, including the *Convention on the Elimination of all forms of Violence Against Women* (CEDAW). Nevertheless, as Abirafeh repeatedly observes, this formal equality with men was not enjoyed in practice by most women in Afghanistan. She (Abirafeh, 2009: 144) notes that prevailing conditions of conflict and hierarchical gender orders ensure that institutions designed to uphold rights and basic protections, such as the police force, often disregard them. Moreover, quite perversely, as rights groups have observed, the police and judiciary hold conservative and, at times, misogynistic views which are prevalent more broadly in Afghanistan. Young girls, who run away from their parents' or in-laws' homes to escape an unwanted marriage, are likely to be charged by law courts with the crime of "running away from home" – a law that does not exist formally (Reid, 2009: 8). Meanwhile, rape is not a crime and women prosecuting their attackers are liable to be charged with committing adultery and sentenced to marry their rapists (Reid, 2009: 35, 46). Furthermore, those in society, including powerful factional leaders and their followers, who commit some of the worst and most brutal crimes, are most often never punished due to their positions of power.

With respect to the democratic process, Abirafeh noted that, while women's involvement was touted in the *Loya Jirga*, these same women suffered continuous fear of harassment and threat on the street and in their homes (Abirafeh, 2009: 142–144). While there was a great deal of jubilation associated with the fact that one quarter of the parliamentary seats in the *Wolesi Jirga* (legislative chamber) were reserved for women, she (Abirafeh, 2009: 72–73) notes that many of the Afghan women working with international NGOs to whom she spoke "were concerned that women were once again being used as window dressing and that their progressive quota served to appease international donors at the expense of laying a foundation for genuine participation". Indeed, what is less discussed is the extreme patriarchal and misogynistic environment in the parliamentary chambers, which poses a continuing threat to women parliamentarians. This was most notably attested to by Malalai Joya (2009: 11), an elected representative from Farah Province, who continuously denounced the presence in parliament of warlords because of their past and ongoing crimes against the people of Afghanistan, until she was eventually banned from parliament by key Mujahedeen leaders, including Yunus Qanooni and Abdul Rasul Sayyaf.

Early in her argument, Abirafeh (2009: 30) also provides one of the most apt portrayals of the gender-focused international aid in Afghanistan when she characterises the mission as an example of "gender and development" (GAD) discourse and a "women in development" (WID) style of implementation. WID is the earlier phase of understanding which shares colonising assumptions of modernisation theory through its emphasis that women in the "developing" world use Western women as examples of subjectivity to which they should aspire in terms of becoming educated and empowered through economic gain. Meanwhile, GAD draws attention to both the politics of gender as well as the way in which understandings of gender identity and gender relations are built upon power and social imbalance. Thus, gender becomes a box to tick off and the theoretical insight availed by GAD into how gendered inequalities exist is obscured from view. This argument has also been made by Marianne Marchand (2009: 922) in relation to the broader incorporation of gender in the field of development studies:

> When, during the United Nations Women's Conference in Beijing, the policy of gender mainstreaming was accepted – and later reaffirmed in

the Millennium Development Goals (MDGs) – the result was that much of the originality and issues raised by GAD were marginalised and excluded from the development (policy) agenda.

Moreover, Marchand observes the way in which the neo-liberal economic agenda of the 1990s influenced the subsequent application of development in the post-9/11 context. This focus, which is characterised by the reincorporation of the public/private myth of economic relations (Becker-Schmidt, 1999), harkens back to the modernisation-inspired approach of Women in Development (WID) from the 1970s (Steans, 1998: 102). This is particularly apparent with the latest neo-liberal classification of women as economic maximising agents who need to be "empowered" by earning money in the public realm instead of being confined to the home (Marchand, 2009: 928). What is missed by this latest reincarnation of modernising non-Western women is that women's labour is already incorporated into the public realm; moreover, this fallaciously reductionist scenario of economic development is unable to account for existing social contexts which would thwart its theoretical propositions (Razavi, 2009: 221).

For instance, on the first point, scholars like Joanne Wright (1997: 80) have noted that women's labour, particularly as farmers, is already incorporated into the public realm. However, as she surmises, although they labour in the public realm in a practical sense in addition to their work of care and child-raising in the reproductive realm, their labour outside the domestic sphere is marginalised and devalued as much as is their domestic labour in the context of the "real" economy (Wright, 1997: 70). This introduces a related second criticism, which is that women will never benefit equally from development initiatives, as is envisaged in reductionist neo-liberal scenarios that posit women as economic maximising agents, because of the host of constraints they face; not least of which is the threat of violence for taking part in the public realm of men. In many homes in Afghanistan, women are already significantly participating in the productive economy whether in agriculture, live-stock rearing or handicraft production, alongside their reproductive duties of child-rearing, cooking, water collection and housework; but their productive work, inside and outside the house, is, with notable exceptions such as poppy harvesting and refining in the northern provinces, underpaid in comparison to that of men and, in nearly all circumstances, does not entitle them to any control of the income earned. A notable example of this is the carpet-weaving industry in Afghanistan in which women receive little or no economic compensation for their skilled labour (Lister and Pain, 2004: 4).

Jill Billaud has also explored the question of gender politics in the context of the international intervention in Afghanistan in her 2015 book entitled *Kabul Carnival: Gender Politics in Postwar Afghanistan*. In this work, Billaud (2015: 12–13) makes an important contribution to understanding the way in which the gendered programming of aid builders intersects with existing dynamics in setting the stage to produce the "carnival of post(war)". Drawing on Mikhail Bakhtin's notion of "carnivalesque", Billaud (2015: 12–13) notes that the carnival exists as a "moment when rules are turned upside down and everything is permitted". She notes that this post-war stage of the "theatre" of Afghanistan currently plays host to a carnivalesque act in which utopian possibilities are imagined. In this way, what Billaud is adroitly doing is juxtaposing the façade of utopian possibilities, such as the promises of women's rights, against the continuation of injustice and an unjust order. To illustrate, Billaud offers two prominent cases, in which acclaimed "transformations" of Afghanistan proved to be a façade. She (Billaud, 2015: 13–14) first observes the disjuncture between the fetishised "rule of law" agenda and the endemic disorder and violence of Afghanistan. Second, she notes the disjuncture between the celebration of Afghanistan as a democracy and the election of many military factions and alleged war criminals who continue to profit from a narco-economy.

The scholarship of both Billaud and Abirafeh serves to powerfully illustrate the way in which gender identities and gender relations play out among women and men in this carnivalesque moment in Afghanistan. They (Abirafeh, 2009: 129–131; Billaud, 2009: 135–136) both make note of the way in which the external gendered ideologies associated with international aid for women have clashed with existing gender dynamics. Both authors agree that this intersection has produced a backlash from conservative power-holders who have moved to equate women's rights agendas as un-Islamic and shameful. This is not a new backlash. Conservative public stake-holders, including the ulema in conservative rural settings, have previously expressed outrage over the loss of traditional values in favour of dishonourable modern ideas of gender relations. This backlash is a reiteration of what occurred most prominently when, during the Soviet–Afghan war and the rule of the PDPA in Kabul, the Mujahedeen argued that the government's PDPA gender programmes were encouraging sexual immodesty and the complete breakdown of honourable society.

Billaud (Billaud, 2009: 229–230) captured this sentiment in her PhD thesis, when she highlighted the work of Asta Olesen who had observed poems and songs expressing popular resistance among different communities in Afghanistan. One particularly insidious song was written by Rafik Jan who equated men's honour, in terms of customary Pashtun tribal codes, with the universal account of honour presented in Islam:

> O, Muslim, modesty, shame and to be in *purdah*
> Is a great *nang wa namus*[5]
> You can't tell her not to go somewhere
> She has the freedom to be at everyone's side
> Whoever she want
> She could spend the night with him
> Everyone has to accept this command
> All of us should taste each other's women
> Khalqis believe that *zar, zan wa zamin*[6]
> Are common things
> O, Muslim! Think about it...

This ongoing tension flares up in the context of the contemporary efforts of the US and the international community to introduce a new wave of gender programming aimed at "empowering" women in Afghanistan. For instance, one of the most prominent examples of this resentment witnessed by Abirafeh (2009: 175–176) and Billaud (2015: 81) in the context of Kabul was that much employment provided by the aid mission was targeted solely at women. As Abirafeh notes, women and men were seemingly open to a change in gender roles which allowed women to seek economic gain. However, men resented the way in which women were prioritised and men were sidelined in the international community's economic aid programmes in Kabul. This move, they argued, was an absolute insult to men's dignity, and a questioning of men's ability to provide (Abirafeh, 2009: 108–109). Meanwhile, Billaud (Billaud, 2015: 1–3) provides an important example of the way in which women have sought to subvert this problem. She examines the practice of *bacha posh* (cross-dressing) in which women in Afghanistan have played masculine characters in order to physically survive in a masculine-dominant world.

Perhaps the most important point these authors raise is that the transformation of gender relations towards greater egalitarianism is an intensely contested exercise which requires great attention to detail. In this regard, the arguments of foreign NGOs about "empowering women", when addressed to conservative male audiences, fall less like pearls of wisdom and more like unpinned hand grenades. Despite this, both authors argue that women's, and men's, ultimate well-being and security lies in the strengthening of social relationships of recognition and respect within communities. This collaborative project is sorely needed because women suffer horrendously from the multiple forms of violence produced by these hierarchical gender relations including physical, sexual, emotional and economic harm. Quite perversely, many of the actions women take to navigate and survive this masculinised world, such as "playing men", running away from home and engaging in prostitution, only lead to their violent punishment.

Conclusion

In the previous chapter I aimed to provide a broad explication of the traditional (pre-1978) ways of being for the various settled and nomadic communities of Afghanistan in addition to showing how it was possible to navigate this extremely heterogeneous, and historically changing, social context through recourse to the way in which groups characterised their own and others' *qawm*s. To further this account of traditional life in Afghanistan, I have used this chapter to reconstruct the historical dialectic between these traditional subjects' local social contexts and larger, more powerful, forces and ideas which were tied up in the process of consolidating and modernising the State in Afghanistan throughout the twentieth century prior to the period of violent contestation that occurred between 1978 and 2001. Moreover, to finalise this chapter, I have attempted to provide an understanding of the way in which the contemporary post-Taliban Western state-building mission has fed into this dialectic of social change. I will next use three provincial case studies of Nangarhar, Bamyan and Kabul in Afghanistan to come to terms with how people's lives have changed in these different contexts. In contrast to this chapter, which focused predominantly on outlining the larger structural forces of this dialectic, the subsequent chapters will delve more deeply into the lives of the subjects themselves. I will be especially interested in focusing on how these processes have made peoples' lives qualitatively better, or worse, and importantly, the way in which people cope with insecurity and struggle against the subjugation that pervades their social contexts.

Notes

1 For an overview of some of these players see Giustozzi, Antonio 2003. "Respectable Warlords? The Politics of State-Building in Post-Taleban Afghanistan". *Crisis States Research Centre*, Working Paper 33, 2003: 1–20.
2 Of this amount $523 billion has been spent through the Department of Defence (DOD), $29 billion through the Department of State (DOS) and the United States Agency for International Development (USAID) and $4 billion through the Department of Veteran Affairs (VA) medical spending. See, Belasco, Amy 2011. "The Cost of Iraq, Afghanistan, and Other Global War on Terror Operations Since 9/11". *Congressional Research Service*: 17.
3 See, Cordesman, Anthony. 2012. "Transition in the Afghanistan–Pakistan War: How Does this War End?" Paper presented at the 2012 Aspen European Strategy Forum, November 16: 3.
4 This figure of $40 billion becomes even smaller when considering the fact that 40 per cent of this amount is returned to donor countries in the form of profits, salaries and allowance. See, Waldman, Matt. 2008. "Falling Short: Aid Effectiveness in Afghanistan", ACBAR Advocacy Series: 9, 18.
5 It is a great honour to keep women chaste.
6 'women', 'gold' and 'land' (Pashtun saying relating to men's possessions).

References

Abbasi-Shavazi, Mohammad Jalal, Rasoul Sadeghi, Hossein Mahmoudian and Gholamreza Jamshidiha (2012). "Marriage and Family Formation of the Second-Generation Afghans in Iran: Insights from a Qualitative Study". *International Migration Review* 46 (4): 828–860.

Abirafeh, Lina (2009). *Gender and international aid in Afghanistan: The politics and effects of intervention*. Jefferson, North Carolina, McFarland & Company, Inc., Publishers.

Becker-Schmidt, Regina (1999). Theodor W. Adorno's Significance for a Feminist Sociology. *Adorno, Culture and Feminism: SAGE Publications*. M. O'Neill. London, Sage Publications.

Belasco, Amy (2011). The Cost of Iraq, Afghanistan, and other Global War on Terror Operations since 9/11. Washington DC, Congressional Research Service.

Billaud, Julie (2009). *Malalay's Sisters: Women's Public Visibility in 'Post-War/Reconstruction' Afghanistan* European Doctorate in Philosophy, Ecole des Hautes Etudes en Sciences Sociales and the University of Sussex.

Billaud, Julie (2015). *Kabul carnival: Gender politics in postwar Afghanistan.* Philadelphia, University of Pennsylvania Press.

Bleuer, Christen Mark (2007). *Uzbeks versus the Center: Mobilization as an Ethnic Minority in the Tajikistan and Afghanistan Civil Wars.* Master of Arts, Indiana University.

Cullather, Nick (2002). "Damming Afghanistan: Modernization in a Buffer State". *The Journal of American History* 89 (2): 512–537.

Dupree, Louis (1980). *Afghanistan.* New Jersey, Princeton University Press.

Emadi, Hafizullah (1996). "The State and Rural-based Rebellion in Afghanistan". *Central Asian Survey* 15 (2): 201–211.

Emadi, Hafizullah (1997). "The Hazaras and their Role in the Process of Political Transformation in Afghanistan". *Central Asian Survey* 16 (3): 363–387.

Fukuyama, Francis (2014). *Political order and political decay: From the industrial revolution to the globalization of democracy.* London, Profile Books.

Giustozzi, Antonio (2004). 'Good' State vs 'Bad' Warlords? A Critique of State-Building Strategies in Afghanistan. London, Crisis States Research Centre – London School of Economics (LSE): 1–19.

Giustozzi, Antonio (2006). Afghanistan: exploring the peacebuilding potential of the private sector. *Local business, local peace: the peacebuilding potential of the domestic private sector.* D. Smith. London, International Alert.

Giustozzi, Antonio (2008). Afghanistan: Transition Without End an Analytical Narrative on State-Making. *Working Paper No 40.* London, Crisis States Research Centre – London School of Economics (LSE).

Goodhand, Jonathan (2008). "Corrupting or Consolidating the Peace? The Drugs Economy and Post-conflict Peacebuilding in Afghanistan". *International Peacekeeping* 15 (3): 405–423.

Goodhand, Jonathan and Mark Sedra (2010). "Who Owns the Peace? Aid, Reconstruction, and Peacebuilding in Afghanistan". *Disasters* 34: S78–S102.

Gossman, Patricia (2005). Casting shadows: War crimes and crimes against humanity: 1978–2001. Belgium, The Afghanistan Justice Project.

Government, Afghan National (2008). Islamic Republic of Afghanistan. Afghanistan National Development Strategy 1387–1391 (2008–2013).

Gregorian, Vartan (1969). *The emergence of modern Afghanistan: Politics of reform and modernization, 1880–1946.* Stanford, Stanford University Press.

Honneth, Axel (2014). *Freedom's right: the social foundations of democratic life.* New York, Columbia University Press.

Hutchings, Kimberly (2000). "Towards a Feminist International Ethics". *Review of International Studies* 26 (05): 111–130.

Hutchings, Kimberly (2013). Universalism in feminist international ethics: Gender and the difficult labour of translation. *Dialogue, Politics and Gender.* J. Browne. Cambridge, Cambridge University Press: 81–106.

Joya, Malalai (2009). *Raising my voice: the extraordinary story of the Afghan woman who dares to speak out.* Sydney, Macmillan.

Lacina, Bethany and Gabriel Uriarte (2009). "The PRIO Battle Deaths Dataset, 1946–2008, Version 3.0. Documentation of Coding Decisions". *European Journal of Population* 21.

Lee, Jonathan L. (1996). *The "ancient supremacy": Bukhara, Afghanistan and the battle for Balkh, 1731–1901.* Leiden, E.J. Brill.

Lister, Sarah and Adam Pain (2004). Trading in Power: The Politics of "Free" Markets in Afghanistan. *Briefing Paper.* Kabul, Afghanistan Research and Evaluation Unit.

Marchand, Marianne H. (2009). "The Future of Gender and Development after 9/11: Insights from Postcolonial Feminism and Transnationalism". *Third World Quarterly* 30 (5): 921–935.

Olson, Lara (2006). "Fighting for Humanitarian Space: Ngos in Afghanistan". *Journal of Military and Strategic Studies* 9 (1): 1–28.

Pain, Adam and Sayed Mohammad Shah (2009). Policymaking in Agriculture and Rural Development in Afghanistan. *Case Study Series*. P. McCann and M. Bonarski. Kabul, Afghanistan Research and Evaluation Unit.

Raj, Anita, Charlemagne S. Gomez and Jay G. Silverman (2011). "Multisectorial Afghan Perspectives on Girl Child Marriage: Foundations for Change Do Exist in Afghanistan". *Violence Against Women* 20 (10): 1–17.

Razavi, Shahra (2009). "Engendering the Political Economy of Agrarian Change". *The Journal of Peasant Studies* 36 (1): 197–226.

Reid, Rachel (2009). "We have the promises of the world": Women's rights in Afghanistan. B. Adams, E. Pearson and J. Saunders. New York, Human Rights Watch.

Rivas, Althea-Maria (2011). Health and Education in Afghanistan: 10 years After – Quantity not Quality. *ACBAR Policy Series*. Kabul, Agency Coordinating Body for Afghan Relief (ACBAR).

Roy, Olivier (1989). "Afghanistan: Back to Tribalism or on to Lebanon?" *Third World Quarterly* 11 (4): 70–82.

Rubin, Barnett R. (2002). *The fragmentation of Afghanistan: State formation and collapse in the international system*. New Haven, Yale University Press.

Schöch, Rüdiger (2008). "UNHCR and the Afghan Refugees in the Early 1980s: Between Humanitarian Action and Cold War Politics". *Refugee Survey Quarterly* 27 (1): 45–57.

Schütte, Stefan (2014). "Living with Patriarchy and Poverty: Women's Agency and the Spatialities of Gender Relations in Afghanistan". *Gender, Place & Culture* 21 (9): 1176–1192.

Smith, Deborah (2009). Community-based Dispute Resolution Processes in Nangarhar Province. *Case Study Series*. L. Kim. Kabul, Afghanistan Research and Evaluation Unit.

Steans, Jill (1998). *Gender and international relations: an introduction*. New Brunswick, Rutgers University Press.

Tapper, Nancy (1973). "The Advent of Pashtun "Maldars" in North-Western Afghanistan". *Bulletin of the School of Oriental and African Studies, University of London* 36 (1): 55–79.

Waldman, Matt (2008). Falling Short: Aid Effectiveness in Afghanistan. *ACBAR Advocacy Series*, Agency Coordinating Body for Afghan Relief (ACBAR). March.

Williams, M. J. (2011). "Empire Lite Revisited: NATO, the Comprehensive Approach and State-building in Afghanistan". *International Peacekeeping* 18 (1): 64–78.

Wright, Joanne (1997). "Deconstructing Development Theory: Feminism, the Public/Private Dichotomy and the Mexican Maquiladoras". *The Canadian Review of Sociology and Anthropology* 34 (1): 71–92.

5 Nangarhar Province

The eastern province of Nangarhar has historically provided a key stage on which Afghanistan's larger dynamics of power have played out. Sitting astride the ancient Silk Road between the Middle East and Asia, this area has long acted as a gateway for imperial conquests, commercial trade and the spread of different peoples and their diverse cosmologies. The province's urban centre, Jalalabad, lies at the mouth of the Kunar and Laghman valleys on the route to Chitral and India north of the Khyber Pass on the Kabul-Peshawar route. Due to its location, the province has long held commercial, military and political importance as is amply demonstrated by several defining moments in Afghanistan's history which have played out here. In the nineteenth century, the province bore witness to the 1838 entry and 1842 retreat cum massacre of British military forces in the first Anglo-Afghan war (Lee, 1996). In the twentieth century, tribes and communities in Nangarhar instigated campaigns of resistance against the centralising regimes of the "liberal" King Amanullah in 1929 and later against the brutal rule of the People's Democratic Party of Afghanistan (PDPA) and their Soviet sponsors from 1978 to 1979, a conflict which continued into the next decade (Keiser, 1984; Rubin, 2002). Finally, Nangarhar provided the space in which Osama Bin Laden's training camps were housed and the Tora Bora escape route through which Bin Laden and his cadre of fighters fled to Pakistan in November 2001 (Jackson, 2014).

In addition to these major political events, Nangarhar has always featured prominently in Afghanistan's social and economic life. Of particular significance is the province's position as a migratory passage for communities of Pashtun kinsfolk and co-religionists across the arbitrary border separating Afghanistan and the North West Frontier Province (NWFP) and Federally Administered Tribal Areas (FATA) of Pakistan. This transit has been vital in sustaining Afghan families both socially and economically as they have sought to struggle with more than three decades of conflict-induced displacement. At the same time, the province is a major economic hub and site of agricultural production. Nangarhar is a major breadbasket of Afghanistan with the Kabul and Kunar rivers providing irrigation to the fertile lands of the province's capital, Jalalabad, and its neighbouring districts. In the twentieth century, these factors ensured that Nangarhar featured prominently as a site of foreign-led modernisation efforts.

This was especially apparent in the decades following World War Two when the USSR provided development aid for a variety of economic projects, such as dams, roads and irrigation canals, to transform the province's traditional pastoral and settled agricultural practices (Dupree, 1973: 57–65).

It is thus little wonder that, in the contemporary period of Western state-building following the fall of the Taliban, in October 2001, Nangarhar emerged as a pivotally important location in the minds of external planners. Nangarhar was often held aloft as an example of the success of development and security strategies taking place in conflictual settings (Kemp, 2010). "Successes" were counted as the major reduction of opium poppy production, the relative abatement of insurgent activity and the implementation of major infrastructure projects (Donahue and Fenzel, 2008: 34–35; Spencer, 2009: 34–40).

The resulting military and aid-fuelled bubble economy in Nangarhar gave rise to massive waves of returning families, numbering approximately 850,000 people, in the immediate years following 2001 (Davin et al. 2009). What became apparent, however, about both these returning families, and the many communities already present, was the precarious nature of their lives in the brave new world of US-led development programming in the province despite the touted "successes". While many families in Nangarhar were able to rise above a technical definition of poverty[1] through employment in the bubble economy, their lives were still characterised by unending cycles of debt repayment and financial adversity as will be expanded upon later.

In this chapter, I will take three main approaches. The first of these will be to examine more closely the story of Nangarhar's "success" by showing the way in which a predominately US-led military and development intervention fed into the province's ongoing dynamics of power. Emphasis here will be placed on the disjuncture between US policy-makers' and strategists' perception of their intervention's benefits and the actual experiences of communities throughout the province. This chapter will second turn to the grassroots level in order to "gender human security". In Nangarhar, as I will attempt to show, the US and the international development mission unwittingly exacerbated pre-existing gendered hierarchies of power which adversely affect women's ability to gain meaningful forms of security and fulfilment in their lives. Finally, this chapter will seek to provide a feminist account of human security (HS), by examining existing struggles for change within communities against these gendered hierarchies of power.

Dynamics of power in Nangarhar Province

In the early months and years following the US-supported 2001 overthrow of the Taliban in Afghanistan, key Mujahedeen commanders and factions from eastern Afghanistan sought to reassert their control over Jalalabad and the province of Nangarhar more broadly.[2] They received strong backing from the US government through the CIA which provided arms and funding for them to establish themselves as de facto armed rulers of Jalalabad and its surrounding districts. This support reflected the Bush Administration's overwhelming desire to kill and capture Al-Qaeda and Taliban fighters during the onset and immediate aftermath of their intervention into Afghanistan. However, by 2004 the dynamics of power and competition began to change in Nangarhar Province as the US's narrow military mission, Operation Enduring Freedom (OEF), was broadened by the international community's engagement with Afghanistan under the auspices of NATO and the state-building mission of the International Security Assistance Force (ISAF) (Suhrke, 2010). This change in strategy was premised upon the notion that, unless the US and the international community could assist in rebuilding the state of Afghanistan, the country would regress into the violent chaos and disorder that had characterised its existence during the Mujahedeen Wars.

A variety of international state and non-state actors were involved in the ensuing programme in Nangarhar, yet the US government remained pre-eminent in terms of the levels of its funding commitments and its military presence (Goodhand and Mansfield, 2010: 13). In addition to the sizeable contingent of US troops in Regional Command (RC)-East, which oversaw Nangarhar, Nuristan, Laghman and Kunar provinces, the US exerted an overwhelming influence on the course of Nangarhar's development through USAID which, between 2002 and 2011, sub-contracted some $344 million in development projects to US-based international development companies in Nangarhar (USAID, 2011). The mission that the US and its international allies would implement in Nangarhar with the help of provincial elites was premised on the three pillars of constructing and consolidating governing institutions, developing the province's economy and providing security for the population (Kemp, 2010: 34–37).

The first of these tasks required appointing a Provincial Governor (Wali) as well as creating governing and development forums such as the Provincial Council and Provincial Development Council (PDC). Much of this governance framework was mirrored at a sub-provincial level with district governors and district development assemblies (DDAs). In the imagination of the Western donors and technocrats who devised this framework, which was formalised in the 2006 Afghanistan National Development Strategy (ANDS), Afghanistan would be one of the "most centralised governments" in the world (Nixon and Ponzio, 2007: 32). The second and third pillars of this agenda were drawn from a contemporary modernisation-inspired programme known as the "security-development" nexus in which security and development were posited as inextricably conjoined elements of a programme to consolidate a central government's authority over its territory. This programme unfolded in Nangarhar, and elsewhere in Afghanistan, through the expansion of counter-insurgency (COIN) and counter-narcotic (CN) strategies in tandem with large scale agricultural development projects. Counter-insurgency and counter-narcotics provided the "security" component of this overarching vision in which it was understood that insurgents would lose control of "human terrain" and lucrative illicit opium crops, as US and NATO troops protected townships in the rural countryside from their influence (Peterson, 2007: 215; Kemp, 2010: 28). Meanwhile, "development" in the form of neo-liberal market-oriented agricultural programmes would develop "value chains" which would expand rural economies and benefit individuals and communities, thereby increasing their buy-in to the holistic programme of US and Western state-building (Spencer, 2009: 34–40). In turn, it was idealised that these measures would consolidate the rule of Afghanistan's government into the furthest reaches of Afghanistan's rural provinces, paving the way for a transformation of communities' identities from tribesmen and tribeswomen into national citizens of Afghanistan.

Under the successive governorships of Haji Din Mohammad (2004–2005), a leader of the powerful Arsala family clan, and Gul Agha Sherzai (2005–2013), a cunning strongman uprooted from his power base in Kandahar, this security and development programme was deployed in Nangarhar (Jackson, 2014: 6). The results from the first three years of its implementation were as startling as they were positive for US policy-makers. Opium poppy cultivation had all but ceased with the United Nations Office on Drugs and Crime (UNODC) showing the province was effectively "poppy free" in 2005 and in 2008 (UNODC, 2008: 8); moreover, from 2009 to 2012 poppy cultivation remained at low levels compared with the rest of Afghanistan (UNODC, 2012: 30). In its place, many centrally-located and highly visible land owners were seemingly successful in making the transition to licit vegetable crops (Mansfield, 2011: 7). They were assisted in this by the construction of vital road and irrigation projects; moreover, centrally located farming districts around Jalalabad benefitted from the construction of a variety of infrastructure projects such as schools, mosques and other public works. By 2008, insurgent attacks against US and Afghan troops deployed in Nangarhar had virtually ceased (Mukhopadhyay, 2009: 14–16). Even if it was only one province of Afghanistan, US policy-makers had provided a strong example to prove that the rule of the central government could be consolidated within the framework of a COIN campaign which focused on civilian protection and economic growth. Such was the belief in the province that US commanding officers of the 173rd Airborne Brigade in 2007 argued that the interagency project, which was dubbed "Nangarhar Inc.", was proof positive of a concept that could be exported to the rest of Afghanistan.

These superficial signs of progress in Nangarhar were not questioned deeply by US policy-makers, which was unfortunate. There was in fact a considerable disjuncture between US policy-makers' framing of the opium-free political order in Nangarhar as a hierarchical expansion of the state's authority and the complex horizontal political dynamics which were necessary to produce this outcome. The province's governor, Gul Agha Sherzai, was able to produce these results during his long tenure in office only through a multitudinous number of reciprocal relationships with different political actors, factions and communities around Nangarhar, with the backing of the immense wealth and coercive power of the US. These patronage relationships extended to: lesser warlord rivals of the powerful Arsala clan, such as Hazrat Ali and Haji Zaman (Jackson, 2014: 6); key communities, such as the Shinwari tribes, which had been isolated by the previous Arsala Governor Haji Din Mohammad; and, finally, the wealthier and well-integrated communities in Jalalabad and its semi-urban surrounding districts such as Surkhoad.

Using these alliances, Sherzai could keep his promise to "Mr America" through the enlistment of maliks, elders and other rural elites across Nangarhar who could be counted on to help enforce the US and international priority of the opium growing ban (Jackson, 2014: 23). Similarly, the promises of development and infrastructure, as a sweetener to these opium bans, and the military presence of US and Afghan National Army forces in the countryside, reduced the activity and presence of insurgents in most remote rural provinces so that what emerges is that the "success" of Nangarhar was not a product of a technocratic development mission expanding the state. Rather, it was a by-product of the successful, albeit temporary, convergence of interests between Governor Sherzai and local actors in Nangarhar to gain power and profit from the booming conflict economy fuelled by the US intervention (Jackson, 2014: 23). In other words, the institutions of governance and development programmes which were supported by the US and its international allies in the years following 2001, actually produced a widespread and lucrative system for rent-seeking behaviour in terms of political power and economic profit, rather than the transformational "success" that had been posited.

As Jackson notes, this programme produced a system of winners and losers among the powerful actors and factions in the province, with those able to tap these lucrative rivers of wealth and power benefitting immensely at the expense of their rivals (Jackson, 2014: 6). The flow-on effects of the competitive dynamic at the village and community level reflected this elite-driven competition with benefits accruing to the tribes, communities and villages with powerful patrons. However, many rural and urban communities, marginalised by geographical distance and a lack of political ties to patrons, missed out on the profits of this Western mission even though they were to experience many of the punitive and destabilising costs. This was particularly apparent for poorer owner-cultivators and sharecropping families whose livelihoods and access to credit for everyday survival had previously depended on their ability to grow opium. Moreover, the creation of an arbitrary system of winners and losers with access to power and profit from the US-driven bubble-economy in Nangarhar exacerbated pre-existing sources of tension within, and between, rural communities.

This was especially true in the case of land disputes between tribes, communities and powerful factions such as former Mujahedeen factions and provincial executives (Jackson, 2014: 24). As contemporary scholars observe, land disputes in Nangarhar have been a longstanding source of latent conflict between communities and are extraordinarily difficult to resolve due to incomplete record keeping, multiple titles and the practice of land-grabbing (Wily, 2003: 62). This confusion and debate over land ownership increased between 2002 and 2005 with the massive flow of returnees to Nangarhar from Pakistan's refugee camps swelling the population of the province to 1.8 million people (Mansfield, 2011: 6). At the same time, various powerful factions, with funding and armaments from the US and newly-minted official titles, were engaging in land grabs in, and around, lucrative areas such as Jalalabad and its neighbouring districts (Glasser, 2002). The effect of the growth in density of Nangarhar's population and the corresponding rise in land prices often transformed latent tensions between communities into open, and often violent, armed conflict as each side sought to force the issue (Foschini, 2012: 1–7). In such instances, US policymakers' inability to read the competitive dynamics which their intervention had occasioned resulted in more insecurity in rural districts.

Gendering human security in Nangarhar Province

As suggested in Chapter 2, human security, in the extent to which it refers to one's personal fulfilment and happiness, is produced through concrete relationships. In other words, a person has security to the extent to which the life and livelihood that s/he desires is recognised and made possible by others' actions within their social context. When examining human security at a grassroots level in Nangarhar against a backdrop of the US-led international intervention, it is vital to unpack the gendered construction of women's and men's lives as a precursor to understanding how relations of recognition have been configured traditionally and how they have evolved over time. Recognition between people can here be seen to undergird the material and ideational considerations which either permit or deny the types of lives to which people aspire as a pathway towards emotional fulfilment and happiness. Social recognition between women and men in Nangarhar, as is the case in many other communities in Afghanistan, has historically been circumscribed by masculinist honour codes within which men are positioned as the defenders of a household's honour which is indelibly inked into the bodies of *their* women (Tapper, 1981: 391).

Previously, in Chapter 4, with the help of the contemporary feminist researchers Lina Abirafeh and Jill Billaud, I demonstrated the way in which the gendered modernisation programme championed by the US, NATO and the international community intersected with, and often reinforced, the existing gender hierarchies of power which disciplined society. What was perhaps most pernicious about this emerging milieu was that it exacerbated the erosion of relationships of respect and reciprocity within a traditional patriarchal context while at the same time it sanctioned, or at best turned a blind eye to, horrific forms of violence and subjugation of women. Moreover, the very acts that women needed to undertake to navigate and survive in this setting of war, poverty and dislocation, such as running away from home, were denied any societal acceptance.

The following section of this case study quotes the experiences of Pashtun women from eastern and northern Afghanistan, though not from Nangahar Province per se. However, since the province is mostly peopled by Pashtuns, and the stories they relate resonate well beyond any specific location, I am including them as being relevant examples of the experiences of Nangahar women in general.[3] In their discussion, the women, from families of different social status, provided complementary accounts of Afghanistan's gender order. Farishta's father had attended university in Kabul and had become a high-ranking public official there. Like many other urbanised men of his generation he had a more progressive view of gender relations and invested in both his daughter's and his son's primary and secondary education. In their home district of Tagab, in Kapisa Province, these modernist views of gender relations, as well as his affiliation with the government, drew enmity from their own family and neighbours. This hostility increased during the civil war to the point that the family was driven out.

> All our villagers and our relatives were angry at my father. They were saying that you're a Kafir (A person who doesn't believe in god or his prophet Muhammad), because my dad let us study and go to school. They even said that you're god's enemy. That's why my father and my family never went to Tagab again. They can never go there anymore because our relatives are Mujahedin and they're working with the Taliban. If anyone of our family goes there, our villagers and relatives will kill them. Because they say that you're a Kafir and unbeliever. Because your daughters are going outside to school and you let them to do so. But my dad never cared about them and he said I want my daughters to study and be educated.

In comparison, both Pashmina and Kashmala were from strict, traditional households in their respective provincial settings of Kunduz and Laghman. They had been married to middle-aged men when they were 14 and 15 respectively in situations in which their fathers held complete and unquestioned authority. Using their own marriages as examples, these women provide a very stark insight into the hierarchy of gender relations in their village contexts.

PASHMINA: Whoever comes and says "would you like it if your daughter married my son?" the girl's family says "Yes" and they're marrying their daughter to that person without knowing who he is and how he behaves. They don't know whether the man is working or he's jobless. The girl's family only thinks about the Walwar (bride price). Fathers were so strict in those times. For example, when my father was sitting in the same room with us, we couldn't even talk. Then when such a father even asked for my opinion on whether I'm agreeing or not about getting married to that person I couldn't say anything because I was afraid of my father that if I said something he would be so angry.

KASHMALA: Your father was good. You know what my father did with me? I was only 14 years old when my dad came inside my room and said "iron the handkerchief". (A customary act in which the bride's family gave the groom's family a handkerchief filled with sweets to indicate their agreement to a marriage proposal.) I was shocked and asked "Why dad? What for?" He told me that I want you to marry this boy. I cried and called my mother. Then my father became so angry and he had beaten me so that I stopped crying and shouting. The boy they wanted me to marry was so much older than me and he was an alcoholic. But in Afghanistan once you marry someone then it's too bad to leave or divorce him. So I had to live with him and I couldn't leave him. In Afghanistan it really rarely happens that a woman gets a divorce. A woman should tolerate any kind of hard situation but she can never get divorced even if she dies she can't.

In their marriages, both women reported physical abuse and psychological torment from their husbands and from their in-laws. Moreover, although they both were aware of the practice of women "running home" to take refuge within their parents' households, they had not undertaken such an action themselves due to the shame such an action would bring on their families. Kashmala offered her own experiences of marriage as a case in point:

> If I give my own example I've tolerated many problems in my father-in-law's family and with my husband. Whether I was sick or healthy I had to do all home chores and even when I was sleeping in my bed if my husband came home, I must get out of bed because maybe he'll beat me and he might be angry that I'm sleeping and nobody is there to put the food on his plate. I couldn't tell anyone even our mother and father.

The stories of these two women serve to highlight the increasingly hierarchical nature of gender relations within families in a changing environment dominated by strict codes of honour. Moreover, in their conversation, these women's recollections also highlight a fundamental perversity inherent in women's ongoing struggles for security and happiness. The perversity here lies in the fact that the actions women were forced into taking in order to survive, such as orphans turning to prostitution after being raped, were denied social recognition and could be punished with death. Farishta, Pashmina and Kashmala each highlighted the dangers and horrors of this hyper-masculinist environment by examining violence against women and prostitution. Farishta noted that, in her home province of Tagab:

> Jihadi officers are going to the people's house and violating the girl they want and in the morning they're telling the elders of the village that the girl in that house is not a good girl and she was violated last night by someone. Then the elders of the village are talking to each other and after that they're sending some people to that house to bring that girl out and they're mostly deciding to stone that girl till she dies, to bayonet her or sometimes they decide to bury her alive.

Meanwhile, Pashmina and Kashmala offered grim accounts of the way in which young girls were often pushed into prostitution after being raped, as a means of survival. Pashmina recalled the story of a 12-year-old girl who had been raped in her own home:

> Once a girl was caught doing this kind of work (prostitution). She was doing it for money and when people asked her why she is doing this work, she said: "I was twelve when people came to our house and they raped me by

force. After that I had no esteem whether in family or in the village. Everyone was taunting me. I tried so hard but I knew that after this I'm not like other girls and I knew that now I'll never be respected in this society. So when I became thirteen I started to do this work and collect money to become rich."

I read the story of this girl in a newspaper and after I read it I became extremely sad. That day I couldn't talk to anyone and I got a really bad headache. I was thinking that how can an Afghan girl do this? Why should she hate her life this much and many other questions were going on in my mind? I couldn't even sleep that night, and all the night I was thinking about her.

Kashmala responded, agreeing with Pashmina, and recounted a similar story she had heard in the news:

Yeah I know how you felt. There was another girl who was doing this work with anyone who wanted to do it and she was taking money for it. When police caught her and they asked her why is she doing this work? She said that "My guardians died during the wars. I had no brothers or any other family member except two younger sisters. No one was there to protect us and to give food or clothes to us. So then I started working in other houses for cleaning and washing the clothes and dishes. Once a day a boy in the family with whom I was working forced me (raped her) and I had no one to ask about me or to tell the police or to punish that boy. I just cried and stayed calm because I knew that I couldn't do anything.

When I started to work as a cleaner in an office, again a man did it with me by force. I couldn't even inform the police about it because I knew that even if I inform the police they won't do anything and they won't punish those men. So I stayed calm and tried to be strong because I knew the more I cry the more will people do such things with me and they won't care about me because I am a poor, weak girl. So then I tried to be strong and to only think about my two small sisters. I thought that my life is already destroyed now but I won't let my other sisters become like me. So I started to do this work to collect money and to make my sisters' lives full of happiness so that they don't need anything in their lives."

Though none of these women lived in the province of Nangarhar, their experiences of gender relations amid societal change and upheaval are highly instructive when assessing similar dynamics both in Nangarhar and in other provinces. Perhaps most importantly, they had all borne witness to the rise, over decades of war, of an ugly, hyper-masculinist order in place of a more traditional conservative society. Each participant in the conversation highlighted the way in which the burdens of poverty, conflict and dislocation fell most heavily on women, a situation which was certainly not restricted to any one part of Afghanistan at that time.

Surkh-Rud and the peri-urban region

Surkh-rud is a district located directly adjacent to the city of Jalalabad on the Kabul river plain in Nangarhar Province and comprises some 40 key villages. Due to its position on a major river plain, which allows 2–3 crops per year to be grown on the lower elevations, as well as its access to markets and non-farm income, the district has become one of the most densely populated in Nangarhar. Alongside other peri-urban districts with large tracts of fertile land, such as Kama and Bihsud, Surkhrod was more easily integrated into the modernising economic programme fuelled by US and international development aid (Mansfield, 2005: 24). Power in this district lies in the hands of the Arsala clan, the Mujahedeen royalty of Nangarhar descended from the Jabbarkhel sub-tribe of the Ahmadzai-Ghilzais, who grabbed much of the district's land in the early 1990s (Jackson, 2014: 29–30). Wealthier families, who own or have access to land as well as non-farm income opportunities for male family members, are characterised by higher levels of security in the sense that women and men from such families experience a greater satisfaction of their everyday needs, as well as increased access to healthcare for girls and young women (Naseem, 2012: 32).

Although many families and communities in lower Surkhrud were able to transition to, and benefit from, the US-led agricultural modernisation programme, it is important to distinguish these groups from farming communities in "upper Surkhrud". Families in the latter grouping are characterised by having smaller, less viable land parcels as well as less access to water and markets (Mansfield, 2005: 10). They could not diversify their crops to higher-value vegetables, due to the perishability of these crops, the lack of water and the high costs of diesel fuel required to run water pumps; they also faced potential exploitation from middle men on whom they had to rely to get their goods to market (Mansfield, 2006: 15). For these families, the US-led agricultural agenda, and the ban on opium growing between 2008 and 2012, necessitated a switch to wheat farming whose returns were not sufficient to meet the everyday survival needs of their households. As a consequence, at least one adult male from each household was required to leave and send remittances from other opium growing regions such as Balkh and Badakhshan.

Other coping strategies for these poorer and more vulnerable households involved selling livestock and household assets and, potentially, migrating to Pakistan or elsewhere in Afghanistan. The ban on the growth of opium fell heavily on sharecropping families for whom the returns from licit agriculture were insufficient for them to afford to lease land, and on those many families who were dependent on their adult males receiving wages from the opium harvest. The coping strategies used by families to deal with these new economic realities often involved practices harmful to women, such as selling their daughters at very early ages to gain money from the bride price (Mansfield, 2011: 8–9).

This increasing trend towards the objectification and commodification of women by poor and impoverished families also became entrenched among other non-agricultural communities in the district. The several thousand people of the brickmaking families of Surkh Rud provide an illustrative story of the problems associated with indebtedness, which are all too common among many poorer Afghans, especially the returnees from Pakistan. These families often had to take out a loan to cover the family's immediate and ongoing needs, including the cost of their relocation to Afghanistan; in many cases, families inevitably needed to take out another loan to pay for further family needs and as a result they became increasingly destined to live out their lives earning wages making bricks (Samuel Hall, 2011: 48–49). In an attempt to pay off their loans more quickly, families often sent their children to work making bricks at a very early age. Though these families have shelter, provided for them by the kiln owner, as well as water and food, there is little quality of life. While the boys and men of a household will spend their entire lives making bricks, girls, upon reaching puberty, will be married off and forever isolated, by strict conditions of purdah, in their small household compounds, a point made clear by the following excerpt from an International Labour Organisation (ILO) (Samuel Hall, 2011: 64–65) report:

> Simingol does not want to get married in a few years. She says that being married is as much work (as making bricks): "I will be working in the home and will be locked inside the home." Her sister got married a few years ago and she does not envy her life. She also says there is nothing good about working in the kilns. Simingol anticipates that they will continue to do this work for many more years to come.

This brief excerpt provides a revealing account of the perspective of young girls in such situations on the realities of their lives. For such families, everyday life is geared towards survival and the never-ending repayment of loans taken from brick kiln operators. In such contexts, girls like Simingol are treated as commodities by their parents, no more than a means of making further inroads on debt repayment.

Achin and the remote rural region

The differentiated rural communities of Achin, located to the south of Jalalabad on the Pakistani border, offer another way of understanding women's human security in contrast to the bubble economy centred on Jalalabad and its surrounding districts. Though Achin is predominately inhabited by different, and often conflicting, Shinwari Pashtun *qawm*s, what is also true is the extent to which this district offers a representation of the life of other Pashtun tribal communities in similarly remote provinces such as Khogayani and Sherzad. As mentioned previously, in contrast to the more low-lying lands of the province where farm sizes are larger, land sizes for many of the people living in this district are very small and offer limited productive value to farmers attempting to grow wheat or alternative crops (Mansfield, 2011: 24). These communities have always preferred to grow opium, because the opium crop is non-perishable, it attracts a high price, it can be sold at the farm gate and, finally, farmers can easily obtain loans in advance for their future crops with little fear of being unable to make repayments (Pain, 2008: 1–2). Moreover, if the crop is grown widely, it offers plenty of reliable, well-paid daily labour for a family's adult males.

In 2005, the impact of the first opium ban by the Western-supported provincial governor was harshly felt across the entire district by the landowners, sharecroppers and day labourers who grew, harvested and processed the crop (Mansfield, 2005: 12–13). The abrupt ban on the crop increased the indebtedness of a majority of farmers and sharecroppers who had already taken out advance loans from opium traders on the future returns of the 2005 crop. The wiping out of some 9.8 million labour days associated with tending to, harvesting and processing the crop was another indicator of the broader impact this ban would have on households and meant that a vast majority of households in the province lost five months of paid labour for at least one member of the family (Mansfield, 2005: 33). The access to informal credit, which had previously been easily available, all but dried up, necessitating more extreme strategies to deal with the situation. Coping strategies employed by indebted families involved migration by working age males to find wage labour elsewhere and, in many cases, the selling of productive resources such as livestock, land and, ultimately, women (Mansfield, 2011: 8–9).

It was this sale of very young daughters into early marriages in order to pay off loans or generate household income that revealed the harsh impact of the opium ban on women and their families. The deleterious consequences of these marriages for the girls involved were stark: domestic violence, emotional trauma and the very real possibility of severe pain, injury and death through early childbearing (Raj *et al.* 2011: 1–4). Opium production briefly bounced back in 2007 but an opium ban was successfully reinforced again in 2008 the effect of which was to constrain poppy growth up until 2012. The 2008 ban brought the same problems as the ban of 2005 although, as Mansfield and Pain (2008: 8–9) show, the effects were felt more in the remote southern rural district of Achin. Factors which balanced out the effects of the ban for some people in other parts of the province that year were the high price of wheat and flour, which led to an increase in the growth of this crop by many households who had previously only been trying to ensure food security as opposed to achieving a marketable surplus. But in the more remote areas of the province, the need to grow opium was vital to household survival. It was in these areas that the aforementioned deleterious logics came into play with farming households selling their productive assets to repay loans and, again, in some cases, selling daughters for the bride price to pay back loans and generate household income. The full expression of this sexualised commodification of women as a means of coping with poverty was also found in the neighbouring district of Shinwar where men sold their wives or female relations into prostitution rings in a bazaar (Azarbaijani-Moghaddam, 2010: 72).

Struggles for recognition in Nangarhar

Many of the problems associated with targeted interventions to improve the lives and security of women in Nangarhar, not to mention Afghanistan more broadly, reside in the reliance of external agents on formal, political and juridical institutions which do not resonate with the existing social and political relationships in which people's lives are enmeshed. The result of this formalistic approach to women's security has been an inability to comprehend the logics which drive exclusionary or inclusive forms of recognition between women and men and their accompanying practices. Instead, state-builder and gender programmers alike have repeatedly fallen back on a belief that the issue of women's rights and security can be resolved through problem-solving institutional capabilities. In Nangarhar, this disjuncture has been particularly apparent in the effort of the US and international community to both secure women's formal rights as well as to qualitatively improve their lives through development initiatives.

In Nangarhar, women can be arrested for crimes which do not appear in the formal penal code, such as "running away from home" (Reid, 2009: 70). If they have been raped, then they can be forced to marry their rapist or can be returned to their families where they might face death in order to restore the household's honour. Thus, women's formal rights and protections have been routinely violated, with the awareness and complicity of the male agents within the institutions ostensibly designed to secure their lives. This is evidenced when examining the policing of the justice system in Nangarhar, a job undertaken by men who often see their positions as the means for their own enrichment and sexual gratification, that is in demanding bribes and in raping young girls and boys and also women (Azarbaijani-Moghaddam, 2010: 39). This is well documented by Sippi Azabaijani-Moghaddam (2010: 75) who explored gender relations in Nangarhar in 2010 with a multitude of women and men. In her interviews with workers from Nangarhar's chapter of the Afghanistan Independent Human Rights Commission (AIHRC) she was informed of the way police were often involved in raping young girls and had this story recounted to her:

> Two policemen under the pretext that they were asking for a girl's hand in marriage for their brother took a 16-year-old school girl from her home and raped her. This came to us and we followed it to the prison and saw that they had been freed. When we asked the directors why they said that the chief of police has ordered them that they were innocent ... They had paid a bribe to the chief of police and walked off scot free. The interesting thing is that the poor girl spent one and half months in prison until she paid 5000 USD in bribes to free herself. You tell me where this girl should go and who she should get help from?

This ugly account powerfully displays the inherent problems associated with improving women's lives and gender relations through formalised institutions of justice in Nangarhar. Indeed, one of the major reasons parents in Nangarhar choose not to send their girls and boys to school is the risk of sexual abuse posed to them by the actions of the police or other armed militant factions of armed men. The technocratic problem-solving endeavours of the US and international community fail to engage with the deeper problematics facilitating this abuse which lie in the distortion of a traditional gender system whereby men abrogate their traditional masculine roles to honour and protect women (Kandiyoti, 2009: 9). What emerges instead is that the worst abuses of this post-traditional gender system are facilitated by the very institutions meant to curtail this behaviour.

Azabaijani-Moghaddam's report also provides empirical insight into the way in which efforts to advance the lives of rural women in Nangarhar through development initiatives face a similar dilemma. This is apparent in the National Solidarity Program (NSP) which provides small direct investments for local communities to build infrastructure, such as solar panels, or to develop business initiatives. The mechanism through which the NSP is extended are Community Development Councils (CDCs) made up of different local decision-makers and these CDCs can be male only, female only, or mixed. In conservative Pashtun areas of Afghanistan, like Nangarhar, female-only CDCs are envisioned as a way of providing women with an opportunity to organise and gain a role in public life; thereby improving their own self-esteem and assisting in positively changing men's ideas about women's roles. Unfortunately, these well-intentioned developmental initiatives do not take place in neutral space but within a hierarchically gendered social context. On this point, Azabaijani-Moghaddam's report (2010: 19) noted that women's projects in Nangarhar were either ignored completely or instrumentally taken advantage of by male family members. In such instances, men, who derided women as stupid and incompetent, would take the bulk of the women's cash grants for themselves and oversee the way in which the women could use the remainder. This is elaborated by one Nangarhar woman responding to interviewers when asked about whether there was a woman's CDC or shura in her community:

> There is no shura here. It's a lie. Two women came here and told us to set up a shura. The head of the men's shura Iqbal Safi was with them and my brother-in-law Commander Abdullah and Abdul Zahir the deputy of the shura. They told me you are the head of the shura ... Then one day they brought eight sewing machines and said find eight women and sew ... When the women came from the NGO we would sit in one room and sew and the rest of the time we sewed in our own homes. They paid me 1800 Afghanis per month as sewing teacher but whenever they felt like it, every two or three months ... They did not tell us anything about NSP. The men in the shura never asked our opinion about anything.

What emerges most obviously from this anecdote is the disconnect between an idealised development forum where women jointly undertake independent projects, with the hierarchical nature of men's authority allowing them to shape such an initiative. What is also evident from the actions of the brother-in-law Mujahedeen commander, and other male CDC members, is an awareness of the need to manage the expectations of the NGO by making sure the women are seen sewing together on their visits.

Struggles for recognition against gender hierarchies

The seeming lack of progress in improving women's lives and, consequently, their human security, does not mean that efforts to engage Afghanistan's communities should be abandoned. Instead, it means that policy-making in Nangarhar requires an even deeper engagement with local actors and communities whereby policy-makers should let go of preconceived notions of what progress should look like and how it should take place. This engagement, which is predicated on the methodological precepts outlined in Chapter 1, should ideally initiate an ongoing conversation between policy-makers, local actors and their audiences, in which protagonists would seek to place themselves in the position of, and learn from, each other's perspective. It is hoped that in such an arrangement, the universal moral positions of both external agents and local actors would give way, through a process of cultural translation, to a shared ethical vocabulary intelligible to both parties.

Attempts to engage in such conversations and, consequently, to further progressive policies for women, would necessarily be driven by different social contexts in Afghanistan and could not be foretold. However, what is apparent is the extent to which such conversations could benefit by engaging with pre-existing struggles for recognition and change by women and men within their own communities. Communities themselves are already evaluating and contesting the conflicting beliefs about gender relations between women and men as well as hierarchical gender social systems. These struggles over a variety of gendered practices harmful to women such as the commodification and objectification of women in marriage, highlight the potential for new relations of recognition to emerge which are more accommodating of the kind of lives to which women aspire.

The existence of these endogenous debates over gender serves to shatter the patronising characterisation of Afghanistan's Pashtun communities as being governed by backward and unchanging patriarchal views. Moreover, it points to immanent revolutionary possibilities, whereby women and men can re-formulate their own gendered identities as well as broader social performances of gender in ways which challenge dominant hierarchical framings. What became apparent from the focus group discussions which I organised among three expatriate Pashtun women living with their immediate families in Delhi, India, was their active pursuit of these possibilities in their own lives despite wider pressures from their community to perform typical gender roles. This was particularly evident from the story of one respondent about the way in which her relationship with her husband was publicly adjudicated for its adherence to accepted modes of behaviour:

> When my husband was at home he was really nice with me. But whenever he was going out with his friends, his friends were telling him that "Oh, your wife is going for study? How can you let your wife go and study with lots of males in her class? When your wife is coming out of the class we're watching her; everyday she is walking with other boys ... and so on."

Then when my husband was coming back home, he was so angry and he was beating me a lot. But I knew that it wasn't his fault because all of his friends were only teasing him because of me. In fact, my husband is a really good man, he went with me himself to the educational centre and registered my name there, but people were not letting him be good with me.

These kinds of thing were always happening in Afghanistan but even in India too it happens. Sometimes he says to me "Don't work anymore". When I ask him why? He says that people are taunting him and telling him that "You're not a man, because your wife is working and going to the office and your daughters are going to school but you're not telling them anything."

Then I am saying to him who cares about people. Don't think about people because they never stop talking. Then he thinks and says: "Yeah, you're right. Because whatever I do, people would never stop talking."

During that time, none of the Pashtun people talked to me but now, when I don't even want to say Salam to them, and I want to ignore them, they're talking to me. Because now they know the truth that education is not only for males and a female can also get educated.

While microcosmic, this example of a struggle for recognition within a hierarchically gendered social setting provides insight into human subjects' underlying resistance to being disciplined by such systems. Moreover, although the relatively safer and freer context of India undoubtedly contributed to the advancement of this struggle, a variety of authorship confirms that similarly revolutionary struggles are also taking place in Afghanistan (Smith and Manalan, 2009; Smith, 2009b; Shirzai, 2013).

This is apparent in Nangarhar where Pashtun women and men are confronted on a daily basis with the disjuncture between traditionally idealised gender relations and the ugliness accompanying the existing hyper-masculine order. Though such forms of resistance should not be romanticised, they are nevertheless a real response by different communities in the fight against the gendered excesses which have been inflicted on women within the post-traditional environment. For instance, one of the most interesting developments in this regard is the extent to which some of the worst tenets and practices of Pashtunwali, which were previously irrevocable, have fallen into disrepute in the eyes of tribal communities. This is especially evident in the case of marriage. As Deborah Smith (2009a: 45–48) shows in a study for the Afghanistan Research Evaluation Unit (AREU), people often display more progressive views on marriage, especially relating to the future happiness of the groom and bride, as well as a tacit acknowledgement of the harm caused by certain types of marriage, including: bride price marriage, exchange marriage and inheritance marriage, all of which are forbidden in Islam. Furthermore, what has become apparent is the extent to which rural Pashtun tribal communities, including *qawm*s from among the Shinwari, Khugiyani and Mohmand, no longer engage in the practice of *baad* to settle disputes involving murders and other serious crimes (Neamat Nojumi *et al.* 2004; Smith, 2009a). According to Smith, among Mohmand and Shinwari women and men in particular, a common reason for people's disdain of *baad* is that a girl, through no fault of her own, was sentenced to live a life as a tormented slave in the household of her husband's family (Smith, 2009a: 47).

What is also apparent, is the extent to which it is possible for women to gain power within wider community decision-making processes that can help to ameliorate some of the worst and most violent excesses targeting women. For instance, as Smith has shown, traditional conflict dispute mechanisms, as found in Jirgas, allow women both to appear as disputants and, in the case of older and respected women elders or "white hairs", to participate in the jirga's adjudication process (Smith, 2009a: 39–42). Moreover, she noted that issues of women's personal, emotional and physical insecurity are addressed by these Jirgas, even where a jirga's outcome contravened the usually incontrovertible tenets of Pashtunwali. This was evidenced in a Jirga working with provincial authorities to issue a divorce for a young girl who had suffered horrendous abuse from her in-laws after being married into their family (Smith, 2009a: 75–76). Smith provides a summary of this case in the following excerpt:

> This case happened about three to four years prior to the research period. It is the story of Janwara, who as a child was taken against her family's wishes to Pakistan by her inlaws, where she suffered terrible abuse. She eventually returned to her own village, and both the *woliswal* and the *jirga* decided she was innocent, that she should be freed from her in-laws and her marriage, and that she should receive compensation.

Meanwhile, as is common among Pashtun communities elsewhere in Afghanistan, women, and some men, argue against injustices of existing gendered hierarchies of the day as they relate to women's personal autonomy, such as the un-Islamic practices (*haram*) of exchange marriage and the bride price, women's reproductive health, and family planning (Huber, N. *et al.* 2010: 227–231), as well as women's ability to gain an education and participate in public life. What is evidenced in Nangarhar is that, even if current circumstances, such as the prevalence of larger scale conflict between opposing armed factions and material deprivation, prevent the full realisation of the transformative aspects of women's and men's resistance to hierarchies of power, they nevertheless still exist. Thus, what should be apparent by the conclusion of this chapter, is that, in spite of multiple sources of insecurity that have arisen as a result of the onset of Western state-building in this province, there are also multiple forms of everyday agency which women and men exercise in resistance to the gendered relations of domination which still characterise their reformulated social contexts. These ongoing acts of resistance demonstrate both resilience against the pressures and constraints which have been brought about by successive periods of war and state-building as well as subjects' creativity in navigating and challenging the gendered hierarchies of power which underpin their socially-embedded contexts.

Conclusion

This chapter sought to show the way in which the US-led Western Intervention attempted to "problem solve" development in the important rural context of Nangarhar province using counter insurgency and counter narcotics programmes. For a short period, this province seemed to demonstrate the effectiveness of the US agenda to transition the province's rural farming communities away from opium poppy to licit agricultural crops. Insurgent attacks in this province were down and from 2008 to 2012 opium poppy bans were observed by almost all the province's farmers.

Unfortunately, behind this façade of modernisation-inspired agricultural "success", ordinary life was greatly jeopardised for poorer farming communities on more marginal land. The opium bans sharply impacted farmers' access to credit as well as incomes derived by household's male members working on processing the crop. Meanwhile, the arrival of US patronage and power in Nangarhar province served to exacerbate inter-communal rivalries between different Pashtun tribes that contributed to heightened levels of militarisation and violence facing families. This conflagration between external state-builders and local structures of power served to exacerbate gendered forms of insecurity facing women but also men.

Nevertheless, what is apparent is the extent to which women, and men, pragmatically and creatively attempt to navigate and challenge broader gendered hierarchies of power within their shared lives. This was powerfully demonstrated by Deborah Smith who conducted fieldwork with Shinwari Pashtun communities in Nangarhar and observed the way in which community-based dispute resolution processes were used to argue against incontrovertible elements of Pashtunwali in favour of women's well-being.

Notes

1 This is displayed in a comparison between two livelihood reports. See: Institute, ICON (2009). National Risk and Vulnerability Assessment 2007/8: A Profile of Afghanistan. B. de Bruijn. Kabul. Also, see (2011). Afghanistan Mortality Survey. Kabul, Afghan Public Health Institute, Ministry of Public Health, Central Statistics Organization, Kabul, Afghanistan, ICF Macro, Calverton, Maryland, USA, IIHMR, Jaipur, India and WHO/EMRO, Cairo, Egypt, 2011.
2 The most prominent of these figures included the following: Haji Hazrat Ali, who was a Mujahedeen commander and member of the minority Pashayee ethnic-group from Northern Nangarhar; Haji Zaman Ghamsharik, a Pashtun and former Mujahedeen commander from central Nangarhar; and finally, the powerful Pashtun family of the Arsalas whose male family members have figured prominently as Mujahedeen commanders since the USSR invasion and have often been referred to as "resistance royalty".
3 Focus Group Discussion between Pashtun women in New Delhi, India, undertaken on 28–29 July 2011.

References

Afghanistan Mortality Survey (2011). Kabul, Afghan Public Health Institute, Ministry of Public Health, Central Statistics Organization, Kabul, Afghanistan, ICF Macro, Calverton, Maryland, USA, IIHMR, Jaipur, India and WHO/EMRO, Cairo, Egypt, 2011.

Azarbaijani-Moghaddam, Sippi (2010). A Study of Gender Equity through the National Solidarity Programme's Community Development Councils. Kabul, Danish Committee for Aid to Afghan Refugees (DACAAR).

Davin, Eric, Viani Gonzalez and Nassim Majidi (2009). UNHCR's Voluntary Repatriation Program: Evaluation of the Impact of the Cash Grant. Kabul, Office of the United Nations High Commissioner for Refugees (UNHCR).

Donahue, Patrick and Michael Fenzel (2008). "Combating a Modern Insurgency: Combined Task Force Devil in Afghanistan". *Military Review* 88 (2): 25–40.

Dupree, Louis (1973). *Afghanistan*. Oxford, Oxford University Press.

Foschini, Fabrizio (2012). Land Grabs in Afghanistan (1): Nangrahar, the Disputed Rangelands. Kabul, Afghanistan Analysts Network: 1–7.

Glasser, Susan B. (2002). "U.S. backing helps warlord solidify power". *Washington Post*, 18 February 2002.

Goodhand, Jonathon and David Mansfield (2010). Drugs and (Dis)order: A Study of the Opium Trade, Political Settlements and State-making in Afghanistan. *Working Paper No. 83*. London, Crisis States Research Centre – London School of Economics (LSE).

Huber, Douglas, N. Saeedi and A. K. Samadi (2010). "Achieving Success with Family Planning in Rural Afghanistan". *Bulletin of the World Health Organization* 88 (3): 227–231.

Institute, ICON (2009). National Risk and Vulnerability Assessment 2007/8: A profile of Afghanistan. B. de Bruijn, Kabul.

Jackson, Ashley (2014). Politics and Governance in Afghanistan: The Case of Nangarhar Province. *Secure Livelihoods Research Consortium*. London, Overseas Development Institute. Working Paper 16.

Kandiyoti, Deniz (2009). The Lures and Perils of Gender Activism in Afghanistan *The Anthony Hyman Memorial Lecture*: School of Oriental and Africa Studies, University of London.

Keiser, Lincoln (1984). "The Rebellion in Darra-i Nur". *Revolutions and Rebellions in Afghanistan: Anthropological Perspectives*. Berkeley, CA: Institute of International Studies, University of California, Berkeley.

Kemp, Robert (2010). "Counterinsurgency in Nangarhar Province, Eastern Afghanistan, 2004–2008". *Military Review* (November–December): 34–42.

Lee, Jonathan L. (1996). *The "ancient supremacy": Bukhara, Afghanistan and the battle for Balkh, 1731–1901*. Leiden, E.J. Brill.

Mansfield, David (2005). *Pariah or Poverty?: The Opium Ban in the Province of Nangarhar in the 2004/05 Growing Season and Its Impact on Rural Livelihood Strategies*. Jalalabad, PAL Management Unit, New Duramsal, Rigisha Mohad Khan.

Mansfield, David (2006). Water Management, Livestock and the Opium Economy. Opium Poppy Cultivation in Nangarhar and Ghor. *Case Studies Series*. Kabul, Afghanistan Research and Evaluation Unit.

Mansfield, David (2011). "The Ban on Opium Production Across Nangarhar: A Risk Too Far?" *International Journal of Environmental Studies* 68 (3): 381–395.

Mansfield, David and Adam Pain (2008). *Counter-Narcotics in Afghanistan: The Failure of Success?* Kabul, Afghanistan Research and Evaluation Unit.

Mukhopadhyay, Dipali (2009). *Warlords as Bureaucrats: The Afghan Experience*. Washington DC, Carnegie Endowment for International Peace.

Naseem, Muhammad (2012). *Determining factors and utilization pattern for normal delivery care in Nangarhar province of Afghanistan.* Master of Public Health, Vrije University.

Neamat Nojumi, Dyan Mazurana and Elizabeth Stites (2004). Afghanistan's Systems of Justice: Formal, Traditional, and Customary. Washington DC, Feinstein International Famine Center, Youth and Community Program, Tufts University.

Nixon, H. and R. Ponzio (2007). "Building Democracy in Afghanistan: The Statebuilding Agenda and International Engagement". *International Peacekeeping – London* 14 (1): 26–40.

Pain, Adam (2008). Opium Poppy and Informal Credit. *Issue Paper Series.* AREU. Kabul, Afghanistan Research and Evaluation Unit.

Peterson, Elizabeth (2007). "Two Sides of the Same Coin: The Link between Illicit Opium Production and Security in Afghanistan". Wash. UJL & Pol'y 25 (1): 215.

Raj, Anita, Charlemagne S. Gomez and Jay G. Silverman (2011). "Multisectorial Afghan Perspectives on Girl Child Marriage: Foundations for Change Do Exist in Afghanistan". *Violence Against Women* 20 (10): 1–17.

Reid, Rachel (2009). "We have the promises of the world": women's rights in Afghanistan. B. Adams, E. Pearson and J. Saunders. New York, Human Rights Watch.

Rubin, Barnett R. (2002). *The fragmentation of Afghanistan: State formation and collapse in the international system.* New Haven, Yale University Press.

Shirzai, Ajmal (2013). Research Report: Engaging Community Resilience for Security, Development and Peace Building in Afghanistan. Kabul, Future Generations.

Smith, Deborah J. (2009a). Community-based Dispute Resolution Processes in Nangarhar Province. *Case Study Series.* L. Kim. Kabul, Afghanistan Research and Evaluation Unit.

Smith, Deborah J. (2009b). Decisions, Desires and Diversity: Marriage Practices in Afghanistan. *Issue Paper Series.* M. Lewis. Kabul, Afghanistan Research and Evaluation Unit.

Smith, Deborah J. and Shelly Manalan (2009). Community-based Dispute Resolution Processes in Bamyan Province. *Case Study Series.* V. Quinlan. Kabul, Afghanistan Research and Evaluation Unit.

Spencer, David K. (2009). "Afghanistan's Nangarhar Inc: A Model for Interagency Success". *Military Review* 89 (4): 34–40.

Samuel Hall Consulting Staff (2011). Buried in Bricks: A Rapid Assessment of Bonded Labour in Brick Kilns in Afghanistan. Kabul, Samuel Hall Consulting.

Suhrke, Astri (2010). The Case for a Light Footprint: The International Project in Afghanistan. *The eighth annual Anthony Hyman memorial lecture.* University of London, School of Oriental and Africa Studies.

Tapper, Nancy (1981). "Direct Exchange and Brideprice: Alternative Forms in a Complex Marriage System". *Man* 16 (3): 387–407.

UNODC (2008). Afghanistan Opium Survey 2008. Kabul and Vienna, United Nations Office on Drugs and Crime (UNODC) and Government of Afghanistan Ministry of Counter Narcotics.

UNODC (2012). Afghanistan Opium Survey 2012: Opium Risk Assessment for All Regions (Phase 1 & 2). Kabul and Vienna, United Nations Office on Drugs and Crime (UNODC) and Government of Afghanistan Ministry of Counter Narcotics.

USAID (2011). Fact Sheet – Nangarhar Province.

Wily, Liz (2003). Land Rights in Crisis: Restoring Tenure Security in Afghanistan. *Issue Paper Series.* C. Bennett, Kabul.

6 Bamyan Province

The mountainous province of Bamyan lies in the heart of the Hindu Kush mountain range squarely between the Middle East, Central Asia and the Indian Subcontinent. Long before the arrival of Islam, the province's valleys provided a prominent central stage in which a variety of different civilisations and cultures crossed paths on the silk road – the ancient trading route which brought together the Western and Eastern hemispheres from the third century BCE until the twelfth century CE. The beautiful valley of Bamyan was initially important for traders as a hospitable *caravanserai* (a Persian word which refers to a roadside inn) during an arduous journey through inhospitable mountain ranges (Liu, 2011: 31). Because of the expansion and interplay of powerful civilisations to the north and south of the Hindu Kush, Bamyan became established as a major spiritual and intellectual centre of the ancient world. This was particularly so during the reign of the Kushan Empire (200 BCE–300 CE), a trading empire which facilitated commerce between the Roman Empire to the west, the Han Dynasty in China to the east, and the Satavahana Dynasty in India to the south (Liu, 2011: 42–43). This Kushan empire was a strong supporter of Buddhism which spread to China along the silk road. The two colossal Buddhist figures carved into the cliffside in the second and third century CE were classic examples of the splendour of the art produced by this empire (Liu, 2011: 64–65). Unfortunately, these two Buddha figures became better known for their destruction at the hands of the Taliban in 2001.

Though empires would come and go, a rich Buddhist culture thrived in the mountain valleys, protected from external marauding armies – a fact testified to by travelling Chinese scholars in the fifth and seventh centuries CE. Buddhism continued to be practised by the communities living in Bamyan up until the tenth century. This was all brought to a halt in 1222 CE by the invading Mongol tribes of Genghis Khan who laid waste to Bamyan, killing every man, woman, child and animal. Following the Mongol's genocide, the valleys of Bamyan were eventually repopulated by nomadic Turkic tribes and Persian-speaking communities who, alongside the remaining Mongols, would produce the ethnolinguistic community of the Hazaras (Mousavi, 1997; Chiovenda, 2014: 414). However, as Nancy Dupree noted, the region's previous importance was drastically reduced in a changing world by the development of sea-based trade routes which robbed Bamyan of its "reason for being" (Dupree, 1963: 21). Nevertheless, in Bamyan and its surrounding provinces, Shiite-worshiping and Dari-tongued agro-pastoral communities of Hazaras lived autonomously up until the early nineteenth century, forging a rich and vibrant culture.

Bamyan Province is important when seeking to understand the broader Western Intervention in Afghanistan because it tells the story of the Hazara people in Afghanistan and, in so doing, reveals the way in which the modern Afghan state has been experienced by one of the ethnic communities most oppressed by it. At the same time, Bamyan is emblematic of the broader failure of an external international coalition to alleviate conditions of endemic poverty through development programmes. Bamyan has one of the highest rates of poverty in Afghanistan and, although there has been a great deal of international concern about the archaeological preservation of the valley, many observers have argued that little to no attention has been paid to the lives of the poor, landless Hazara families living in caves in the cliffs of the Buddhas (Mariani, 2006: 6–8). International aid has benefitted certain socio-economic groups in Bamyan, primarily the wealthier and more educated families, and development spending is most likely to be given to communities with powerful patrons in the Afghanistan government. Moreover, gender-focused development measures have often exacerbated conditions of insecurity, as will be demonstrated by exploring the impact of micro-credit loans. The dynamic of this growing poverty has affected the basic human insecurity of men, women and children but, in many ways, women have been the most greatly affected.

These differences point to the tensions which exist within, and between, different communities as well as the fact that people's visions of a moral society are often very different. While there is a strong sense of an Hazara identity and nation revolving around a shared struggle against their historical subjugation in Afghanistan, there is also a strong sense of injustice. This is primarily articulated by poorer families who are often forced into exploitative labour arrangements with wealthier and more powerful families in order to ensure their basic survival. It is also broadly recognised that many of the largest beneficiaries of state-building and development processes are the former militant leaders of Hazara Mujahedeen groups whose members have gained power in the new institutional infrastructure of the Afghan State in Kabul and in Bamyan Province (Ibrahimi, 2009: 11).

In this chapter I will repeat the three main arguments of the previous chapter. To begin with I will explore the way in which the arrival of the US and NATO mission in Afghanistan affected communities. In this reconstruction, I will outline the broader political changes associated with the intervention as well as the socio-economic impact of international aid on local districts. Second, I will use feminist theory to gender the concept of human security to provide insight into the gendered dimensions of security at a local level. Finally, I will explore the creative ways in which women and men in Bamyan attempt to navigate and resist the contemporary gendered hierarchies of power which discipline their lives. What should be noted here is that, while Hazara women's lives are still largely tied into a gendered universe which corresponds, to some extent, to a variety of other settled Afghan communities, in many ways the severity and rigidity of hierarchies within Hazara gender dynamics have been changing historically through processes of social transformation such as large scale migration to Iran, Pakistan and further abroad, which has led to changed understandings of both masculinity and femininity.

Dynamics of power in Bamyan Province

What should be noted when discussing Bamyan is that at least 25 per cent of the province's estimated population of 500,000 people is landless. Moreover, most farming families hold less than five *jeribs* (2,000 sq. metres) of agricultural land (Central Statistics, 2012: 16). According to a recent report, based on the 2007/2008 National Risk and Vulnerability Assessment (NRVA), the poverty rate in Bamyan stands at roughly 56 per cent of the population compared to the national rate of 35 per cent (Bank, 2011: 16–17). Alongside decades of violent conflict, the major reasons for this relate to the large influx into Bamyan province, during the twentieth century, of families from other regions of the Hazarajat conquered by Abdur Rahman Kahn and the generational division of land into small plots among families over time (Lety, 2006: 46–47). The agriculture in this mountainous province is also far more marginal due to the scarcity of flat arable land and the distance to major markets outside the Hazarajat.

The contemporary onset of the Western Intervention in Afghanistan has fed into the previously articulated historical dialectic of social change in this provincial context, as well as for the Hazarajat and the Hazara people more broadly. What also needs to be considered is the major change brought about by the removal of the Taliban in 2001. The party of Wahdat, under the leadership of Mohaqiq and Khalili, rose in tandem with the Northern Alliance forces of Dostum, Fahim, Massoud and Ismail Khan and, with the help of US air support, was able to drive the Taliban out of Bamyan Province (Ibrahimi, 2009: 8–9). This period marked the return of autonomy across the Hazarajat, ending the direct Pashtun rule which was occasioned by the Taliban's conquest of Bamyan in 1998. For many Hazaras, this freedom from violent conflict at the hands of militant factions, from the pervasiveness of Pashtun control and intervention into their communities, and from the seasonal arrival of nomadic Pashtun tribes or the Kuchi were the most tangible benefits of the contemporary Western project (Winterbotham, 2011: 67–68).

Another clear benefit was the efficient and commendable delivery of aid following the fall of the Taliban. Several aid agencies had previously worked in the region, including Oxfam (Johnson, 2000: 6, 10) and Solidarites (Solidarites, 2002: 5) and were well-placed to provide emergency aid to a large portion of the population. Their work, between 2001 and 2004, was important in ensuring the survival and basic needs of many families in the province who were particularly vulnerable as a result of drought and the violence of the Taliban (Solidarites, 2002: 5). What was also evident, in contrast to the conflictual period of nominal autonomy in the Hazarajat from 1979 to 1996, was a marked absence of major internecine violence between competing Hazara militant factions. Indeed, as Ibrahimi suggested, the Wahdat party itself was weakened as an independent militant actor (Ibrahimi, 2009: 1). However, despite the absence of armed conflict and direct oppression and humiliation by Pashtun outsiders, the onset and evolution of Western Intervention in Bamyan Province have had mixed effects upon people's lives depending on their social context.

What should be noted is the politicised and self-serving nature of much of this aid. Not only was the overall amount of aid spent on Bamyan far lower than in more insurgent-prone provinces, but also, within Bamyan, the allocation of aid spending favoured particular districts, such as Bamyan District and Yakawlang District, which were represented by the powerful political leaders Mohaqiq and Khalili of Wahdat (Lety, 2006: 28). This was a point made explicitly in a survey, conducted by a non-profit development analysis organisation called Collaborative Learning Projects (CDA), which undertook a series of recorded interviews with local communities in Bamyan (CDA, 2009: 14). As one farmer from Bamyan Province argued:

> Impact of assistance? Where it has come, it has been good. But there is imbalance: if we knew powerful people we would get more. Bamyan centre and Yakawlang are getting much more because the previous governor was from Yakawlang. The current governor does not pay much attention. People demonstrated about the [road being not wide enough], but nothing has been done.

In many ways, the impact of the West in Bamyan has been indirect, through the creation of a miniature bubble economy based in Bamyan District Centre and, to a lesser extent, Yakawlang District, in which foreign and local expatriates involved with the project generate a significant proportion of growth, which then generates a subsequent influx of poorer inhabitants seeking work (Mariani, 2006: 7–8). Moreover, of the aid that is "spent" on the province, much goes into the salaries and operating costs of NGO offices. Major graft in repeated rounds of contracting and sub-contracting often results in a very small amount of funding being spent on physical infrastructure (CDA, 2009: 12).

The contradictions in this Western Project were perhaps most wittily and incisively highlighted for a wider local and international audience by Jawad Zahak. Jawad was the former head of the Bamyan Provincial Council and, until his death in 2011 at the hands of Hezb-I-Islami militants in Parwan province, he instigated a series of community protests (Karimi, 2011). These included the construction, in 2009, of a road from a material called cor or Kaahgel, which is essentially hardened mud, to highlight the lack of any improvement in the Kabul to Bamyan road (Karimi, 2011). He also awarded a certificate of service to a donkey in 2010, claiming that it had done more for Bamyan than had the Karzai government (Karimi, 2011). The popularity of Zahak was evidenced by the fact that at least seven thousand people attended his funeral procession when his body was brought by helicopter to Bamyan City (Karimi, 2011).

While the onset of emergency aid programmes in 2002 provided the basic needs of the province's large proportion of landless sharecroppers and smallholders, the underlying problems of the province remained. These problems related to the pressures put on the already marginal agricultural productivity in Bamyan's valley plains and pastures by a dense, and rapidly growing, population and, additionally, the trend towards hierarchical organisation among the province's different communities, in which poor landholders and the poorer landless were susceptible to exploitation from more powerful landowners and external agents. Furthermore, although development in Bamyan was implemented by a variety of agencies, such as the Ministry of Rural and Regional Development (MRRD) National Solidarity Program (NSP), as well as by other large development agencies, broad ideas of modernisation tended to underpin the development process holistically. Despite competition between the different individuals and groups, this strand of state-building taps into a long-standing Universalist position, based on the advancement of all Hazaras in Bamyan, and the Hazarajat more broadly, to redress their historical persecution and subjugation.

After this broad outline of the way in which some of the key agencies associated with Western state-building have fed into a social dialectic of historical change in Bamyan province, I will provide more specificity through an examination of the two district-level contexts of Bamyan District and the Kahmard/ Saighan region.

Gendering human security in Bamyan Province

My approach here to gendering human security in Bamyan will be like that previously applied to the context of Nangarhar. As before, I will invoke a thoroughly social conception of human security. Security in this account is determined by the extent to which a person's well-being and happiness are supported or denied in their relationships with each other. When assessing the impact of the Western Intervention in Bamyan, it is useful to understand how societal relations of recognition have been configured traditionally and how they have evolved over time. As I suggested previously, recognition refers to the way in which a person's life is variously permitted or denied social recognition by a community, based on that person's adherence to societal values and practices.

Societal dynamics of recognition in Bamyan offer an interesting contrast to Nangarhar. Though social recognition between women and men in Bamyan was circumscribed by masculinist honour codes, the formulation of gender roles and gender identities did not match the explicitness of the hierarchies within the conservative settled Pashtun contexts in Nangarhar. Though life was gendered in a way that privileged masculine subjects, this did not mean that women were without their own recognised power in the social system. This argument has been made in various historical, anthropological, and contemporary sociological accounts of Bamyan Province.

A good starting point is to explore the nature of marriage practices within, and between, different *qawm* communities. As Robert Canfield (1973: 70–71) noted, marriages concretised processes of alliance-making with existing families within a *qawm* as well as those among other new communities. In contrast to *qawm* relations among hierarchical Pashtun tribes, affinal relationships in Bamyan were cultivated after marriage in ways which expanded the *qawm* beyond consanguineous relationships. This network was a way of distributing perishable economic goods like foodstuffs through communal feasts in a series of reciprocal relationships (Canfield, 1973: 72). In doing so, this process of transforming economic goods into social capital, provided an adroit way in which Hazara communities in Bamyan adapted to the challenge of many families sharing a marginal agricultural setting. Although women and men operated within different gendered spheres, each played a vital role in the reproduction of the household and the *qawm* more widely (Canfield, 1973: 81–82).

This relatively more horizontal form of social configuration, as well as women's agency within it, was highlighted in a variety of discussions between Hazara women and men within my Delhi focus group discussions. Ahmad Nasir, who had previously surprised Reza with his revelations that women could escape abusive relationships and gain divorce, also observed that it was possible for a woman and man to elope and send a message to both their families that they were married in common law.

AHMAD NASIR: In some situations, the girl and boy who are in love with each other escape from their village or city as their families do not agree with their marriage. They run away and go to another city or mostly to the areas in which a shrine is located and spend some time together and then return to their village or city sometime after and send a message to both their families that they are married.

Then their families gather and, with the presence of a Mullaha or Sayed, they accept their marriage and legitimise it with a small party. To prevent any kind of hostility the family of the man will accept that their daughter or any relative marry the brother or cousin of the escaped girl. By the second marriage they create a kind of unity and prevent the hostility.

Later that same afternoon, my colleague Ankita Haldar raised a similar question when she engaged with the women of the Hazara group by asking them about women's roles in resolving crises associated with the scandal of romantic love. The answer provided by women attested to the enduring role of women's solidarist agencies in contributing to the health and well-being of families.

ANKITA: Suppose, a girl had hidden her relationship with a man and then the family got information about it; then what was the reaction of that family?
LADIES: If our daughter loves someone and has a hidden relationship with him and the man loves her, then we try to hide this relationship and do not let people know about it. We then ask the other family to come and we speak to them and solve the problem by allowing them to marry each other. Subsequently, we announce that the couple will marry each other and invite

relatives to the marriage party. They will marry without people knowing that they had a relationship before. We try to make both sides happy and prevent any kind of hostility.

Alongside the historical existence of a more horizontal distribution of power in gender dynamics, what also became apparent was the more explicit embrace of progressive changes towards gender equity among a wealthier socio-economic grouping of Hazara communities. As Alesandro Monsutti observed from his extensive fieldwork research with Hazara communities in Iran and Afghanistan, this has been driven by a variety of historical factors.

To begin with, one of the ways in which Hazara families have coped with the threats of disruption and poverty is through migration and the transfer of remittances within families and among communities. There are several large and established Hazara communities in Iran, Pakistan, India and elsewhere around the world. During Afghanistan's decades of war and revolutionary upheaval between 1979 and 1989, Hazara men provided a valuable source of labour in Iran during that country's own period of war with Iraq. Not only did this provide valuable economic support for the Hazara men and their families, it also provided vital remittances for Hazara communities still in Afghanistan. At the same time, Hazara families in Iran were exposed to, and positively embraced, broader ideas relating to modern gender relations in which women and men had equal rights to education and employment. Thus, one of the effects of this period of migration for Hazara people was that it changed gendered roles substantively. In the absence of their menfolk, who were sending remittances from abroad and or fighting, many Hazara women became the heads of households in charge of both the productive and reproductive labour required to sustain their families. At the same time, in their travels abroad, men in diaspora communities in Iran and Pakistan assumed responsibility for reproductive work like cooking, cleaning, sewing, and so on, in to their paid labour.

This change has been highlighted by both Hazara and non-Hazara scholars and it was widely acknowledged by the Hazaras who participated in my FGDs. In both their mixed and segregated discussions, women and men acknowledged the presence of this progressive reformulation of gender roles and relationships. These views were presented in a very matter of fact way by my research collaborator Ankita, in the women's FGD.

ANKITA: What were women's responsibilities and what kind of power did women have in the time of your parents and grandparents?
DELARAM: In that time the women did not have freedom in their own works. They even did not have authority to object to their parent's decisions. Their parents were making decisions about who should marry their daughters. This was happening without asking their daughters. The daughter had to work in the house and help her mother and later after her marriage, she was responsible to her new house and had to be a good wife for her husband and a good mother for her children. Some women were helping their husbands

with working in the farms. To sum up, I should say that the women were totally responsible for the house affairs.

ANKITA: Did women have power on any matters in their own lives?

MARJAN: Yes of course but not in the way that they could overwhelm their husbands. The women's power was limited to within the house and not outside or in their husband's personal issues. They had to work in the house; cooking, cleaning, washing clothes and preparing food for guests. They would even go to the farms and help their husbands. They had to listen to their father or mother-in-law and respect them.

ANKITA: Is this the same in the Hazarajat today as it was in the time of your parents? Are women still forced to do all these forms of work in households?

DELARAM, MARJAN AND SALMEH: Not now; times have changed and people do not think the same as their parents. Many of the Hazaras are educated now and they do not force their women to do those works today.

As part of this discussion, the participating women suggested that, despite the prevalence of customary notions of honour and shame, many families sought education for both their daughters and sons. This conversation spoke to the previously highlighted process of change among Hazara communities towards more progressive gender relations, especially for the families and communities from a wealthier socio-economic position. This was succinctly captured by Delaram when she recalled that even gender relations in the "past" weren't settled.

DELARAM: In the past, the girls were not allowed to go to the school and the mothers' advice was ignored by the men. So, the women's decision was not important. But this was not widespread as there were some families who allowed their girls to go to the school.

The reason was simple as their men were educated they liked to see a better life for their children. In contrast, there were some people who would interfere in other family's affairs and would try to deprive the children from going to school by gossiping. They would say to other families why do they let their daughters go to school. They were saying that school is not a safe or good place for a girl. But the situation is changed now.

This message of progressive change was highlighted by one of the ladies present moments later when Ankita asked the women if they could recount their own experiences from their provincial locations within the Hazarajat and if they shared such experiences.

MARJAN: I am from Ghazni and I had a chance to study but had to go to the mosque for Islamic studies first. I remember my father was keen to send us to school as he was saying that my children should be educated and have a good future. Other ladies say that they are not happy with their parents as they did not let them to go to study. To them education remained a wish.

I could study under my father's protection and with his support I could complete my high school. Then I married but still wanted to continue my studies. I could even convince my father and mother-in-law but it was not in my destiny as the Taliban arrived and captured our areas and deprived the girls of studies. But I am happy that I can read and write and I encourage my children to study and fulfil their wishes.

Despite a broader societal change among wealthier and more educated Hazara communities, the women and men participating in this group all identified a difference in their own gender relations in poorer and/or rural communities. This was illustrated by Nasrullah, a young Shia Ismaili man from Shibar District in Bamiyn who, during the mixed focus group discussion, commented on a recent news story he had seen on television.

NASRULLAH: I would like to add something to this issue. I am young but I saw a clip that recorded some cases where the girls are given for marriage in childhood. I think the tradition is still continuing in some villages in Bamyan that an aged man marries a very young girl. (Ladies are attesting by saying yes, yes). The clip shows other marriages in which the bride and groom are two little children. They do not even understand what is happening around them and what marriage is for. The groom was asked why he is marrying? And he replied that he is taking his bride only to help his mother in the house! That is it. This is their motivation for getting married!

This points to the inequities experienced by a poorer class of Hazaras. Faced with the daily task of survival, families must forgo the education of their children to survive. Moreover, it is the women making up this poorer class of Hazaras who suffer the most pernicious effects of broader gendered hierarchies of power.

While many poorer women and men are similarly desirous of a better, more progressive and equitable future for their sons and daughters in society, their marginalised positions constrain them from participating in, or benefitting from, Western state-building. This is true for the landless, whether they be sharecropping families or casual workers, as well as for the many landed families who often own no more than two to three jeribs of land (Ministry of Public Works, 2009: 23). For this large majority of poor people in Bamyan, livelihoods are geared towards basic survival, with many being unable to meet their basic caloric and protein needs (Bank, 2011: 9). This has been demonstrated by contemporary surveys which reveal the widespread prevalence of stunting in Hazara children (Sabawoon, 2012: 4).

Though Hazara families in Bamyan face different degrees of poverty, what is common to them all is the susceptibility to external events, such as worsening environmental conditions through drought or flooding, disputes over land or inheritance, as well as the exploitative actions of wealthy landowners and traders. In recent times, the drought of 2010–2012 caused a rise in food prices and a major shortage of water for families in the more remote and higher districts of the region such as Panjao, Waras and Saighan (Affairs, 2012: 155). A contributing factor here is that, owing to the ongoing environmental degradation of the hillside scrub of the valleys throughout Bamyan, which have been over-grazed and over-culled for firewood, flooding is a frequent problem which jeopardises the livelihoods of many people (Mojumdar, 2012: 22–24). Meanwhile, the intergenerational sub-division of land has resulted in a general trend towards smaller and smaller landholdings, which cannot meet a family's basic needs and whose ownership is often subject to dispute by others, leading to the potential loss of the land itself.

To more deeply illustrate how the dynamics of human (in)security for women and men have changed, I will examine the specific developmental processes taking place at a district level in Bamyan District and Kahmard and then offer broad suggestions about the way these processes produce gendered insecurities for poorer women and men.

Bamyan District

As was observed in the previous overview of Bamyan district, these historically rural, farming valleys are moving towards semi-urbanisation. This process accelerated dramatically from the fall of the Taliban onwards as the longstanding aid agencies moved to the central district of Bamyan to conduct emergency humanitarian programmes. Moreover, as the years wore on and international agencies began to shift their attention to a more developmentalist agenda, the area became something of a bubble economy, attracting some 31,000 displaced Hazaras from outside the province (Mariani, 2006: 29). A large majority of these poor migrant families have relied for their basic survival needs upon finding casual daily labour in the growing bazaar or in other activities such as carpet weaving. However, alongside this growing constituency of semi-urbanised poor, the wealthier and "middle class", educated families have benefitted from the contemporary period of Western aid flows and development projects.

Wealthier families with, or without land, have been able to profit from the increasing trade brought to their farms, market shops and transport businesses by the international presence (Mariani, 2006: 38). Also, wealthier and more educated Hazara families have been able to benefit through direct employment with foreign NGOs and by receiving favourable microcredit loans, while their communities have enjoyed better infrastructure as well as access to schools, universities and healthcare centres. What emerges overall in the case of Bamyan district is that, even though a majority of women and men, regardless of their socio-economic position, favour development, increasing gender equality and participating in a democracy, Western aid and development tends to benefit the comparatively well-off in society even as it simultaneously exacerbates exploitative tendencies in societies which constrain the poor. These themes are highlighted by a brief examination of the following two developmentalist technologies which are employed in this region and province more broadly under the auspices of the NSP: micro-credit loans and community development projects.

It is worth noting that micro-credit has been consistently touted by many Western academics and policy-makers as an excellent pro-poor initiative, especially as it relates to women becoming entrepreneurs (Weber, 2002: 539–540). The actual story of micro-credit in Bamyan and Afghanistan more broadly, however, is somewhat different. This is illustrated by a brief overview of the experience of microcredit borrowers from different socio-economic positions, conducted by Erna Andersen (2008: iv) of the AREU in a village in Bamyan district. As Andersen (2008: 50) pointed out in this study, contrary to popular Western (mis)conceptions, access to credit has always been available within Afghanistan. Whether in the form of money or other forms of assistance, credit has constantly been available to individuals and families through agreements with their relatives or their broader *qawm* communities. Thus, the entrance of micro-credit into Bamyan, and Afghanistan more broadly, did not take place in a vacuum but instead fed into a complex web of financial and social reciprocity.

As Andersen (2008: iii–iv) notes in the context of Bamyan Valley, while some types of micro-credit are highly useful to families, those based on a favourable combination of grace period of the loan, interest rates and loan size, these types of micro-credit tend to go to the wealthier families who have the means to profit from them. The micro-credit loans that the poorest families can access are those with the worst loan conditions, vis-à-vis very small grace periods, higher frequencies of repayment and smaller loan sizes. As mentioned, contrary to the beliefs of Western advocates, these loans do not take place in a social vacuum inhabited by equally positioned rational entrepreneurs, but instead feed into a complex array of societal relations in which people hold different degrees of power over each other. Thus, women and men from poorer households can be pushed to take on loans for the benefit of other family or more powerful community members. Andersen herself offers examples of the way in which availability of micro credit can feed into exploitative tendencies within both subjects' familial relations and their patron client relations. In the case of familial relations, she observes the way in which a relatively wealthy male household head, with prior access to micro credit, was able to compel his sister-in-law's husband to take out and then hand over, a micro credit loan (Andersen, 2008: 56). Meanwhile, Andersen (2008: 57–58) observed a similar situation in which indebted and dependent sharecropping families working on their patron's land could be coerced into taking out loans for the benefit of their patron. Thus, rather than offering a means for poor people to "break the cycle of poverty", micro-credit may reinforce the exploitative relations of power that constrain and jeopardise their livelihoods.

In addition to the use of micro-credit targeted at family units, another aspect of Western-backed processes in Bamyan involves community level development through the implementation of the National Solidarity Program (NSP) whereby Community Development Councils (CDCs) are established to build larger communal projects such as schools, hospitals, wells, and so on. However, as was true in the case of micro-credit, this form of development tends to benefit wealthier communities composed of land-owning families who have strong social networks and can lobby effectively for various types of aid to be brought to their communities, at the expense of the poorer families who make up a majority of the population of the district and the province. For these women and men, whether living in the caves surrounding the Bamyan Buddhas or living as sharecroppers in overcrowded houses provided by their landlords, Western state-building at the local level, as enshrined in the CDC programme, in many ways serves to formalise their exclusion from society. This is because the marginal and potentially temporary status of these families ensures that they are effectively excluded from participating in the developmental process (Wily, 2004: 67). Shawna Wakefield (2004: 7–8) observed this disjuncture in a village called "Obtoo" in Panjao district, which offers similar rural contexts to those found in Bamyan district. In this village, she observed that adult women and almost landless men tended to be excluded from any meaningful engagement in community decision-making within formal CDCs or in traditional Shuras. In contrast, she noted that in a nearby wealthier village comprised of both land-owning women and men, community decision-making was more egalitarian between the sexes as well as between different, relatively wealthy households. On this point, she (Wakefield, 2004: 9) notes:

> The women were much more outspoken in this village, and in fact held the male representative accountable for failure to address the main concerns of the villagers. When the research team enquired why this village seemed more active, they were told by the Oxfam Team Leader that it was because the village was made up of more landowners than in Obtoo. In fact, he relayed that it had been much easier to organise village organizations (VOs) and implement community development projects in areas where there are more resources and landed people. This is presumably because those without land may pick up and leave at any time in search of cheaper land, and as a result are less included in community decision making.

Similarly, in Yakawlang, David Lety (Lety, 2006: 9) observed this same phenomenon among wealthier land-owning families who had historically held the larger and more productive lands of the valley. These examples do not, of course, suggest a universal experience across all land-owning families of Bamyan Province. Another consideration is that, as Jo Grace (2005: 20–21) notes, the social norm of the majority of landowning families is for the women to gift their shares of land to their brothers in return for the latter's support later in life, so that there tend to be many more land-owning men than women. However, what is still shown is a significant demonstration of more equitable and egalitarian gender relations than is usually seen among people from the settled *qawm*s of Afghanistan's other ethno-linguistic groups.

Kahmard

Kahmard is an interesting case to highlight in an overall account of human (in)security in Bamyan Province. What is apparent in this district is the extent to which creative community development programmes by a Western NGO, working through the National Solidarity Program (NSP), have helped improve parts of the natural environment of the district, while also improving the livelihoods of many of the local Tajik women and men. However, as will be explored subsequently, many of these gains are threatened by the 2012 district-wide ban on informal coal mining that was enforced by the government of Afghanistan in order to satisfy the terms of a mineral resource contract signed with a Chinese consortium.

Historically, the land in Kahmard, watered by the plentiful supply from the Kahmard River, has always been a very fertile and prosperous valley where a variety of agricultural crops have been grown. However, as is the case elsewhere in Afghanistan, the district's formerly wooded rangelands high above the valley, which serve as water catchment areas, have been significantly degraded for the last two decades by families cutting scrub for firewood to bake bread, and by the over-grazing of livestock (Azami, 2010: 3). As part of a solution to this overarching problem, many of the district's NSP CDCs worked with the Swiss NGO, Helvetas, to rejuvenate damaged water catchments and rangelands through the planting of a variety of environmentally restorative trees and grasses, fruit and spice trees, as well as vegetables. To reduce a family's need for firewood for bread-making, Helvetas built community bakeries in 13 villages which were fired by the rich coal deposits in the valley (Azami, 2010: 3). Previously, families had to either purchase wood or send children and men to collect it from the depleted scrub and vegetation of the watersheds. Baking bread was especially onerous for women who would spend four hours daily standing over a hot oven and suffering from the consequent smoke inhalation. With the construction of these community bakeries, families would simply leave their dough with the village baker each morning and collect it in the afternoon. Importantly, this service cost only 250–300 Afghans for the entire month which was equivalent to what it had previously cost for a single day's supply of firewood. Men and, far more emphatically, women from the communities expressed joy about the reduction in their work burden as well as the benefit of extra money, which often went towards tuition fees for their children's schooling (Azami, 2010: 10). This programme significantly reduced the amount of scrub collected from watershed areas and led to noticeably improved vegetation cover; thus, floods between 2010 and 2012 were noticeably diminished.

However, although this project was largely beneficial to the relatively better off households from more tightly-knit, land-owning communities, this overarching development programme foreclosed a vital source of income for the relatively poorer, landless and sharecropping families – informal coal mining. The broader economy of the district was severely affected by the Afghanistan government's 2012 ban on this activity, (which was the primary occupation of some 1,000 people) to pave the way for a Chinese Mining Consortium's coal mine construction. In addition to these 1,000 jobs in Kahmard, a *Wall Street Journal* report estimated that a further 5,000 to 10,000 people across the provinces of Bamyan, Samangan and Baghlan also lost their primary source of employment because of the imposition of the ban (Maria Abi-Habib and Sultani, 2012). A less direct consequence is that many families suffered over the most recent winter due to a lack of access to coal for household heating. This has caused many younger and older Sunni Tajik men of the district to fight for the Taliban locally and abroad, to earn the substantial sum of $30 per day. Interestingly, neither the local nor non-Afghan Taliban fighters, interviewed by the *Wall Street Journal* reporters, expressed opposition to mining in principle. While the latter group argued vehemently against mining development under the Karzai regime, the new local Taliban recruits expressed anger mostly because the mining project was not being built quickly enough:

> The Taliban say they oppose the Chinese investment because the concession was awarded by a government they consider illegitimate. "We are against any foreign company extracting the mineral [wealth] of Afghanistan as long as Afghanistan is under occupation," Taliban spokesman Zabihullah Mujahid said.
>
> Many locals say they are turning to the Taliban for the opposite reason: Anger at the Chinese for failing to move ahead with a project they say would have given stable, better-paid jobs to the displaced miners.
>
> "The brave insurgents will fight against the Chinese if they don't start their work and hire the poor labourers they have kicked off the land," said Khaliqdad, a driver from the area who used to transport labourers to the coal mines.

Though the overviews of women's and men's human (in)security provided in these two districts are only cursory, some important points can be made. First, the women and men of relatively more wealthy and well-positioned families in Bamyan have seen marked benefits from aid and economic development in the region. This is doubly true for Hazara families among whom there are strong tendencies towards more equitable and egalitarian gender relations. However, what is also true is the extent to which women and men from the many poorer families of society tend to suffer the worst effects of the gendered hierarchies of power into which they are embedded.

Furthermore, what stands out about these contemporary, gendered social contexts is the extent to which their commodification of a family's livelihood, in which work is tied to wage-earning and survival, can exacerbate underlying patriarchal tendencies, to the detriment of women's and children's lives. This point is evidenced both indirectly, with the increasing pressures of survival leading families to commodify their daughter's bodies, vis-à-vis the bride price as was described for Nangarhar, and also directly with some wealthier landowners reportedly demanding that women from the families of their sharecropping tenants be made available to them (Wily, 2004: 67). At the same time, because of a poorer family's more marginal position, their children are likely to be engaged in work from an early age, especially in carpet weaving, which has adverse health effects and also denies them the chance to receive an education

(Standal, 2008: 44–45, 62, 66). The strains placed on families in such situations contribute to the prevalence of violence within the family itself; and, unlike in relatively wealthier families, the poorer women, suffering from this domestic abuse, especially after marriage, are less able to seek refuge from their paternal kinship networks.

Struggles for recognition in Bamyan Province

In the final section of this chapter I will attempt to reconstruct the struggles for recognition in which local subjects of Bamyan are engaged to secure a better life for themselves and their families. When exploring these struggles, there is not just one story to tell for all women or men. Instead, when seeking to understand how the Western state-building project has affected women's and men's lives, as well as gender relations more broadly, it is worthwhile returning to two moral visions for societal change in Bamyan and the Hazarajat.

The first vision is Universalist in nature and articulates a discourse of shared Hazara unity and the need for the advancement and modernisation of Bamyan, and the Hazarajat, as well as the permanent establishment of freedom for the Hazaras from the oppression of outsiders. Although this vision resonates with most Hazaras, regardless of their socio-economic background and political or religious worldview, its most ardent proponents are an historically growing number of wealthy and educated Hazaras, both inside and outside Bamyan and Afghanistan.

When exploring this agenda, what emerges is that many Hazara women, and men, are waking up to a brighter future in which traditional patriarchal ideas of women's and men's roles are changing to produce a more equitable state of affairs (CDA, 2009: 8–9). Women and men from this growing section of society, in both urban and rural locations, are able to both participate in, and receive the benefits of, the Western state-building project. In many ways, their struggles in this regard revolve around advancing a more democratic and legitimate form of government which can advance an agenda of non-corrupt modernisation of the province (Ibrahimi, 2009: 9–11). This has been evidenced by the previously articulated case of Jawad Zahak but perhaps more tellingly by the protest of educated women and men to the 2009 Shia marriage law, championed by Ayatollah Asif Mosheini (former Iran-supported Mujahedeen leader and Shia cleric), that attempted to formalise a crude form of patriarchal authority (Oates, 2009: 18–22). Additionally, even in what could be considered to be more conservative rural areas, such as Panjao District, what is apparent is that in wealthier families and in wealthier communities there is a greater degree of egalitarianism between women and men.

In contrast to this Universalist position, which could be summarised in the saying "We are all Hazaras now" (Wakefield, 2004: 10), a second moral vision of society highlights ongoing historical oppression and the struggle by the most marginalised in society against pervasive inequality in Bamyan Province and the Hazarajat more broadly. For many of the province's landless and small-holding families, this inequality, which became evident in the decades prior to revolution in 1979 and the formation of the Shura (Ibrahimi, 2006: 6–7), relates to the exploitative nature of the society, whereby the bare survival of poor families has been tied to their capacity to work for wealthier landlords, be they Hazara or Pashtun (Wily, 2004: 3).

Alongside the continuing persistence of poverty, the loss and breakdown of kinship relations among these marginalised families may be the worst aspect of their experiences within broader gendered hierarchies of power. Though these relations themselves can be gendered in a hierarchical fashion, they represent the primary sources of an individual's physical, economic and emotional security. This has been displayed by the insightful reporting of Deborah Smith in three different research papers for the Afghanistan Research and Evaluation Unit (Smith, 2008, 2009; Smith and Manalan, 2009). These reports were based on extensive fieldwork interviews which Smith organised in Bamyan in a variety of rural and urban communities. In them, Smith highlights a variety of issues which relate to the overall well-being of women and men in their gendered lives, specifically relationships of love and discipline in child-raising practices, decision-making practices associated with marriage, and community based dispute resolution processes.

Her research on violence in child-rearing techniques found practices such as beating widespread among women as well as men in Bamyan and other parts of Afghanistan. Moreover, Smith's finding that this violence was prevalent regardless of a family's socio-economic position, spoke a great deal about generalised attitudes towards violence. Using her participants' own comments, she highlights the way in which much of this violence was intended to ensure that children are respectful (and fearful) of their parents as well as to ensure their honorable conduct per gender norms. Indeed, similar points were raised during the mixed Focus Group Discussion in which Ahmad Nasir, Delaram (and the broader group) observed these practices:

AHMAD NASIR: yes, it (beating) was common among some families and some fathers would beat their children. Sometimes the children would not obey their fathers and that would make the father angry and the result was beating the children. But there were some cases in which the child was liked by the parent a lot and usually would not be abused or beaten by his father. But other children would play with him or sometimes would bother him/her so he was beaten up by his parent because he played with those bad children. So, this was a punishment to make him understand that he should not play with those children anymore. It is possible that this way of treating the children is continuing in some Hazara areas.

REZA: Would mothers also beat their children.

WOMEN AND MEN: Yes, even mothers would beat children sometimes but fathers would beat children more often.

DELARAM: Nowadays the children are fine and the parents are not beating them as our parents would beat us. Now in Hazara areas the parents are speaking to the children instead of beating them as they think it is more effective. They realised that if they beat the child for each and every thing then their child would be growing up with violence and this would make them resist everything and not respect others. But in our grandfather's time as we heard they would say "*if you do not beat the child then they will become NATARS* (without fear)." They would think that this fear should always be with the children but they would not understand that this fear will destroy the child's character.

One of the most interesting findings to come out of this research into child-rearing was that poorer and less educated women and men did not object to the idea of their daughters being educated past primary school. However, these families noted that broader conditions of insecurity associated with girls travelling long distances posed threats to their physical safety as well as to a household's reputation under the prevalent masculinist honour codes. In this way, gendered hierarchies of power can be seen to pose particularly formidable barriers to girls' education in poorer rural families.

This point carries over in relation to marriage practices among Hazara women and men in Bamyan Province. Though gendered hierarchies of power affect all Hazara communities' decision-making practices with regard to marriage, what is apparent is the extent to which Hazara women and communities have influence over these practices. As highlighted by Deborah Smith and attested to in the statements of Hazara women and men in my focus group discussions, the fact remains that the women who have tended to gain the most say in their own lives and that of their communities come from wealthier families and from communities with stronger social bonds. In contrast, families from poorer communities tend to face the dilemma of their children's marriages being a task of basic survival and reproduction rather than the idea of two consenting adults agreeing to marry each other.

Struggles for recognition and human security in Bamyan

Despite the presence of these gendered hierarchies of power, not to mention broader conditions of economic hardship, women and men have found ways to navigate, and challenge, these hierarchical configurations of life. In so doing, these individuals provide a strong account of what human security means and how it can be improved. Essentially, what these people show is the way in which they secure their own lives and well-being with each other. In this regard, it is possible to discern two notions of struggle. The first one refers to the notion of the very struggle to survive and maintain a family household.

As Alessandro Monsutti (Monsutti, 2004: 219, 221) has noted, though poorer families face a variety of constraints and exploitative tendencies across Bamyan, in their attempts to improve their livelihoods, it does not necessarily follow that these families are helpless victims. Women and men from poorer families have a variety of ways in which they attempt to improve their situations. Migration plays a key role whether in the movement of an entire household to seek a safer and more secure location, or through the labour migration of a household's adult and younger male members to pursue economic opportunities, either elsewhere in Afghanistan or among a broader Hazara diaspora outside the country in Iran, Pakistan and, for educated and wealthier families, even further afield in Europe, Australia and the US (Monsutti, 2008: 68–69). In these cases, the *Hawala* system allows families to send remittances safely and reliably to their families inside Bamyan and elsewhere in Afghanistan.

Moreover, nearly all Bamyan's poorer families possess some livestock, particularly goats and sheep, and they consider their future to be invested in these animals since the extent of their livestock ownership, especially of draught animals such as oxen, can allow them to come to more equitable crop-sharing arrangements with their landlords (Wily, 2004: 67–68). Here, it is important to highlight again how important credit relations are in enabling families to meet both their basic needs as well as to make productive investments to improve their household's economic position. As was previously noted in respect to Erna Andersen's study of micro-credit and informal credit practices in a rural village in Bamyan district, at times, credit relations can verge on being exploitative. However, at the same time, the giving and taking of credit undergirds people's everyday livelihood strategies regardless of their socio-economic status. As Andersen (2008: 56) suggests, credit arrangements between relatives are very common and it is a normal occurrence for individuals to be in debt to relatives in a complex web of reciprocity. In this situation she notes:

> Debts may or may not be expected to be repaid but form the basis on which reciprocal relations of help and cooperation are built, involving both the giving and taking of money and other types of assistance.

For the poor and very poor families of Bamyan, this access to credit is often characterised by charitable relations in which loans or assistance are given by wealthier households, in accordance with the Islamic practices of *zakat* (obligatory alms) and *khairat* (voluntary alms) (Pain and Klijn, 2007: 13, 28; Andersen, 2008: 49–50). These practices are very beneficent, enabling poorer families to survive through the goodwill of wealthier households in their family and community. At the same time, especially in the context of increasing capitalisation of rural economies in Bamyan, there is evidence to suggest that, here also, charitable relations can become exploitative. This is especially true between wealthier land-owning patrons and their client sharecropping families where the former can withhold shares of a harvest or even demand a family's daughter in marriage as payment of a loan.

The second notion of struggle refers to the acts and practices which directly challenge gendered hierarchies of power in society. As Deborah Smith observed, Bamyan is interesting in this regard because there are opportunities for progressive change occurring in different parts of society. As already mentioned, there is the increasing trend among a wealthier, more educated class of Hazaras towards egalitarian gender relations in which women and men are valued equally. However, what she noted as even more striking was the way in which women could take part in customary forums aimed at implementing community-based dispute resolution. Many of these adjudications improved the well-being of women, including: upholding inheritance rights, divorce rights, and responding to violence against women. What was evident was the extent to which women's presence in community dispute resolutions gave them broader agency and recognition of that agency.

For instance, consider one of the stories of conflict resolution which emerged from a report by Smith and Manalan (2009: 54–55), a young girl named Aquela had run away from her father's home to marry the young man she loved called Nasir. This elopement triggered an initial furious response from Aquela's father, and her male cousins, due to the shame such an action brought, namely the patriarch not being able to control "his women". With the help of the community's white-beards (men), and white-hairs (women), Nasir's father was able to meet Aquela's household and defuse a potentially violent situation. In the adjudication process, as one white-beard recalled, when Aquela was asked if she was brought to Nasir's home by force, she replied: "I have the right to one husband from God. I wasn't brought by force. I came of my own free will. I will marry this boy" (Smith and Manalan, 2009: 55). Subsequently, the elders decreed that, based on the girl's testimony, she made a legitimate choice in a marriage partner and that Nasir's father would have to pay a bride price of three cows as well as the costs of the wedding ceremony and feast. This was a much smaller bride price than her father had originally asked for but he accepted the proposal and, after the marriage, relations between the two families were reportedly very good. What is very revealing about this story is it shows that, despite the underlying presence of a patriarchal code of honour, this gendered order of power is not immutable and that it can be challenged and that women were included in the decision-making process.

A similar sentiment was also strongly expressed by Hazara women in a focus group I conducted in Delhi in July 2010, as is apparent in the following exchange between the female interviewer and the five women in attendance:

INTERVIEWER: If your own son or daughter wants to marry someone who loves him/her and both are in love and the person is from a good family then will you allow them to marry based on their own choice?

HAZARA WOMEN: Yes, why not, they can marry the person they really love. They should live together and not us. What we want is a good life for them. *"When you agree and I agree then no need to go to the court"* and also there is another proverb saying *"when the two pieces of wood fit then there is no need for carpenter"*.

What emerges from both excerpts is the potential for women's agency in both an individual woman's decision-making abilities, including the right to choose a marriage partner and, additionally, in the ability of the women of different households to act in unison to keep secret such matters and to expedite resolutions that are in the interests of the woman involved.

Conclusion

This chapter aimed to show the way in which the US-led Western Intervention in Afghanistan affected the lives and well-being of rural communities in Bamyan. As I suggested previously, in contrast with Nangarhar Province, Bamyan received far less development aid in this intervention because of its lesser strategic importance in the mind's eye of Western policy-makers. This contemporary neglect of Bamyan, alongside the historical persecution of the Hazara communities living there, has given rise to a highly visible campaign by Hazara politicians and an educated class of young Hazara women and men. This struggle revolves around a variety of issues, such as food assistance and important infrastructure like roads and electricity, relating to the underdevelopment of the province.

Alongside this broader struggle relating to a universal Hazara identity, there are also a myriad of ways in which different women and men navigate and struggle against the gendered hierarchies of society. In dealing with the material pressures of a household's reproduction, families creatively and pragmatically adapt by sending some of their members to work abroad and return remittances through the *Hawala* money system. However, more fundamentally Hazara women, and men, are challenging gendered hierarchies of power associated with masculine control. This is evidenced in the way in which women are again in an increasingly recognised position as claimants within community-based dispute resolution forums that have traditionally been the preserve of men.

References

Abi-Habib, Maria, Yaroslav Trofimov and Ziaulhaq Sultani. (2012). "Delays at Chinese-Run Afghan Mines Raise Security Fears". *Wall Street Journal*, 17 December 2012.

Andersen, Erna, Paula Kantor and Amanda Sim (2008). Microcredit, Informal Credit and Rural Livelihoods: A Village Case Study in Bamyan Province. *Case Study Series*, Afghanistan Research and Evaluation Unit.

Azami, Khalid M., Sanjeev Bhuchar, Sylvaine Rieg and Frank Wiederkehr (2010). Results Survey Community Bakeries Kahmard District, Bamyan Province, Afghanistan. Bern/Kabul, Helvetas Afghanistan.

Canfield, Robert (1973). *Faction and conversion in a plural society: Religious alignments in the Hindu Kush*. Ann Arbor, University of Michigan.

CDA – Collaborative Learning Projects (2009). Listening Project. *Field Visit Report*.

Central Statistics Organisation (2012). Socio-Demographic and Economic Survey Highlights of the Results. Kabul.

Chiovenda, Melissa Kerr (2014). "Sacred Blasphemy: Global and Local Views of the Destruction of the Bamyan Buddha Statues in Afghanistan". *Journal of Muslim Minority Affairs* 34 (4): 410–424.

Dupree, Nancy Hatch (1963). *The Valley of Bamyan*, Afghan Tourist Organization.

Grace, Jo (2005). Who Owns the Farm? Rural Women's Access to Land and Livestock. *Working Paper Series*. Kabul, Afghanistan Research and Evaluation Unit. February.

Ibrahimi, Niamatullah (2006). The Failure of a Clerical Proto-State: Hazarajat, 1979–1984. *Working Paper no. 6*, Crisis States Research Centre.

Ibrahimi, Niamatullah (2009). The Dissipation of Political Capital Among Afghanistan's Hazaras: 2001–2009. *Working Paper no. 51*, Crisis States Research Centre.

Johnson, Chris (2000). Hazarajat Baseline Study – Interim Report, UN Co-ordinator's Office.

Karimi, Ali (2011). "Abductors killed Bamiyan's head of Provincial Council". https://alikarimi.ca/2011/06/07/taliban-killed-bamiyans-head-of-provincial-council/2016. Accessed 20 February 2017.

Lety, David (2006). Land Development in the Central Highlands of Afghanistan: Case Study of Shaman Plain Flood Control Project (Bamyan Province). *Linking Relief, Rehabilitation and Development Programme (Lrrd) in Afghanistan*, Urgence Rehabilitation Development.

Liu, Xinru (2011). "A Silk Road Legacy: The Spread of Buddhism and Islam". *Journal of World History* 22 (1): 55–81.

Mariani, Claire (2006). Is Building a City an Appropriate Response to Development Issues in Bamyan?, Urgence Rehabilitation Development.

Ministry of Public Works, Islamic Republic of Afghanistan (2009). AFG: North-South Corridor Project. *Resettlement Planning Document*.

Mojumdar, Aunohita (2012). 10 stories – 10 years of SDC Engagement in Afghanistan. Kabul, Swiss Agency for Development.

Monsutti, Alessandro (2004). "Cooperation, Remittances, and Kinship Among the Hazaras". *Iranian Studies* 37 (2): 219–240.

Monsutti, Alessandro (2008). "Afghan Migratory Strategies and the Three Solutions to the Refugee Problem". *Refugee Survey Quarterly* 27 (1): 58–73.

Mousavi, Sayed Askar (1997). *The Hazaras of Afghanistan: an historical, cultural, economic and political history*. New York, Routledge.

Oates, Lauryn (2009). *A Closer Look: The Policy and Lawmaking Process Behind the Shiite Personal Status Law*, Afghanistan Research and Evaluation Unit.

Pain, Adam and Floortje Klijn (2007). "Finding the Money: Informal Credit Practices in Rural Afghanistan". *Kabul: Afghan Research and Evaluation Unit (AREU)*.

Sabawoon, Dr. Mohammad Akbar and Óscar Serrano Oria (2012). Report of Nutrition and Mortality in Bamyan Province Afghanistan from 9th to 16th of May 2012. *SMART Nutrition Assessment Report*, Save the Children.

Smith, Deborah J. (2008). Love, Fear and Discipline: Everyday Violence Toward Children in Afghan Families. *Issue Paper Series*. Kabul, Afghanistan Research and Evaluation Unit.

Smith, Deborah J. (2009). Decisions, Desires and Diversity: Marriage Practices in Afghanistan. *Issue Paper Series*. M. Lewis. Kabul, Afghanistan Research and Evaluation Unit.

Smith, Deborah J. and Shelly Manalan (2009). Community-based Dispute Resolution Processes in Bamyan Province. *Case Study Series*. V. Quinlan. Kabul, Afghanistan Research and Evaluation Unit.

Solidarites (2002). District of Bamyan – Bamyan Province Central Afghanistan. *Food Security Assessment in Afghan Rural Areas*. EU Solidarity Fund.

Standal, Karina (2008). "Giving light and hope in rural Afghanistan: the impact of Norwegian Church Aid's barefoot approach on women beneficiaries". Master thesis, University of Oslo.

United Nations Office for the Coordination of Humanitarian Affairs (2012). Afghanistan Consolidated Appeal Process. Geneva, United Nations.

Wakefield, Shawna (2004). Gender and Local Level Decision Making: Findings from a Case Study in Panjao. *Case Studies Series*. Kabul, Afghanistan Research and Evaluation Unit. November.

Weber, Heloise (2002). "The Imposition of a Global Development Architecture: The Example of Microcredit". *Review of International Studies* 28 (3): 537–555.

Wily, Liz Alden (2004). Land Relations in Bamyan Province Findings from a 15 Village Case Study. *Case Studies Series*. Kabul, Afghanistan Research and Evaluation Unit.

Winterbotham, Emily with Fauzia Rahimi (2011). Legacies of Conflict Healing Complexes and Moving Forwards in Bamyan Province. *Case Study Series*, Afghanistan Research and Evaluation Unit.

World Bank (2011). "Afghanistan Provincial Briefs". www.worldbank.org/en/country/afghanistan/publication/afghanistan-provincial-briefs. Accessed 20 February 2017.

7 Kabul Province

From ancient to modern times, Afghanistan has been regarded as a "highway of conquest" for migratory peoples, such as the Mongols, and for those expanding empires, including the Indian Mughals, the Turko-Mongols and the Safavid Persians (Gregorian, 1969: 10). It has also been regarded as a "crossroads of civilisations and religions" and a "roundabout" for trade routes linking Europe, the Middle East, the Indian Subcontinent and the Far East (Gregorian, 1969: 10). In this broad historical milieu, the countryside and city of Kabul, like Kandahar, served as the "Gates of India" which were used by contending empires for the defense of India or as a springboard to invade the subcontinent (Gregorian, 1969: 11). Historically, the city and region were predominately inhabited by Persian-speaking Tajiks and Turkic-speaking people as well as other minority communities, including Hindus and Sikhs, Jewish people and Armenian Christians. However, during the reign of Ahmad Durrani Shah from 1747 to 1772, Kabul would become a centre for the powerful Durrani tribal nobility and their communities who would increasingly evolve throughout the nineteenth and twentieth centuries into an urbanised class who ran, and were served by, the bureaucratic state machinery of the city (Ahady, 1995: 621–622). What was interesting about the Pashtun communities who lived in Kabul, as well as other urban centres in Afghanistan throughout this period, was the extent to which they became Persianised in both their customs, celebrating Nu'rooz (Nader, 2011: 3) and increasingly speaking solely in Persian with many Pashtuns losing their Pashto language altogether (Giustozzi, 2009: 3).

The province and city of Kabul are integral to understanding Afghanistan's modern history. This city and its people formed the very core of Afghanistan's modernising state throughout the twentieth century. Moreover, as I observed in Chapter 4 regarding Barnett Rubin's scholarship (Rubin, 2002: 75–77), Kabul was the site in which conflicting revolutionary ideologies, whether Islamist, Communist or nationalist, were formed and these ultimately led to the "fragmentation of Afghanistan". Kabul was at the epicentre of this fragmentation in the horrific internecine violence of different Mujahedeen factions following the fall of Najibullah's government in 1993.

In 2001, the US and its coalition allies helped the Northern Alliance seize control of Kabul and Afghanistan more broadly from the Taliban. Following this initial military victory, Kabul became the site for forging an emerging government between a variety of warlords, Afghan elites and Western technocrats and donors. Perhaps the most dramatic effect of the Western Intervention basing itself in Kabul has been the creation of a bubble economy which has resulted in a large influx of people from all parts of the country and abroad. This trend has seen Kabul's predominately urban population swell from 1.2 million people in 2001, to 2.3 million people in 2002, 3 million people in 2005 and, finally, to a population that has been estimated at 3.5 million people today (GOIRA, 2015: 11).

While the growth of this bubble economy has entailed development in Kabul for the wealthy, as evidenced in the construction of new malls, mansions and infrastructure for certain neighbourhoods, it has also given rise to a drastic urbanisation of the poor and an attendant rise in urban tenements without access to infrastructure, such as water, sanitation or electricity, and with informal housing that is not protected from demolition by city planners (Metcalfe et al. 2012: 28). This major urbanisation of the poor since 2001 is illustrated by the fact that two thirds of those living in Kabul do so in informal tenements where families' survival is dependent on lowly paid casual wage labour (Metcalfe et al. 2012: 19–21). This large inflow of people from within and outside of Afghanistan to Kabul has also been driven by people's need to escape conflict, whether in the past, present or likely future. Others are unable to return to their homes of origin due to the changes wrought by ongoing conflict.

The context of Kabul, and especially Kabul City, is important to understand because it illustrates some of the most prominent ways in which the Western Intervention has fed into existing gender dynamics. Unlike much of rural Afghanistan, which lies beyond the administrative control of centralised authorities, the urbanised context of Kabul offered Western policy-makers more opportunity to advance women's empowerment programmes. Indeed, urban women are inherently envisioned as best suited to become modernised and freed from cultural traditions.

As Julie Billaud (2015: 8) eloquently observed, urban centres like Kabul provide the primary sites in which symbolic battles over gender play out between Western developers and local entities of power be they individuals, groups or broader communities. Moreover, Billaud (2015: 12) very plausibly makes the case for understanding the unfolding dynamics of intersecting gendered ideologies in this urban setting with Mikhail Bakhtin's conception of the carnival.

> Bakhtin describes the carnival as a moment when rules are turned upside down and everything is permitted. It is shaped according to a pattern of play. It is a type of performance that is communal, without boundaries between performers and audience.

As Julie Billaud (2015: 13–15) has argued, Kabul presents a carnivalesque stage in which the West has staged its gender intervention to empower women. In this carnival, gender programming and women's empowerment initiatives appear as a dazzling array of endless opportunities for positively changing society. However, there is a darker side to this carnival for, while new possibilities are opened up for women they also face a variety of new constraints and vulnerabilities in playing the roles of empowered women. Nevertheless, Billaud (2015: 15–16) notes that it is ordinary Afghan women and men who are most aware of this carnivalesque period of life during the Western Intervention. These subjects have gotten used to variously navigating and resisting the gendered hierarchies of power produced in this conflagration of external and local forces.

In this chapter, I will follow Billaud's lead and use this idea of "the carnival" as a way of understanding how women's, but also men's, lives have been affected by the onset of the Western Intervention in Kabul. I will add detail to this carnival by first exploring the dynamics of power which emerged in the city following the Taliban's fall from power. In the second move of this chapter, I will provide insight into the gendered dimension of human (in)security at a local level. Here, I will show the constraints and insecurities facing women and men within broader gendered hierarchies of power. To finalise this chapter I will explore the existing ways in which women, and men, creatively navigate and struggle against these hierarchies of power. Kabul is an interesting case for this exploration because it offers a microcosm of Afghanistan's broader social heterogeneity. What becomes apparent when exploring this heterogeneity is the existence of a variety of struggles which challenge dominant gendered ideas and practices.

Dynamics of power in Kabul Province

The idea of a carnival is an apt way of framing the Western Intervention which descended on Kabul in the years following the Taliban's fall in 2001. This metaphor neatly illustrates the fundamental disjuncture between the rhetorical face of a Western Intervention designed to promote democracy and human rights and the way in which this intervention was experienced by the people themselves. On the one hand, Kabul offered a stage in which "utopian" possibilities could be imagined by Western policy-makers in their efforts to bring freedom to ordinary people. On this stage, it was imagined that women, alongside men, could enjoy the fruits of being liberated, modern individuals equally protected by the rule of law, upending social and political structures of injustice.

As Julie Billaud (Billaud, 2015: 13) noted, the festivities of this carnival serve to mask its "continuity of injustice" in a series of Janus-faced propositions which ultimately serve to sustain the dominant order. Though Afghanistan has a very progressive and secularised constitution on paper, the protection of Afghan citizens per their "rights" under the "rule of law" is revealed as a farce by the endemic disorder and violence in society across Kabul. Most recently, this was horrifically demonstrated by an Islamic State (IS) affiliate bombing in Deh Mazang Square which killed 80 young Hazara protesters and injured some 230 people (Constable, 2016). One year previously, similar protests had taken place in Kabul against the beheading of a nine-year-old girl and six members of her family in the Southern Province of Zabul by an IS affiliate (Constable, 2015).

Alongside these grotesque public acts of violence, the endemic disorder was laid out in plain view through the cronyism and corruption of the judicial institutions designed to "uphold the law". This ugly disparity is evidenced by an examination of Pul-e-Charki prison where a majority of the women imprisoned have been sentenced for "moral crimes", such as *zina* or adultery (including being raped) or "running away from home" (Reid, 2009: 70). The prosecution of these crimes contravenes Afghanistan's nominal constitutional obligation to protect women and men equally before the law. Indeed, the crime of "running away from home" does not exist in Afghan Law or in Sharia Law. Despite the dazzling façade of human rights, "law and order" continued to be overseen by conservative masculine figures who were influenced by customary tenets associated with male honour codes.

The injustices of the "Kabul Carnival" become even more acute when examining the process of "democratisation" which allowed former warlords and Mujahedeen commanders to pursue profit and power in the country's booming war economy. In addition to maintaining their own private militias, these figures could enrich themselves through their involvement in both the licit economy, such as in construction and shipping, as well as in the narco-economy involving Afghanistan's drug trade (Lister and Pain, 2004: 3; Goodhand and Mansfield, 2010: 17). Moreover, as foreign money, militaries and aid organisations began to pour into Kabul, the leaders of the victorious Northern Alliance association were quick to claim all of the land in an area that was to become most prized and valuable in the Sherpur District (Maykuth, 2003). To do this, they had to evict hundreds of families, many of whom were Tajik and had already been displaced from the Shomali plains to the suburbs following war with the Taliban in 1997. Thus, as Marc Herold (2006: 1) and a variety of other media commentators, including Walter Mayr (2010) and Farah Stockman (2005), have incisively noted, what emerges when examining the evolving dynamics of power following 2001 was the Janus-faced nature of the bubble economy in the city and wider region. For some, such as Western and Afghan expatriates, wealthier Afghan families and those connected with powerful political figures or groups, this life was characterised by excess, for instance, malls, hotels, and expensive "Western lifestyles"; however, for others, life was much harder in the new context of informal tenements with only lowly paid informal labour available to families in their struggles to stave off crushing poverty.

As was the case in the province of Nangarhar, which has the second highest rate of return after Kabul, the massive amounts of foreign capital pouring into Kabul have led to vast migrations of individuals and families to the city and province in search of jobs and economic survival. The city of Kabul was ill-prepared to meet this massive human influx; it had suffered horrendous physical damage during the civil war of the 1990s and had gone for a decade with little to no investment in basic public infrastructure (Metcalfe *et al.* 2012: 7). Moreover, while the "formally-recognised" centre of Kabul, which houses wealthier Afghan families, key Afghan elites and Western expatriates, has experienced a reconstruction boom and an expansion of vital services and luxury amenities, some 80 per cent of the city's inhabitants have taken up residence in "informal" slums with no access to basic infrastructure and with no security of tenure (Metcalfe *et al.* 2012: 7).

This picture of excessive greed, inequality and injustice is on display everywhere throughout the city of Kabul – the heart of the Afghan State and the Western state-building mission. This was poignantly captured in 2005, following the previous year's elections, by Farah Stockman (2005) of the Boston Globe who noted that a rich trans-nation crowd of internationals, foreign expats and local power-holders benefitted from the presence of luxury malls and luxury consumer goods, could frequent the hidden brothels of Chinese restaurateurs and lived in expensive and newly constructed hotels and large mansions. As she noted:

> Warlords who once destroyed the city fighting one another in ethnic turf wars now duke it out at the ballot box. Larger-than-life billboards left over from the recent parliamentary election show female candidates, now free to participate in politics. They gaze down on burka-clad women begging for money below.

The "Green Zone"

It is useful to remember that the large holistic Western Intervention into Afghanistan, which has come at a total cost of $800 billion since 2001, has predominately been based in Kabul and in the city's nearby environs. Thus, all the component parts of different Western governments' missions in Afghanistan, including their military forces, their diplomatic staff and other civilian advisors and specialists, are located in what is variously called the "Green Zone" of Kabul or the "ring of steel" (International Crisis, 2011: 8).

Within this fortified Western Green Zone, many other major Western agencies have been based, including the following: international organisations such as the United Nations, the World Bank and the Asia Development Bank; International Humanitarian Non-governmental Organisations such as AKDN, OXFAM, Solidarites, CARE; and finally a host of other Western and Non-Western NGOs chiefly concerned with profit-making in both security, as highlighted by the Private Security Companies (PSCs) Blackwater and Dyncorp, and the development aid industry, which is exemplified by companies like Chemonomics. As was the case in Iraq, the large international presence which has descended upon, and occupied, the central districts of Kabul exists as an island unto itself. Embassies, banks, hotels and NGO offices are ringed with multiple layers of concrete barriers, barbed wire fences as well as PSC and Afghan Army guards (Anyadlke, 2012). From within these fortified warrens, Western expatriates can earn large amounts of money, whether in salaries or corporate profits, without ever having to meet the masses of ordinary Afghans whose lives they are ostensibly meant to be improving (Herold, 2006: 67–68).

Nowhere, is this bifurcated reality more evident than in various Western agencies' ad-hoc attempts to collaborate with the Afghan Ministry of Urban Planning (MUP) in dealing with the exponential rise of people living informally in the city. Urban development in Kabul has been haphazardly driven by the cycle of donor conferences in which these donors have inevitably produced wish lists that nominate several highly ambitious, if not completely unrealistic goals. For instance, consider the 2004 National Urban Programme (NUP), developed by various Western donors and implementing agencies as part of the Afghan National Development Strategy (ANDS) (Jolyon, 2012: 126–128).

A senior non-governmental planner who worked on the NUP noted that there was a scant two-week timeframe to finalise this enormous urban policy document; moreover, within this plan, virtually every type of urban development had been registered as a core priority (Esser, 2009: 15). This was true even though tackling even one of the sub-programmes in the context of Kabul's massively expanding population would have been highly ambitious. Unsurprisingly, as Leslie Jolyon (2012: 127) noted, the 2004 NUP and its fantastical vision for urban development comprising an array of highly ambitious sub-programmes has been forgotten by civil servants and donors alike. Instead, he argued that urban development in Kabul has proceeded in an ad hoc fashion or not at all. Thus, while some progress has been made in improvement of services in the historically established "formal districts" of the city, such as reconstruction of major water pipe networks as a result of German-funded investments (Jolyon, 2012: 127), there is little understanding or agreement between Afghan stakeholders, such as Kabul City municipalities and the Ministry of Urban Planning, Western donors and international organisations on an overarching framework. In this situation, spending on urban development by the Afghan government has effectively been sidelined with only 2.5 per cent of the government's annual budget of $4.75 billion having been earmarked for the MUP; a sum which becomes even smaller when considering how much of this money would have actually been disbursed (Jolyon, 2012: 127).

Moreover, in this morass of uncertainty on how to marry urban development goals with the existing messy reality of millions of people living in informal tenements within the city, increasingly fantastical dreams of modernised cities have been forwarded and rhetorically supported by Western and Afghan actors. This is highlighted by the current idealised plan to build a second city, replete with the necessary infrastructure but also "eco neutral", beside Kabul City in the adjoining rural district of Deh Sabz which is currently used for pastoralism, brickmaking and farming. The plan, entitled *The Kabul Metropolitan Development Cooperation Program,* was completed by the Japan Investment Cooperation Agency (JICA) in 2009 and has been subsequently endorsed by Hamid Karzai's cabinet (Watanabe, 2010). Entailed within this plan is the idea for a city which might house three million people by 2025. As Joylon (2012: 127) notes, oft-made claims that this scheme will be funded from sales of residential and commercial land are implausible, while it still remains extremely difficult to secure resources for the rehabilitation of Kabul's threadbare infrastructure networks. He similarly dismisses the idea that "recycle-oriented" resource use might prevail in what he terms a "brave new urban world".

Kabul City's urban districts

Though Kabul can be typified as a bubble economy, this bubble centres on the very small central area of Kabul. Though the rise of this bubble has doubled the cost of living for everyone living in Kabul, it is the masses of urban poor who suffer most hardship (Doherty, 2011). The research of Metcalfe *et al.* (2012: 19), Stephan Schütte (2009: 471) and Marc Herold (2006: 50), among many others, captures this dynamic very aptly when exploring the different earning potential of Afghans and Westerners working in salaried and casual positions in Kabul. According to this research, at the top of the food chain are those Westerners in the employ of the international mission who earn $4,000 per month (Herold, 2006: 66); Afghans in the employ of aid organisations can earn up to $1,000 per month (Herold, 2006: 49) and those Afghans working to lay pipe in the formal economy can earn $700 per month (Metcalfe *et al.* 2012: 20); however, teachers and civil servants working for the government of Afghanistan earn a mere $100 to $150 per month and $50 per month respectively while casual day labourers' wages range from $75 to $250 per month for work which can be sporadic and will end each winter (Metcalfe *et al.* 2012: 20).

Against this backdrop of daily struggle, inflation is on the rise in Kabul and affects all the basic necessities of life such as water, food, fuel and clothing as well as the cost of rents which have risen dramatically. Rental payments can range from $25 (Schütte, 2009: 486) to $200 (Herold, 2006: 50) a month and, it was observed by Schütte (2006: 32) that rental payments typically make up 30 per cent of families' yearly costs. However, owing to the informal or "illegal" communities in which they live, these families have no security over their tenure and could at any stage be evicted by government authorities (Metcalfe *et al.* 2012: 33). This was illustrated dramatically in Sherpur when factional leaders of the Northern Alliance and those associated with Hamid Karzai bulldozed the homes of dozens of poor squatters to make way for the redevelopment of the suburb. Writing for the *Philadelphia Inquirer* at the time, Andrew Maykuth (2003) relayed the following story of the way in which this process affected ordinary residents:

> As Kabul's police stood by, a backhoe clawed into Sediq's house, collapsing the tin roof and mud walls, knocking over his portable TV in a cloud of dust. While children wailed and women waved copies of the Koran, the machine took a bite out of 11 other houses in the cramped enclave.
>
> In a thin gesture of charity, Kabul Police Chief Basir Salangi gave residents 24 hours to clear out before he finished demolishing their structures to make way for a development of luxury villas.
>
> "It's not fair," Sediq said. "We suffered under the Taliban, who were cruel people, yet they never did anything like this to us."

In this exercise in raw greed and power, 300 plots totalling about 120,000 square metres were distributed among senior governmental officials and commanders and the many businessmen linked to them (RAWA, 2003). Miloon Kothari, a special housing rapporteur for the UN Commission on Human Rights, noted that the government sold 4,300-square-foot lots to the officials and commanders for about $1,000 each but that these same lots were then resold for more than $80,000 in Kabul's hot real estate market (Maykuth, 2003). Kothari noted the following about this process in a public interview for which he was later rebuked by Special Representative Lakhadar Brahimi:

> essentially what we have found there is that ministers and people at the highest level are involved in occupying land and in demolishing the homes of poor people ... In fact a number of ministers, including the minister of defence [Marshall Fahim at the time], are directly involved in this kind of occupation and dispossession of poor people, some of whom have been there for 25 to 30 years.

When providing detail of the everyday economic pressures facing the majority of families living in informal tenements, it is also important to highlight the economy of water in this city. The Kabul water basin is being severely stressed by the exponential increase in people living in the city, coupled with the increasing effects of climate change which are predicted to result in a warming trend for south-western Asia (US Geological Survey, 2010: 1–4). The authors of contemporary hydrological reports for the US Geological Survey on Kabul noted that the water levels of a number of urban wells had decreased considerably as a result of increased pumping and climatic factors (US Geological Survey, 2010: 3). Moreover, while some improvements in water infrastructure had taken place within the formally registered districts, on the whole over 50 per cent of people lack access to a water source (Metcalfe et al. 2012: 24).

In these situations, families living in informal communities would often have to travel great distances or over dangerous routes to obtain water from major communal pump stations. Meanwhile, for many other families, access to water is dependent on shallower wells, which run the risk of drying up, or from 30 litre drums of water that are delivered by water tankers around the city. These tankers are owned by relatively wealthier families who can earn $30 per tanker day or approximately $850 per month by filling up their tankers at particular wells for which they have the monopoly (Beall and Esser, 2005: 12). Rather than allowing international organisations and humanitarian NGOs to dig deeper wells to facilitate the needs of the city's inhabitants, the Kabul municipal authorities, in tandem with the government of Afghanistan, have often worked to prevent any new water infrastructure, which could lend a degree of permanency to informal communities' tenements (Metcalfe et al. 2012: 36–37). Thus, access to water, which is a basic requirement for human life, has increasingly become a right for the well-situated wealthier urban inhabitants of the formal city and a privilege that must be paid for by the majority of poor families.

Gendering human security in Kabul

A consistent argument that I have made throughout this book is that human security, characterised by personal well-being and happiness, is a product of concrete, social relationships. A person has security to the extent to which the life and livelihood that s/he desires is recognised and made possible by others' actions within their social context. In Kabul, perhaps more than anywhere else in Afghanistan, women, and women's bodies, represent the symbolic, and literal, battle ground which is fought over by Western state-builders and the many supporters of a traditional honour-bound society. In this urban space, Western policy-makers and aid workers have targeted women with strategies aimed at economic empowerment and political participation. While women possess these freedoms nominally, their pursuit of such "opportunities" is not without extreme risk to themselves and their family. The unabashedly political nature of aid has provoked a backlash from many men and women in Kabul's society who agree with conservative religious and traditional figures of power that programmes aimed at women are shameful and dishonourable.

At the same time, by sheer economic necessity, many women must work to ensure their family's survival needs. This is especially true for some 300,000 widows who live in Kabul. For these female-headed households, the lack of male labour means that women, and their children, become engaged in different forms of informal employment to sustain their families. Such forms of work include begging, washing clothes, tailoring and carpet weaving. Perhaps most horrifically, some poor families push their young girls, and boys, into sex work to meet the household's economic needs (land of the unconquerable, sex trafficking report). Such work is highly hazardous to women as well as young girls and boys. They face the threat of violence from their extended families and communities and at the same time these individuals are also pursued as moral criminals by the police and courts. At the same time, sex work is dangerous because of the severe health risks due to the spread of sexually transmitted diseases like HIV – widespread because of the use of unclean intravenous needles by the country's one million opiate addicts.

The life of the urban poor of Kabul is not only characterised by crushing poverty but also the threat posed by clashing ideologies over women's roles. By prioritising urban women as individual economic agents in need of empowerment, Western agencies were engaging in a highly political series of actions which challenged dominant conservative attitudes based on honour. Aid was not only being given to help the vulnerable but also to socially transform gender relations through development programmes targeting women. Unsurprisingly, this focus on women's empowerment has provoked a conservative backlash among Kabul's political and religious elites who have railed against this programme as shameful for turning women into godless and honourless individuals in the mode of Western women (Abirafeh, 2009). Women therefore face a dual challenge in navigating this gendered minefield. On the one hand, out of economic necessity, women seek paid employment in some capacity. Yet, in undertaking these actions, women bear the public and private backlash, often involving violence, of men who are resentful and angry about the dishonour such actions bring their family and community.

As a variety of researchers and journalists have observed, Kabul's unskilled male labour force is oversaturated meaning that work opportunities for the city's displaced rural poor men are intermittent and insufficient for survival. Men consider that their inability to provide in such circumstances and the need to be supported by their wives is an assault on their masculinity. They consider that they should be the providers of a household and the defenders of its honour. In her extensive research, Abirafeh repeatedly drives home this point by arguing that a clear majority of the 121 Afghans she interviewed in Kabul (44 men and 60 women expressed an opinion) argued that Western aid programmes had failed because they didn't take men and men's views into account (Abirafeh, 2009: 116). Moreover, in her many interviews and focus group discussions, she reveals a multitude of personal anecdotes from these women and men attesting to the increase in conflict and violence within urban families' homes.

> Some women expressed this new violence as a result of men's insulted honour. A married woman in her late 20s put it this way: "We don't want our men to be backed by any other man in the world. It is this that causes violence." She elaborated to explain that Afghan men are feeling dependent on others and as a result their dignity was under question...
>
> ...Another woman reinforced the point, explaining that "men are more aggressive and angry" because they lack employment. A few women were vocal in their blame of aid institutions and their focus on women. One said: "They increased violence between men and women and it will increase more." An Afghan woman elaborated: "The men, they have become more angry, more violent. Much more violent."

A Tajik man named Donesh, who lived in Kabul both before and after the fall of the Taliban, made a similar point to me in Dehli. During the mixed FGD among Tajik women and men, I asked about the prevalence of domestic violence in families. Donesh, himself a university-educated professional and former teacher in Kabul in post-Taliban Afghanistan, argued initially that a lack of education was to blame for such violence. Then moments later, he gestured towards the fact that violence was also arising out of economic insecurity which threatened men's sense of self-worth as providers of a family.

> DONESH: I believe that the economic factor is equally as important as education. The bad economic condition of a family could create serious problems between husband and wife, no matter how much they love each other.
>
> Today after so many years of war, the economic basis of the society has broken down, and it is difficult for men to maintain their family's expenditure. Undoubtedly the bad economic condition of life distracts men from being tolerant, and this uneasy condition directly impacts on their family

life. If a man could not maintain the expectation of his kids, and his family obviously it creates problems in their families.

Stefan Schutte, who worked as a researcher for the Afghanistan Research and Evaluation Unit (AREU), also observed the prevalence of violence in urban families in which men were under or unemployed. This was illustrated in an anecdote provided by a woman in Kabul speaking about her family's violent and precarious home life.

SALIMA: In summer, my husband waits at the roadside for work, and sometimes he finds employment for a day or two. In winter, it is harder, and we have no income at all. When my husband has work and income he behaves normally, but when there is no work he becomes rude. He beats me and the children; my little daughter has suffered the most. Even her brothers started beating her and she became mentally very sick as a consequence.

In this broader context of poverty and unemployment, the decisions by Western donors and aid agencies to use aid politically to "empower" women fuelled new forms of violent resentment against women by men. Thus, far from being "liberated", women's need to pursue training and employment, while simultaneously upholding "traditional" roles in the household, placed new constraints and burdens on their lives, not least of which are the conflicts and violence which they confront in their own households and communities because of this work. This is not to say that women's right to work is not important or should be discouraged; rather it is to say that the Aid priority should be focused on alleviating families' crushing experiences of poverty by providing reliable paid employment opportunities for working age men.

One of the best illustrations of this is offered by Anila Daulatzai (2008: 420–421) in a critical assessment of gender-focused aid by the Western Intervention. To make her argument, Daulatzai (2008: 19) provides the example of the World Food Program's (WFP) 86 bakeries run by widows which provide subsidised bread to Kabul's 170,000 mostly female-headed households. Daulatzai doesn't belittle or dismiss the important work these bakeries do by providing work for women and feeding vulnerable families. However, she (Daulatzai, 2006: 300) is keen to note that this programme is an example of Western agencies' views about their own role in "empowering women" and their complete misperception of the roots of Afghan women's, and men's, hardship which has been brought about by war, dislocation and impoverishment. Daulatzai (2008: 430) uses the story of Hila, a 25-year-old woman working at one of the WFP's community bakeries, to convey this disjuncture. Hila was the only remaining member of her family alongside her mother. Her three brothers had died from violent and natural causes in 1990, 1997 and 2000. According to Hila, it was the impact of this cumulative loss which caused her father to die from grief shortly after his eldest son died in 2000. Hila worked nine-hour per day shifts at the bakery to support herself and her mother.

One day during an interview, I asked her about the circumstances surrounding her husband's death. She had never mentioned anything about him to me, even though other widows would often speak about their own married life.

Hila looked at me and began crying, as she said in Dari: "I am a widow, dear sister, but I was never married." I was confused, and initially thought I was misunderstanding her, because although Hila used the common word for widow (*biveh*) in Dari, widowhood is also expressed with a range of terms that literally mean "woman without (protection, husband or male head of household)" or "vulnerable woman".

But I continued to listen and quickly realised that her statement was not linguistically confounding. Hila was not merely expressing her current status as a female head of household, in using the term *biveh*, she was making a profound gesture toward her relationship to loss, as well as to her particular perspective of the future.

In this way, Hila had become a "widow" out of economic necessity to comply with a Western perspective of a vulnerable woman in need of empowerment. Yet taking on this classification is not liberating. Rather it is confining. Hila's position as a permanently employed unmarriable woman occurs precisely because of the destruction of her primary kinship relations who would otherwise have supported her and her mother. Although Hila had previously tried to get married several times, the prospective grooms and their families could not afford to provide for her and her mother. For this reason Daulatzai notes:

> For Hila it was not an oppressive system of gender imbalance that took away her husband before she ever had one – it was her life in a war-torn, poverty-struck, neglected environment, and the pressure to submit to scripts that others had written for her, those who had come to 'liberate' women like herself. Kinship structures and social networks had to be redrawn for her to inhabit something like ordinary.

In her critique, Daulatzai (2008: 432) therefore argues that the international community determines the conditions of "possibility" whereby Afghans can or cannot "make ends meet". She notes that these conditions are not experienced as "liberating" but rather as "very stringent, very limiting, and very arbitrary." Indeed, while working within the WFP sponsored bakeries, Daulatzai would sometimes be asked by the women to translate the conversations of the UN officials and foreign dignitaries who visited these programmes. When she described the conversations the foreign officials were having she noted that the women were annoyed to hear that their daily work was a heroic political struggle.

> As a matter of fact, some of the widows even wondered why they were not treated with more consideration by the international organizations, especially since they were presented to visitors as heroines of resistance against

oppression. Why could aid institutions not make daily life less of a struggle, for example, by increasing the salary the widows received from the bakery?

One of the bakers expressed herself with tears: "One day we are heroines for them, the next day something else, at the end we are useless." Another baker continued by saying "they know nothing about our lives yet they tell our stories on our behalf", while other bakers found it disturbing that the visitors never tried to speak with them and only wanted to take their photographs.

In my Pashtun women's focus group discussion, a similar sentiment was expressed by Farishta, on the broader aims of the West to socially transform Afghanistan.

HOST: In making Afghanistan's government like Western governments, do you think it's been better for females' life or it's been worse?
PASHMINA: It's been worse. People are buying women with 100 dollars.
FARISHTA: If Western countries and its politicians want to change the culture and customs of Afghanistan then it's a really bad thing even to think about. We never want to tell their women to be like us or to live like us. Then how can they think or do so?

And even if we do so will they accept it? Or will they even care about what we are telling them? The answer is of course they won't.

Then how can they come and change our culture and customs and exchange it with their culture. They shouldn't do or even think so. I'm agreeing with them that females should live their life the way they want and it's true that a woman can live like a man but not as they do. We never want to work or live like them. Especially I would never like to accept their culture. When we're not imposing them to live like us or to do as our culture. Then they can never impose us to accept their culture.
KASHMALA: Even now life for females is not safe. They can work and study but they aren't safe and if they unhide their face their families would never let them go out or work outside. Because people won't let them and they won't be safe.
FARISHTA: When a woman works in an organization or institute she's being very shameful and her life won't be safe. Her relatives will never go to her house and no one will be good with them.

To provide some specificity to this account of the gendered dynamics of human (in)security, which face different families in Kabul, I will explore contrasting urban districts which have been profiled in contemporary reporting on the city's poor families. As I have already indicated, the gendered battleground of Kabul has tended to exacerbate the hierarchies of power which discipline women and men's lives alike. Even though many women and men have moved to the city in the hope of a better future for their families, especially their sons and daughters, these idealised hopes are thwarted by the everyday realities they face to survive.

For instance, as opposed to sending their children to school, families are driven to send these children out to work to help supplement their household's income and, when faced with a severe shock, such as the loss of a male breadwinner's earnings, they may need to resort to drastic measures such as arranging the marriage of young daughters for the bride price.

Life, death and toil for the urban poor in Kabul City

There is perhaps no better explanation of the core of material insecurity faced by the urban poor in Kabul in the contemporary context of Western state-building than that offered by Stefan Schütte (Schütte, 2009: 465–467). He has done considerable research on urban contexts in Afghanistan, regarding the scholarly work of Geoff Wood (Wood, 2003: 455), on the economic choices made by poor people because of chronic insecurity. Schütte argues that the dynamic of insecurity which encapsulates poor people's lives in urban contexts in Afghanistan, especially in Kabul, relates to the need to invest their energies in immediate strategies of survival at the expense of their future prosperity and happiness (Schütte, 2009: 468). This dilemma is neatly captured using Wood's (2003: 455, 468) very simple, but powerful, argument that the poor are engaged in a "Faustian Bargain" in which they often act to engage with the "devil they know" vis-à-vis the immediate requirements of work to enable survival rather than attempting to pursue an unknown and hazardous future livelihood by striking out on their own.

While urban families in Kabul earn slightly more than their rural counterparts, they are also paying more in household rents, food, products and services (Schütte, 2009: 32). Moreover, as Schütte (2009: 471) notes, the everyday burdens of the poor in Kabul are exacerbated by the saturated state of the urban labour market which means that job-seekers' opportunities for work are limited to informal employment which is unreliable, lowly paid and subject to high seasonal variance. Schütte (2009: 471) also notes that families' situations become particularly dire during the bitter season of the Kabul winter when work opportunities shrink further, yet families' costs of living rise because of the freezing cold.

District 5 – South-West Kabul

This district is located on the western outskirts of Kabul and contains different informal settlements as well as the largest of Kabul's approximately 40 displaced persons' camps, Charahi Qambar, which is considered an "illegal" settlement. In addition to the district's longstanding population of a variety of ethno-linguistic groups, the number of families living in this area has continued to expand with the influx of displaced people from the southern provinces of Helmand, Uruzgan and Kandahar. Returnees are predominately composed of different Pashtun tribes but also include some Baluch, Tajiks and a smaller number of "Kuchis" (Metcalfe *et al.* 2012: 8). While long-standing residents of District 5 tend to have moderate access to infrastructure, such as electricity from the city mains, and services, as well as the municipal waste collection, the recently-displaced fare far worse than many other informal communities around Kabul.

When suggesting what the overarching effect of Western state-building has been in this area, particularly on the most vulnerable recently displaced residents, what emerges is a story in which Western war-fighting in the south and the rise of Kabul's aid-driven bubble economy have compelled many families to head to the city. However, as has been previously highlighted by Stephan Schütte, rather than being able to pursue idealised livelihoods, these families are more likely to find themselves living in squalid informal slum towns with their adult male workforce unable to find any stable work or fair remuneration in Kabul's saturated informal labour markets. Thus, although these families migrated to Kabul in the hope of a better life in which their families could access healthcare and their daughters and sons could go to school, the reality for these families is a life geared towards basic survival. The pressure of this "brave new urban world" (Jolyon, 2012: 127) on these recently arrived families was compounded by the contempt of long-standing residents and authorities for these rural Pashtuns. Newly arrived Pashtun men from Southern Afghanistan faced discrimination and prejudices which made their efforts to find casual work even more difficult in a saturated labour market. This is notably highlighted in the following responses from Pashtun men to a 2009 Listening Report Survey (CDA Collaborative Learning Projects, 25):

> Kabul was the only place we could be secure and get aid. We were driven off our land. All during the war we were secure, but now that the US military is here, we're not secure because we can't negotiate with them.
> (Internally displaced person from a southern province speaking in Kabul)

> From a bag of assistance, we don't need very much. We need peace. If we have peace, we can even eat grass and stay in our own place.
> (Internally displaced person from a southern province speaking in Kabul)

> [The US military] arrests our young people without reason. They say we are Talib. We are not. So we left because of security. We want to work, but there are no jobs, so we send our children to beg.
> (Internally displaced person from a southern province speaking in Kabul)

Consequently, many households' women and children have turned to begging despite the risks and harassment this brings from the authorities and from the wider community. At the same time, the mixed and densely populated urban settings exacerbated the communities' gendered honour codes to the detriment of women's and girls' lives. This was especially apparent in *Charahi Qambar* where the demands of *Purdah* meant that women and girls could not leave the home without a Mahram and, subsequently, often could not access water, sanitation facilities or healthcare (Metcalfe *et al.* 2012: 16). Meanwhile, rather than sending their children to school, families must send their children into the streets to engage in casual labour, such as weaving carpets or selling gum, newspapers and cigarettes, to attempt to meet families' basic needs (Metcalfe *et al.* 2012: 16).

As was noted, winters in Kabul are very harsh, particularly for those communities who live in tents within the *Charahi Qambar* camp (Metcalfe *et al.* 2012: 25). Though there is a desire by the international aid community to establish more durable solutions for the community, such as the installation of more water pumps, the Afghan government and Kabul Municipal authorities have blocked any projects which could give greater permanence to these settlements (Metcalfe *et al.* 2012: 36–37). Consequently, aid agencies respond each winter on an ad hoc basis by supplying fuel, tarpaulins and blankets, food rations and cooking oil. As many news agencies have noted, while people living in these desperate circumstances in Kabul's winter will accept whatever aid is being offered, inevitably the cold season outlasts whatever supplies they may be lucky enough to get. Rod Nordland, writing for the *New York Times* in Kabul, observed in December, 2012 that the United Nations High Commission for Refugees, having abandoned its preoccupation with distinguishing "refugees" from "internally displaced persons", had provided some 40,000 cold weather packages, consisting of fuel, tarps and warm clothing, in Kabul and 5,000 to Kabul's camps at a cost of $6 million (Nordland, 2012). However, he noted that UN officials themselves had acknowledged this fuel would be insufficient to heat families' mud and tarp huts through the season and that there were no plans to distribute food to the families. Of the Afghans who received these winter packages, Nordland relayed the following impressions:

> "We are happy to receive this," said Tawoos Khan, one of the camp representatives. "But we want food, and we need more fuel; we have all run out of firewood and charcoal." He and other camp officials said large sacks of charcoal were distributed to every family more than two weeks ago, but supplies had run out…
>
> …Taj Mohammad, the father of the child who died, Janan, said Sunday that he believed that his son might have survived if the cold-weather kit had arrived earlier. But like many of the refugees, he was critical of its contents, which he said were hard to sell in exchange for food.
>
> "I didn't know a package costs $150," he said. "It's a lot of money. It would have been much better if they had given us the money, and we would have spent it on what we need the most."

While the pressures fall heavily on the families' men, women and children what is also true is the extent to which women in particular suffer in these reformulated patriarchal contexts. As was observed previously in Nangarhar and Bamyan, economic pressures influence families' decisions to sell their child and young teenage daughters in order to obtain a bride price. This gendered form of insecurity means that it is more likely for girls to become pregnant and give birth at dangerously young ages, which is evidenced by Afghanistan's exceedingly high maternal mortality rate. Moreover, in Charahi Qambar, only 20 per cent of women gave deliveries in safe healthcare clinics and many found it difficult to access post-natal healthcare (Metcalfe et al. 2012: 26).

District 13 – North-West Kabul

This district is comprised of the community of Pul-i-Khushk (Hunte, 2005: 4), which is 14 kilometres west of the city centre as well as the communities living in the surrounding hillsides of Afshar, on the way to Paghman Province (Winterbotham, 2011: 15). While the district was formally recognised as a city district by the Kabul Municipality in 2003, it was settled decades ago but was deserted during the reign of the Taliban. After 2001, many returning families, as well as more recently displaced migrant families, settled here. The majority of these families are Hazara but there are other minority communities within the district including Tajiks, Qizilbash, Sayyeds and some Pashtun "Kuchi" nomads (Metcalfe et al. 2012: 9). In this region, there exists a broadly shared communal ethic of tolerance among the different ethno-linguistic groups who predominately share an affiliation with Shiism and/or being Hazara. However, while different groups, for the most part, live in harmony with each other, major inter-communal cleavages, notably between Hazaras and Pashtun "Kuchi" nomads, have often sparked violent and armed conflict (Metcalfe et al. 2012: 9).

The socio-economic status of these different communities varies from the more prosperous neighbourhoods of Pul-Khushk to the more insecure communities of Afshar. Prior to exploring this dynamic further, it is worth presenting the view of one of the *wakils* (community representatives) of district 13 as noted by Metcalfe et al. (2012: 20). This Wakil identified three broad economic groups in the informal settlements as follows:

> A wakil in District 13 interviewed in this study identified three broad groups in informal settlements: families with a relative working in Iran or a breadwinner who is a civil servant, with a monthly income of 12,000 Afs ($249); a middle strata of residents with a monthly income of 5,000 Afs ($104); and the poorest, forced to sacrifice medium-term security to deal with immediate survival: "they burn the shoes of their children to keep the room warm in winter, saying tomorrow God will help us."
>
> (HPG interviews, 2011)

In contrast to District 5 and many other informal and insecure areas around Kabul City, many of the residents in the communities of Pul-i-Khushk have embraced and taken advantage of the opportunities created by the Western mission with corresponding quality of life improvements. This stems in no small way from the strength and solidarity of the broader Hazara community, whose aim is to promote a more progressive and equitable future for Hazaras in Afghanistan. Moreover, as was previously discussed in the Bamyan case study, there is a growing group of Hazaras who could very loosely be termed "middle class" given the rise in their level of education and economic positions; this process was fuelled by the education of a younger generation of Hazaras in Iran as well as the financial and social ties with a large Hazara diaspora. Metcalfe *et al.*, highlight this qualitative improvement in the livelihoods of Hazaras in this neighbourhood with reference to the fact that a majority of families have breadwinners working in the formal economy in some of the following occupations: pipelaying, welding, teaching and working in the armed forces and civil service (Metcalfe *et al.* 2012: 19). Additionally, she noted that District 13 is the only district which met the stated target of the Afghan National Development Strategy (ANDS) that 50 per cent of people in Kabul have access to piped water by 2010 (Metcalfe *et al.* 2012: 24). In this case the system was installed by a private contractor and paid for by wealthier members of the community. Residents who are connected pay a nominal fee of 400 Afghans per month.

Nevertheless, even with these relative improvements in families' livelihoods, life for the better-off but especially for the poor is beset by economic pressures and hardships. For instance, in the suburb of Pul-i-Khushk, while some less wealthy residents have access to deep-well hand pumps that were installed by the Danish Committee on Action for Refugees (DACAR) (Hunte, 2005: 4), a great many rely on privately dug shallow wells which are both expensive and tend to run dry because the level of water in the Kabul Basin is falling (Hunte, 2005: 4). Furthermore, as Rebecca Gang (2011: 10) noted, access to water in the hills of Afshar was even more difficult, with families needing to buy water from tanker delivery points at the bottom of the hills prior to hauling it up on foot or by donkey. This task of hauling water, which would often be delegated to the children of a household, is particularly treacherous in winter when passages are icy, muddy and slippery. According to one survey in the similarly hilly context of Deh Mazang in District 3, it is a common occurrence for children to slip and break their bones when carrying out this task (Zimmermann, 2011: 9). In the context of Afshar, Gang (2011: 10) also observed a chronic lack of access to electricity, sewerage and garbage removal as well as health and education facilities. However, due to the pressing conditions of poverty and complete mistrust of the municipal and national government, communities here are loath to be formally incorporated into the Kabul Municipal plan which would require each family to contribute $120. In Gang's report (2011: 10), a community leader in Afshar and a participant in an AREU focus group discussion noted:

> The government comes here sometimes to tell us that we should pay some taxes for our houses, but we are very poor people. We tell them: "From hungry people, what can one take to eat?" (Az goshna che bana, ke gada bokhora?)
>
> (Mullah, 60, FGD 3)

As was the case in District 5, in spite of the majority of parents wanting an education for their children, economic pressures result in the children of many poorer families being sent out on the streets to look for work instead of going to school. Moreover, while it has been observed that Hazara communities have evolved towards more equitable and egalitarian gender relations, families are sometimes pressured to act in ways completely contrary to this ethic. This can occur when families need to marry off their daughters at a young age despite the irreparable harm and suffering such marriages can bring or when they are compelled to make their sons, but especially their daughters, work in home-based industries such as rug weaving (Hunte, 2005: 22–24). This is captured quite poignantly in a focus group discussion conducted by Pamela Hunte in an extended Hazara family household in the Pul-i-Khushk neighbourhood of District 13:

> The mother of Ali Jon, a widow, sat there with ruffled hair and a pale face. She seemed to be an experienced woman who had spent a life full of troubles.
>
> "If I send my grandchildren to school, then we won't have any food. And our water well is dry – the children fetch our water every day. Shah Wali added, I have many economic problems and so I can't send my daughter [who weaves rugs] to school. She's very willing, though, and she cries every day for me to enrol her in school."
>
> Tears welled up in the eyes of his daughter who was sitting nearby, and she got up and ran away. As the conversation went on, there were a few children sitting at the nearby loom weaving rugs – barefooted, with ruffled hair and chapped lips.
>
> Another father continued: "Our children are obliged to weave rugs. They work day and night to make a living, and they suffer from the dust and pollution of weaving. If I had a job to do, I would never force my children to weave rugs or labour – we would then enrol them in school."

Struggles for recognition in Kabul

Having broadly outlined the gendered dynamics of power which have been produced in Kabul's "carnivalesque" moment of Western Intervention, I will now attempt to explain the way in which ordinary people creatively struggle to secure better livelihoods for themselves and their families. This investigation will first focus on finding the ways in which women and men respond to the practical material challenges related to their family's daily and future needs before second showing the way in which these subjects attempt to resist gendered larger hierarchies of power.

In the previous rural case studies of Nangarhar and Bamyan, what was evidenced was the presence of similar coping strategies used by families to ensure their household's basic survival. Two strategies in both cases were the use of labour migration, whereby a household's working-age males would work abroad and send home remittances, as well as the use of a variety of informal credit relations, which could be issued on very low, or completely free, interest rates.

Similarly, in the urban context of Kabul, both labour migration (Metcalfe *et al.* 2012: 5, 20–21) and informal credit practices (Schütte, 2009: 20, 24, 31) are vital coping strategies which households employ to help cope with the material burdens of everyday living. As these particular strategies have been dealt with previously, I will not investigate them further in this context. Instead, I will focus upon the informal strategies which the urban poor use to strengthen their own family's and their community's tenure against the external pressures brought to bear on them by Kabul's governing authorities.

When tackling this issue, what should be noted is that the context of Kabul presents a picture of a completely heterogeneous social context in which a variety of ethno-linguistic groups live in a shared urban space albeit with well-demarcated exclusionary boundaries between different groups. Though these larger inter-group boundaries have become firmly cemented, what is also apparent is the extent to which the many different local boundaries, relating to families' traditional *qawm* affiliations within their particular ethno-linguistic grouping, have been worn down, paving the way for the emergence of spontaneous constructions of community. These newly-arisen communities often act to provide a basic safety-net for their most vulnerable members as well as to pursue strategies which ensure the security of the group more holistically through attempts to resist the threats posed by external authorities like the government of Afghanistan and the Kabul Municipality. The strategies used demonstrate a high degree of creativity and innovation and help these communities mitigate, or even successfully counteract, the external threats and material pressures being brought to bear.

For instance, in one informal community, displaced families who were "illegally" constructing houses without the permission of the municipality, only did building work at night in order to avoid having to pay bribes to the police (Metcalfe *et al.* 2012: 33). Similarly, Stefan Schütte (2005: 20) has observed, in a variety of newly emerging informal settlements in Kabul, such as Brishna Kot, people are investing in building solid houses to make their community more permanent and ward off future eviction. Meanwhile, in the case of one western district in Kabul, wealthier members of the community autonomously engaged with a private contractor to install piped water to their community, benefitting some 50 per cent of the families in the area (Metcalfe *et al.* 2012: 24).

Moreover, as part of this process, Schütte noted that communities would encourage their extended family and *qawm* networks to migrate to their area in an effort to strengthen the community more holistically; in fact, in District 7, established community members would build housing to accommodate the influx of new families from their traditional rural backgrounds (Metcalfe *et al.* 2012: 41). More fundamentally, different communities lobby powerful patrons within the upper ranks of the government of Afghanistan to ensure their protection. Thus, as Metcalfe *et al.* observed in the context of Charahi Qambar in District 5, displaced Pashtun women from Helmand were facing the threat of eviction made by businessmen from Kandahar. After having received no response from a letter sent by the community to their local member of parliament, the community then enlisted the support of a high-ranking official in the Afghan National Army with whom they had ethnic ties. He lent support by summarily destroying the walls that these businessmen had erected in their attempt to reclaim the land from its informal residents (Metcalfe *et al.* 2012: 28).

Struggles for recognition against gender hierarchies

In her own analysis of Kabul's "carnival", Billaud (2015: 13) notes that the Janus-faced nature of the Western Intervention has influenced the widespread societal rejection of, and resistance to, this governance project. On this point, she argues that, as "'democratisation' efforts" have been accompanied by sharp increases in crime and violence and a regime that has brought lawlessness, "Afghans' mode of engagement with the 'public sphere' has been marked by a general feeling of suspicion, mistrust, and resentment." Despite this, Billaud (2015: 16) argues that the carnivalesque moment has created a sense of togetherness among Afghans based on a "non-Western public life".

> Because the carnivalesque creates a sense of togetherness, a lived collective body that is constantly renewed, non-Western public life challenges the moral assumptions that underpin the liberal public, especially in the domain of gender relations where "emancipation" is often thought of in terms of a public "coming out" and a break-up with "tradition".

This argument by Billaud essentially points to the fact that Afghan women and men, despite the challenges posed in postwar Kabul, find ways to creatively navigate or resist hierarchies of power. However, in exercising this agency, women and men strive towards a moral vision of society in which traditional gender relations are reconciled with changing societal attitudes rather than arbitrarily made redundant. In many of my Delhi focus group discussions, similarly strong sentiments were expressed that women's "emancipation" was meaningless without broader societal recognition of women's roles. Donesh expressed this view in the mixed Tajik FGD when he pointed out that even well-educated, democratic and open-minded women refused to exercise their full freedom because of the current societal context in which they lived.

> Since, the society is not ready for it. Let's first make our society ready for accepting and respecting these values. To bring security, peace, remove poverty and hunger, build schools and support education among people, these changes automatically bring freedom itself. What does it mean to set a few women in parliament, or create a ministry for women and assign a few women there! These are all formalities without having any practical benefit for women in Afghanistan.

When exploring women's, and men's, struggle against gendered hierarchies of power in Kabul, what is apparent are the contrasting situations which different families face. This is evident in the case of relatively well-off Shia and Hazara families living in more tightly knit communities in District 13 compared with the relatively poor Pashtun families of Charahi Qambar Camp in District 5 where the complete heterogeneity of *qawm* affiliation precludes a holistic solidarity among displaced Pashtuns. The reason for highlighting these differences in wealth and community solidarity is that these phenomena have a very strong bearing on the resulting forms of struggle for a positive progression of women's roles within households and communities.

Though such forms of struggle are evident in both of these social contexts, what is also apparent is the extent to which the particularly strong qualities of community in District 13, which extend across ethno-linguistic lines, contribute to a far stronger and more visible dynamic of change than occurs in District 5. This is evidenced in a comparison of markers of gender egalitarianism in the two districts. In District 13, women tend to have greater mobility within their community and, increasingly, an acknowledged decision-making authority within both the household and the public sphere; this is evidenced by women's participation as disputants in community-based dispute resolution processes (CBDR) in which they can influence proceedings (Gang, 2011: 52, 54, 58). Moreover, there is an increasingly prominent conversation in these communities which argues that the improvement of gender relations and women's positions is beneficial to families and communities (Gang, 2011: 38).

In contrast, although there is an evident desire among Pashtun families in District 5 for progressive change regarding family dynamics, there are many constraints because of the more conservative social context. Owing to the prevailing sense of a household's honour and, given the fact that there are a multitude of *qawm*s whose members consider each other strangers, women have far less mobility in the district and city and a far smaller role in public (Schütte, 2006: 48; Metcalfe *et al.* 2012: 16). Similarly, although it is quite possible that women could appear as disputants in CBDR, as Smith has observed of Shinwari Pashtuns in the context of Nangarhar Province, it remains to be seen whether the issues discussed in such forums would extend beyond the realm of the private sphere and "women's issues" into more practical public demands by women such as in the pursuit of inheritance rights or marriage rights.

Having said this, gender relations within families and the community are in a constant state of flux, as is the case in District 13, and exhibit immanent potential for moral progress. This is apparent in the conversations in Pashtun households relating to the improvement of their sons' and daughters' future lives. A variety of Pashtun households in Charahi Qambar explicitly stated that one of the overriding reasons they fled the war zone of southern Afghanistan, apart from basic physical security, was the potential opportunity for their children, whether girls or boys, to receive an education (Metcalfe *et al.* 2012: 23). This means that families are putting faith in the idea that their daughters, as well as their sons, can take on roles in the public sphere and earn wages to support the household (Smith, 2008: 20–21). Though seemingly of only minor importance, this emphasis by families on their hopes and dreams for their children's future heralds the potential development of a major argumentative thread in society challenging overarching gendered hierarchies of power which constrain women's and men's pursuit of the good life.

Furthermore, what is apparent in urban social contexts in Kabul is the growing strategic use of Islam's tenets, as well as a re-emphasis of its core themes of peace and tolerance, as a means of struggling against gendered hierarchies of power. As observed by Rebecca Gang (2011: 31), this is particularly evident but not necessarily limited to District 13. In many of the CBDR cases in this district, she noted that Sharia law was consistently used to support the rights of women and their children in inheritance claims, to gain access to financial maintenance in cases of divorce, in child custody negotiations and even in support of marriages between members of different ethnic groups. This is notably demonstrated in the following story related by Gang:

> My mother had a dispute with my father when he remarried and kicked her and her children out of the house without any money or household items. Although my mother believed that it was not appropriate for women to go to the district or to the whitebeards with this kind of problem, she still went to the whitebeards and asked that they organise a jalasa. My mother and father both sat in the jalasa. The whitebeards said to him, "This is a respectable woman. You remarried and kicked her out of the house with nothing. Aren't you afraid of God?" Then my father agreed to give my mother financial maintenance (naqafa) for herself and for us.
> (Qizilbash woman, 25, FGD 5, participant B)

The importance of using Islam as a way of arguing for change was apparent among many of the Afghan women and men who participated in my focus group discussions in Delhi. In the Tajik women's focus group this point was illustrated by Soraya Emadi, a university-educated mother of five who worked at a women's shelter providing support and training for women who had run away from their homes. When explaining the way in which she and her organisation argued for change in attitudes towards women's education she said that they contacted members of the Ulema in Kabul.

> Our organization wanted to advocate for women's rights through religious sermons by asking the preachers to support education of women by quoting Prophet Mohammad's kindly behaviour to his daughter Fatima. Once Prophet Mohammed said that if my daughter is contented and happy, it means that I am contented and happy. For such aims, some religious Mullahs also helped us by supporting women's rights in their religious sermons with religious justification.

Similarly, in the Tajik mixed discussion between women and men, Ghadir pointed towards the Khatam-al Nabyeen Islamic University, founded by Ayatollah Mohammad Asif Mohseni (former leader of the Shia Mujahedeen group *Harakat-i-Islami*) with funding from Iran. Though this university is undoubtedly controversial, owing to Iran's political influence through this institution, Ghadir praised the value of its multi-sectarian approach to teaching an Islamic education. Moreover, he argued that the construction of the mosque by Mosheni, who was a former Mujahedeen commander in the 1980s, was a significant development in and of itself.

> The Khatam-al Nabyeen madrassa was built at a cost of thirteen million US dollars … I remember an interview with "Sheikh Mohseni" who was asked, where and how he got thirteen million dollars, that he was able to build the Khatam-al Nabyeen Madrassa? Abdul Rasul Sayyaf (former leader of the Sunni Mujahedeen group *Ittihad-i Islami*) was there too. I think this question was asked by Sayyaf.
>
> In reply, Sheikh Mohsini looked to Sayyaf and said, "The money that you received during 1980s, you spent it for purchasing guns, ammunition and killing people, but I kept it and now build a Madrassa."
>
> Though, Khatam-al Nabyeen is a Shia madrassa, it has many other departments for Sunnis too. I think the existence of madrassas such as, Khatam-al Nabyeen is very significant for Afghanistan. It can bring different religious prospects, such as, Shia and Sunni close, and remove the wall of pessimism and hate which is the result of wrong interpretation and understanding of each other.

Though Islam is highly contested in Kabul, and Afghanistan more broadly, what is evident among women and men who are struggling to change societal attitudes is the value this body of knowledge has in contentious moral debates. This is particularly apparent in the value Islam holds in fighting harmful traditional practices such as revenge killings, *baad* (the exchange of women to settle a dispute) and extreme corporal punishment. For instance, in her study of community-based dispute resolution institutions in Kabul, Rebecca Gang (2011: 26–28) observed the way in which a flexible, and pragmatic interpretation of Islam and differing societal customs, informed a multi-ethnic *shura* (community governance body) called the *shura-i-mahal* (literally "shura of the location", i.e. a community-wide shura) in the Afshar neighborhood of District 13. This body was comprised of elders and *wakils* (community representatives) from each of the neighborhood's different ethno-linguistic *qawm*s which included: Hazaras, Tajiks, Sayyeds, Qizilbash and Pashtuns.

The ingeniousness of this local form of community governance is that it can flexibly draw on Sharia, Customary and State law to tailor dispute resolutions in the most appropriate manner to individual and inter-communal disputes. In addition to providing a community-derived council that lobbies external agents like the Kabul municipality and the Afghan government, the *Shura-i-mahal* also promotes inter-communal cooperation with the broader aim of bringing about *Islah* (the promotion of peace and social cohesion through mediation and reconciliation) (Gang, 2011: 29, 51). In so doing it offers a highly instructive example of the potential ways of fostering inter-communal solidarities that dampen ongoing rivalries and tensions between different communities.

Conclusion

When concluding the book's third empirical case study, what should be observed again is the extent to which the process of Western state-building has produced an artificial state apparatus dependent on foreign aid flows alongside an aid-driven bubble economy within the city of Kabul. This, in turn, has led to the massive influx of different families from Afghanistan's rural provinces and beyond the city who are drawn by the thought of economic opportunity as well as safety from war and violence. However, as was shown, life for these newly-minted urban poor communities in sprawling informal tenements and slums around the city of Kabul is defined by hardship and constant economic need. While the Western mission has brought untold benefits to individuals and families at the centre of power in the political-economy of Kabul, millions of people living informally face the inverse and oppressive side of living in this bubble economy where families' lives are based around earning enough to enable bare survival.

This does not mean there is no struggle on the part of the poor and oppressed majority to improve their lives and the world around them more broadly. Perhaps the most interesting form of resistance was the way in which different sections of a community banded together against the pressures of external threats like the Municipality of Kabul and the government of Afghanistan. In these situations, families that usually would not have been affiliated produced new, more inclusive, forms of membership with different communities. Moreover, within these new formulations of community, traditional gendered precepts of a household's honour have also begun to be debated and changed in ways that signal qualitative moral progress towards more equitable relations between women and men. While this was very evident in the case of the Hazara and Shia communities of District 13, it was also apparent in the context of communities who would typically be considered conservative and staid in their views on gender relations. For instance, in Charahi Qambar, in addition to wanting their daughters to receive an education, many newly arrived Pashtun families from the southern countryside suggested that they could envisage future communities in which their daughters could also pursue important economic employment to benefit their paternal households.

References

Abirafeh, Lina (2009). *Gender and international aid in Afghanistan: the politics and effects of intervention.* Jefferson, North Carolina, McFarland & Company, Inc., Publishers.

Ahady, Anwar-ul-Haq (1995). "The Decline of the Pashtuns in Afghanistan". *Asian Survey* 35 (7): 621–634.

Anyadlke, Oblnna (2012). "Living in the Kabul Bubble". *IRIN News*, 16 April 2012.

Beall, Jo and Daniel Esser (2005). "Shaping urban futures: challenges to governing and managing Afghan cities". *Issues Paper Series.* Kabul, Afghanistan Research and Evaluation Unit.

Billaud, Julie (2015). *Kabul carnival: Gender politics in postwar Afghanistan*. Philadelphia, University of Pennsylvania Press.
CDA – Collaborative Learning Projects (2009). Listening Project. *Field Visit Report*.
Constable, Pamela (2015). "Beheading of third-grade girl 'was just the spark' for Afghan minority group". *The Washington Post*, 28 December 2015.
Constable, Pamela (2016). "The bomb that killed 80 Hazaras in Kabul also upended their nonviolent reform effort". *The Washington Post*, 5 August 2016.
Daulatzai, Anila (2006). "Acknowledging Afghanistan". *Cultural Dynamics* 18 (3): 293–311.
Daulatzai, Anila (2008). "The Discursive Occupation of Afghanistan". *British Journal of Middle Eastern Studies* 35 (3): 419–435.
Doherty, Ben and Kate Geraghty (2011). "Kabul: the best of times, the worst of times". *Sydney Morning Herald*, 30 July 2011.
Esser, Daniel (2009). "Who Governs Kabul? Explaining urban politics in a post-war capital city". *Working Paper No. 43*. London, Crisis States Research Centre – London School of Economics (LSE).
Gang, Rebecca (2011). Community-Based Dispute Resolution Processes in Kabul City. *Case Study Series*, Afghanistan Research and Evaluation Unit.
Giustozzi, Antonio (2009). The Eye of the Storm: Cities in the vortex of Afghanistan's civil wars. London, Crisis States Research Centre – London School of Economics (LSE).
GOIRA (2015). State of Afghan Cities 2015. Kabul, government of the Islamic Republic of Afghanistan.
Goodhand, Jonathon and David Mansfield (2010). Drugs and (Dis)order: A study of the opium trade, political settlements and state-making in Afghanistan. *Working Paper No. 83*. London, Crisis States Research Centre – London School of Economics (LSE).
Gregorian, Vartan (1969). *The emergence of modern Afghanistan: Politics of reform and modernization, 1880–1946*. Stanford, Stanford University Press.
Herold, Marc W. (2006). Afghanistan as an empty space: The perfect neo-colonial state of the 21st century. University of New Hampshire, Department of Economics and Women's Studies.
Hunte, Pamela Anne (2005). *Household decision-making and school enrolment in Afghanistan: Case Study 2, District 13 Pul-i-Khushk, Kabul City*, Afghanistan Research and Evaluation Unit.
International Crisis Group (2011). The Insurgency in Afghanistan's Heartland.
Jolyon, Leslie (2012). "Urban recovery, or chaos?" *Snapshots of an Intervention: The Unlearned Lessons of Afghanistan's Decade of Assistance (2001–11)*. Kabul, Afghanistan: www. aan-afghanistan.org. Accessed 20 February 2017.
Lister, Sarah and Adam Pain (2004). Trading in Power: The Politics of "Free" Markets in Afghanistan. *Briefing Paper*. Kabul, Afghanistan Research and Evaluation Unit.
Maykuth, Andrew (2003). "Facing land grab by elite, Kabul's poor turn to U.N." *The Philadelphia Inquirer*, 20 September 2003.
Mayr, Walter. (2010). "Exotic Birds in a Cage: Criticisms of Afghanistan's Bloated Aid Industry". *Der Spiegel*, 22 September 2010.
Metcalfe, Victoria, Simone Haysom and Ellen Martin (2012). Sanctuary in the city? Urban displacement and vulnerability in Kabul. *HPG Working Paper*, Humanitarian Policy Group.
Nader, Alireza and Joya Laha (2011). Iran's balancing act in Afghanistan, Rand Corporation National Defense Research Institute.

Nordland, Rod. (2012). "Afghan camps receive winter aid, but officials say it isn't enough". *New York Times*, 30 December 2012.
RAWA (2003). "Crime and barbarism in Shirpur by Afghan ministers and high authorities". *RAWA News*, 16 September 2003.
Reid, Rachel (2009). "We have the promises of the world": Women's rights in Afghanistan. B. Adams, E. Pearson and J. Saunders. New York, Human Rights Watch.
Rubin, Barnett R. (2002). *The fragmentation of Afghanistan: State formation and collapse in the international system*. New Haven, Yale University Press.
Schütte, Stefan (2005). Emerging trends in urban livelihoods, *Working Paper Series*. Afghanistan Research and Evaluation Unit.
Schütte, Stefan (2006). Searching for security: Urban livelihoods in Kabul. *Case Study Series*. Kabul, Afghanistan Research Evaluation Unit.
Schütte, Stefan (2009). "Informal (In)security in Urban Afghanistan". *Iranian Studies* 42 (3): 465–491.
Smith, Deborah J. (2008). Love, fear and discipline: Everyday violence toward children in Afghan families. *Issues Paper Series*. Kabul, Afghanistan Research and Evaluation Unit.
Stockman, Farah (2005). "Afghanistan: Few haves and so many have-nots". *The Boston Globe*, 9 October 2005.
US Geological Survey (2010). Availability of water in the Kabul Basin, Afghanistan.
Watanabe, Takeshi (2010). JICA's assistance to Afghanistan: Introducing the Kabul Metropolitan Development Cooperation Program. JICA Afghanistan Office, Japan International Cooperation Agency.
Winterbotham, Emily (2011). Legacies of conflict: Healing complexes and moving forwards in Kabul Province. *Case Study Series*. Kabul, Afghanistan Research and Evaluation Unit.
Wood, Geoff. (2003). "Staying Secure, Staying Poor: The 'Faustian Bargain'". *World Development* 31 (3): 455–471.
Zimmermann, Robert, (ed.) (2011). *Afghanistan Human Development Report 2011.* Centre for Policy and Human Development, Kabul University.

8 Conclusion

At its heart, this book has attempted to show that it is possible and vitally necessary to illustrate what human security means to people in Afghanistan. The story I have told here with the help of feminist and critical theories is that security is an inherently relational proposition. Peoples' lives are variously enabled or constrained and permitted or denied recognition through social relationships. This means that ultimately we are only as secure as we make each other.

For this reason, I argued that it was important to understand how subjects sought to struggle against hierarchically gendered forms of social recognition. Here, I was interested in the way in which women, as some of the most insecure persons in Afghanistan, struggled against such hierarchies with men. These struggles are not without risk to those who are engaging them because they do so in a violent context which is dominated by hyper-masculine ideas.

Anyone who has been in a serious relationship before will have experienced conflict with their partner. Those who have had these experiences will also know that conflicts are not necessarily a bad thing. Indeed, through conflicts, we can learn to better understand and recognise each other's perspectives and feelings to build a happier and more fulfilling relationship. Yet, if conflict does occur, we all know that it is best when it takes place in a safe and respectful environment. Otherwise, there are very real risks of such conflicts becoming violent and causing physical and emotional trauma to both partners.

In Afghanistan, right now, there are a multitude of conflicts taking place within and between different communities on important issues which speak to people's security and well-being holistically. As I have demonstrated throughout the book, regardless of local context, there are a variety of ongoing debates and struggles about gendered inequality and inequality more broadly. The problem is not that these conflicts are occurring but that they are not happening in a safe environment. Afghanistan is a warzone in which dynamics of violence, displacement and impoverishment continue to make daily survival a struggle for many families. Meanwhile, Afghanistan's social context is pervaded by gendered hierarchies of power that jeopardise both the lives and well-being of women and men.

Throughout this book I have been highly critical of the enlightenment-inspired beliefs that informed a US-led Western Intervention in Afghanistan and the effects of this intervention itself. Indeed, I have also written two similarly critical articles of the Western Intervention exploring the deleterious effects of its neo-liberal agricultural programme (Walter, 2016) and its application of counter insurgency techniques in Nangarhar Province (Walter, 2017). This does not mean I think that Western policy-making is inherently doomed to fail in Afghanistan. Rather, it means that changing Western policy-makers' views so that they can comprehend the world of Afghanistan as people there see it is a very difficult task. Yet it is only with such vision, that Western policy-making practitioners could realise the complexity of conflict in Afghanistan and their own roles in fuelling it.

At this point, it is useful to draw on a contemporary historical anecdote to illustrate the disjuncture between the Western developer and the local Afghan subject. Quite serendipitously last year, I found a video taken by a *Guardian* news team in 2008 (McHugh, 2008) regarding the Afghanistan–Pakistan border which very succinctly captured this perspectival challenge. In this video, a US platoon, which has come under rocket fire from a Taliban position, travels to a village nearby where the rockets were fired. There, a US sergeant and his translator impatiently talk to a lone elder to find out where the rockets came from. What emerges from this exchange is the gulf in understanding between the translator and the local elder as well as the US sergeant.

VILLAGE ELDER: I can only speak Pashto.
TRANSLATOR: That is okay. How is the security here?
VILLAGE ELDER: There is no security
TRANSLATOR: No – what I mean is: how's the security situation here?
VILLAGE ELDER: I just told you! There is no security here. We've yet to see any security around here.
TRANSLATOR: (In English) We are fine; there are no problems here.
VILLAGE ELDER: I agree with you on the cooperation; the Taliban are over there – not far away (he points off camera).

Then the Pashtun Elder attempts to sketch out the broader cultural picture in which the US and its allies are attempting to bring change to Afghanistan.

VILLAGE ELDER: I would like to tell the American a story. In our country, we grow wheat and we have ants. There is no way we can stop little ants from stealing the wheat. There are so many little ants it is almost impossible to stop them. I've told this story to help the American understand the situation in Afghanistan.
  Yes, the Americans built this road and they would do more to help us if we cooperate with them. Of course, we know that! And we would like to cooperate with them. It's just that we can't!
TRANSLATOR: (In English) He gives many examples; the main point is that if you want to get the ACM (Anti-Coalition Militia). They are behind this road; behind this mountain.

The nuance and detail of Afghanistan's politics are hidden in the translator's account but even if he provided them it seems unlikely the sergeant could comprehend this knowledge as is demonstrated in the following exchange. Sergeant Adams tells his translator to ask when the man last saw the Taliban.

TRANSLATOR: (In English) I asked him; he said one year ago.
SERGEANT ADAMS: One year! Oh, for fucks sake are you kidding me! Hey, tell him he's full of shit, first of all. One week ago, we took four rockets from a hilltop 800 metres from here. They didn't hear that? Didn't see it?
TRANSLATOR: (In English) One week ago sir?
SERGEANT ADAMS: Yeah, it was a week ago, right?

The translator relays the question in Pashto to the man as Sergeant Adams excitedly asked, "What did he say, what did he say?"

TRANSLATOR: (In English) They are afraid: two months ago they [the Taliban] came and took all their young guys and beat them.
SERGEANT ADAMS: Ask them if they've got any guns here? I don't want to take them I just want to know why he didn't shoot them in the fucking face!

Later, standing around with his platoon in the village, Sergeant Adams collected himself and tried to summarise the situation he and his platoon were in, to the *Guardian* photo journalists.

SERGEANT ADAMS: It's the same thing again you know. They are ... they're afraid of the ACM and no matter how many times you tell them or how you tell them they don't want to seem to understand that until they ... well they're allowed to have an AK per household. If they put an AK in dude's face and shot him knowing he's a bad guy. They would stop coming here and they won't understand that. So, basically, they support the ACM by not supporting anyone.
SERGEANT ADAMS: (To his translator) What's he saying?
TRANSLATOR: I hate these people sir! When I ask them something else, they give me the wrong answer!

It is worth repeating this exchange in full because of the depth of insight this account provides of the inability of the American and his translator to comprehend the story which the Pashtun Elder elucidated. This account also demonstrates a greater level of blindness in the broader Western Intervention itself. In its actions, to support some political factions in Afghanistan like the Northern Alliance but not others, like the Afghan Taliban, it has fuelled conflict dynamics more broadly.

This does not mean that conflict resolution and conflict transformation is impossible in Afghanistan by US and Western policy-makers. Merely, it is a very hard act to engage in when some of the principal actors engaged in this dialogue cannot apprehend the world through the eyes of the "other". If policy-makers can begin to more thoroughly question the premises of their own positions which depict Afghanistan's conflict in a binary fashion, then they will be well served. Moreover, there are signs that this is possible and that the power of certain "regimes of truth" regarding the Western Intervention in Afghanistan has been destabilised.

Indeed, this was demonstrated to me early in 2016 when I presented a conference paper on a panel discussing intelligence and national security at the 2016 ISA Annual Convention in Atlanta. The paper, which was entitled "Data-driven fantasies and maps of human terrain", directly addressed the question of the plausibility of the US Military's instrumental use of social science research to inform Counter Insurgency (COIN). In my critique of the US's perception of Afghanistan I highlighted the way in which the broader "interpretive lens" associated with implementing development and security missed a great deal.

As I argued, it failed to apprehend the complete and complex story of Nangarhar with regards to the horizontal politics of power and patronage between tribes and their governing elites. Moreover, the US's efforts to hasten the logics of capitalisation and modernisation directly fueled violently competitive and exclusionary processes among different communities residing in the province. This has been demonstrated in the rise in number and severity of conflicts between different communities over land and land tenure.

This presentation was well-received by the attending audience who were largely comprised of US military officers and intelligence professionals. Many of those attending, who had direct experiences with post-9/11 conflicts in Iraq and Afghanistan, recognised the disjuncture I was highlighting. On this matter, they suggested that institutional problems, such as the cultural memory loss brought by frequent rotations of military units as well as institutional inertia in responding to local intelligence reporting, were the main reason for poor outcomes. However, they were entirely receptive to the idea that policy-makers' were unable to see the world of Afghanistan as it actually existed.

Indeed, one audience member elucidated on this point by relaying a story that was presented in Bob Woodward's (2011: 347–351) "behind the scenes" book entitled *Obama's Wars*. The anecdote related to President Obama receiving a briefing from his national security principals in early 2009 on the expansion of the US counter insurgency campaign into Kandahar Province. President Obama was provided with a map of Kandahar by General Stanley McChrystal which laid out in detail the social and political complexity of the region by delineating 20 tribes their overlapping linkages and mug shots of major power brokers. As Bob Woodward (2011: 350) recorded:

> The president reflected on the Kandahar map and the power broker chart.
> "This reminds me of Chicago politics," Obama said. "You're asking me to understand the interrelationships and interconnections between ward bosses and district chiefs and the tribes of Chicago like the tribes of

> Kandahar. And I've got to tell you, I've lived in Chicago for a long time, and I don't understand that."
>
> ...
>
> Afterward, the president indicated to several close aides that the briefing had a clarifying effect on him. "What makes us think," he asked, "that given that description of the problem, that we're going to design a solution to this?"

This excerpt is interesting because there is a tendency among some critical scholars to treat the US liberal empire as a hegemonic and unchanging order whose key policy-makers unreflectively support its reproduction. This instance demonstrates that even high officeholders in US policy-making exhibit unease and uncertainty with the aims of intervention itself.

As Rajiv Chandrasekaran (2012: 223) observed in his analysis of the US Intervention in Afghanistan, entitled "Little America", the idea of making a peace deal with the Taliban appealed to Obama. However, at the same time Chandrasekaran (2012: 223) pointedly highlighted the institutional pressures such a change in policy faced where predominant emphasis was placed on COIN and war fighting.

> Less than two months after he took office, the president said he was open to seeking reconciliation with the Taliban, comparing such an effort to a U.S. initiative to work with former Sunni militants in Iraq who were willing to break with al-Qaeda. His comments alarmed top military and intelligence officials. Admiral Mike Mullen and General David Petraeus thought it was too soon even to talk about talking. They wanted to implement a COIN strategy first and then talk, but only to Taliban leaders who wanted to surrender; they were reluctant to make any meaningful concessions to the enemy.

This anecdote captures the tensions inherent within US policy-making in Afghanistan. On the one hand, there are certainly policy-makers who appreciate the complexity of Afghanistan's conflict and the need for inclusive forms of power-sharing. At the same time, there are strong institutionalised preferences towards seeing the US Intervention in Afghanistan in a hierarchical and polarised view of a conflict between "us" and "them". This mentality obviously is a problem for US policy-makers across the world in the multitude of conflicts they are engaged in under the broad auspices of a global war on terror.

While I am under no illusions as to the likelihood of drastic changes in US policy-making, I feel it is always worth highlighting spaces for change. US and other Western policy-makers could become more circumspect and reflective of their own ideas of affecting change in the context of Afghanistan. In so doing, they would have a far better understanding of this conflict and the alternative approach needed to resolve it. Failing this, policy-makers are likely to continue to misread Afghanistan and entrench the existing dynamics of conflict.

A good starting point, should policy-makers decide to approach Afghanistan as a complex case of conflict resolution – rather than a counter insurgency war – would be a report recently conducted by the Centre for International Cooperation. In this report, authored by Borhan Osman and Anand Gopal, they note a broad pragmatism among the Afghan Taliban towards resolving war in Afghanistan. Quite tellingly, they note that the Taliban's grievances have less to do with the Western-designed national state apparatus and more to do with the ongoing US occupation of the country. Moreover, contrary to popularly held beliefs, they noted that the Taliban were not anachronistic and misogynistic men intent on denying women their rights. For instance, Taliban leaders suggested that they had no problem with girls' education in principle just that it should occur in ways that ensure purdah is upheld. In this way, the authors argued that the Taliban's views on women were no more advanced or regressive than many of Afghanistan's other political factions.

Obviously, the Afghan Taliban represent just one of a multitude of militant factions currently engaged in violent conflict with the government of Afghanistan and the US. Nevertheless, if there are spaces for change in transforming this particularly hostile and long-running feud then there are also likely to be possibilities in engaging positively to de-escalate other violent conflicts. This is always a challenging task and the way in which such engagements and conversations would move forward could not be foreknown. They would need to emerge organically in a situation in which protagonists in a conflict find a shared language with which to debate what progress should look like and how it should be attained.

The transformation of armed violence in Afghanistan would be a starting point for advancing human security but it would not be sufficient in and of itself. For instance, even in the absence of public violence, that is a negative peace, women's and men's lives are still jeopardised by the presence of a masculinised and militarised environment. What good would it be if power-sharing between Afghanistan's conservative masculine armed factions resulted in the reproduction of gendered hierarchies of power which oppressed women and men? Instead, meaningful forms of security in Afghanistan can only be assured if gendered hierarchies of power can be transformed in such a way as to ensure the well-being and happiness of those who are most vulnerable. This process of transformation encapsulates what is meant by a positive form of peace.

As I have shown in three provincial contexts in Afghanistan, women, and men, are already engaged in a variety of actions which challenge dominant masculine hierarchies built on male honour. For instance, in Nangarhar, what was apparent was the extent to which previously fundamental tenets of the patriarchal honour code of Pashtunwali were being cast aside by many Pashtun communities because of the harm they caused innocent women. This was evidenced in the case of communities avoiding the usage of *baad*, or the payment of a virgin girl as a blood-price to the family of a man killed accidentally or purposefully. Moreover, to varying degrees throughout these provinces, women are gaining agency and recognition of their voice in both public and private spheres of life. Though such processes of struggle are often fraught they reveal progressive ways to transform gendered hierarchies in an ugly environment. This is evidenced in women's increasing access to traditional community-based dispute resolution like *jirgas and jalasas* forums as both disputants and, in some cases, adjudicators. Similarly, women's increasing role in households' productive labour has gained wider social recognition in a variety of different communities.

These struggles and broader moral debates can be engaged with but not in the exclusionary manner that has typified the West's effort to transform gender dynamics in Afghanistan. Engagement in these existing moral debates needs to happen in a sensitive fashion which is inclusive to both women and men and which unfolds with a logic and a language that they share. It is only once this shared language and logic is established that it is possible to articulate critique of the contemporary societal ideas and practices which do not harmonise with holistic moral principles.

For this reason, it is once again important to highlight the radio soap opera, which was co-founded by John Butt, "New Home, New Life", as an exemplar of how such issues can be engaged with. As I mentioned in Chapter 2, this drama used stories of love, comedy and human suffering told in a generalisable and contemporaneous rural setting. In its storylines, the drama provided useful information to men and women on a variety of issues relating to their basic health and safety. Thus, there were stories about land-mine identification, women's health issues associated with childrearing, and developmental issues like environmental management. However, what was even more important were the moral stories about society. In these stories, critiques were obliquely made of existing societal injustices, especially those that targeted women like the Taliban's ban on women from working. In an interview I conducted in 2011, John recalled that the impact of the show was such that it even changed the perceptions of the Taliban ruling class towards these issues. I was highly interested in this matter and pushed John to elaborate:

BEN WALTER: Here, the Taliban members you were talking to. They had learned from listening to your show? Is this essentially how it happened? They changed their minds?

JOHN BUTT: They changed their minds I know it. One Talib was saying to me, one senior Talib, was saying that you know there was a ... two people talked to me. Senior level Taliban. And one of them told me that actually top people in the Taliban are listening to your New Home, New Life.

He was in the municipal corporation in Kandahar. He was the deputy head of the Kandahar City Council during the Taliban time. He said to me that your soap opera is *tarbiyah munza* which means "home education". It's a Qur'anic term. He used a Qur'anic term with reference to our soap opera. He said it's home education.

Another told me that there were actually two groups among the Taliban in the ruling council of the Taliban which is about 18 people. He said that one group had said, "This should be stopped because it's education and that's our job we're the government of Afghanistan so the BBC shouldn't be doing this."

And then the other people said, "Yes, very well but what they're doing is good isn't it? And we don't have the resources to do it do we? Or the know how? So let them do it."

And that is the view which prevailed and this was someone sitting at this conversation who told me.

It was not just the ruling classes of the Taliban who listened to "New Home, New Life", it was also widely popular among women and men more broadly across Afghanistan, reaching some 80 per cent of Afghanistan's population via families' radios. Indeed, all the women and men of the focus group discussions I conducted had positive memories of the show. This was particularly evident in the responses of the Pashtun women who observed the drama's impact on men's negative attitudes towards women. Their discussion of the breadth of this drama's impact on their own families and wider communities is worth repeating in full here:

HOST: What do you think about this drama "New Home, New Life"?
KASHMALA: Yeah, it was a really good programme and its dramas were just like it's made for the people of our village. The sounds they used, the songs, the space they made and the sounds of the different animals like cow, sheep, cock and etc were just like it was (the drama) happening in our own village. It seemed really good when we were listening to this drama.
PASHMINA: Yeah, you're right. And the language and their pronouns was just like our own pronouns and the way they were calling for example their daughter in the drama was just like it was happening live in our village. Oh my god when we were listening to them, the feeling we had was really nice. (Laughing)
KASHMALA: And it had a really good effect on our people. I mean most of the cruellest people became better day after day when they were listening to every episode of this drama. Because the situations and conditions they made was just like it was happening in our own family and our own area. So, I think it was the biggest reason why people liked this drama that much and why the cruellest people become better after they listened to it. They thought it's like their own life and they were agreeing with everything they said on that drama.
FARISHTA: In rural areas most of the young girls were listening to this drama because they really wanted to study and get educated but when their families did not let them then they were listening to this radio without their families knowing it and then they could learn some really good things from this radio and its programmes.
KASHMALA: Some men who were really bad guys, became really good. My uncle was always listening to this drama; and after he was listened it then he was going to the city to bring some chargul (an ornament worn on the nose

by women) for his wife and daughters. It was all because of this drama. Because it had a really good effect on such men, and when they listened to it they could realise what they are doing wrong with their family, wives and daughters and then they wanted to be good to their family.

Concluding thoughts

There are a variety of gendered forms of violence which jeopardise women's, and men's, lives in contemporary Afghanistan physically and emotionally. Nevertheless, there are very strong and persuasive moral arguments that can be made about why such gendered violence, and the hierarchical gender dynamics sustaining it, is wrong. This argument can be made with reference to Islam's universalist message of egalitarianism and peace but it can also be made with respect to customary beliefs and practices among different communities.

When turning to future research that would logically flow on from this book, what should be apparent is that my proposed revision of human security aims to restore the emancipatory potential entailed in the concept of Human Security. The implications of this proposition are that it is possible to comprehend both the insecurity caused to human beings around the world by the clash of global and local forces as well as human beings' own ways of surviving, and challenging, the hierarchies of power produced in this intersection. Moreover, I believe, in the same vein as Hutchings and Honneth, that a phenomenological and genealogical approach to normative reconstruction allows researchers to begin to put their finger on the potential mechanisms of societal change which may advance qualitive forms of human security. These twin tasks enjoin researchers to understand how it is possible to frame an argument against the injustices caused by existing societal beliefs in a way that is rational for those on the other side of a moral debate.

Contrary to the many critical naysayers, who believe Human Security is a fundamentally flawed conceptual paradigm that is beyond revival, what I have demonstrated is that the emancipatory potential is within reach of future practitioners. If scholars undertake human security research that is informed by these principles, then they are likely to discover a very rich world of emancipatory struggles towards human security across a wide swathe of "fragile" post-colonial and "developing" states. Furthermore, it should be noted that, although the voices of vulnerable and subaltern groups are eulogised in critical theory, there is often a lack of engagement with the subjects themselves. This phenomenological methodological innovation offers a clear path for these critical theorists to move beyond an overly detached normative and meta-theoretical critique of the ways in which a hegemonic Western mono-culture dominates post-colonial subjectivities towards actual engagement with the subaltern subjects whose struggles against this hegemony they espouse.

Though it could be argued that the overriding emphasis that I have placed on particularity and difference in the grassroots context of Afghanistan would preclude the transferability of my proposed phenomenological methodology to other contexts, what must be remembered is that, while subjects and the social contexts in which they are embedded will always exhibit difference, what will always be present are everyday acts of struggle and resistance by people to improve the world around them. This insight is highly useful to the shared larger contemporary project of various strands of critical theory in coming to terms with the way in which a hegemonic Western mono-culture of neo-liberalism and modernisation affects the insecurity of humans and the ways in which these subjects resist these dominating tendencies. Furthermore, the struggles of these subjects to gain security and emancipation against this hegemonic project are likely to reveal insight into a host of creative and progressive movements in different social contexts that illustrate the dynamism in supposedly "timeless" and "traditional" cultures. As I have suggested, in the case of Afghanistan, far from being oppressive and monolithic structures, traditional forms of knowledge, based around Islam and custom, are in a constant state of flux with many women and men creatively using tenets from these bodies of knowledge to argue for and act towards more progressive futures.

References

Chandrasekaran, Rajiv (2012). *Little America: The war within the war for Afghanistan*, New York, Random House LLC.
McHugh, John D., Teresa Smith, Alex Rees, Michael Tait and Lindsay Poulton (2008). *Afghanistan: Lost in translation*. London, *Guardian*, 12 June 2008.
Walter, Ben (2016). "The Securitisation of Development and Humans' Insecurity in Nangarhar Province, Afghanistan". *Global Change, Peace & Security* 28 (3): 271–287.
Walter, Ben (2017). "Interpreting the 'Human Terrain' of Afghanistan with Enlightenment Philosophy: The Instrumentalisation of Social Science in US Counter-insurgency Planning" *International Studies Perspectives* 18 (1): 1–16.
Woodward, Bob (2011). *Obama's wars*. New York, Simon and Schuster.

Glossary

Arbab   Persian word which means "master" or "landlord". In Afghanistan, this word usually designated a villager leader and interlocutor with the State.

'Aql   This Arabic word from the Qur'an, which literally translates to "reason", relates to an individual's ability to balance their passions (*Nafs*) and display reason (*'Aql*).

Baad   The practice of compensating a murder (or even an accidental killing) by the family of the killer by giving either one or two never-married girls in marriage to the victim's family.

Bacha Posh   Persian saying which literally means "dressed up as a boy" and refers to a practice in which families would raise their daughters as sons by dressing them as such.

Badal   Marriage conducted by exchanging two girls for each other.

Burqa   From the Arabic *Burqu* this word refers to a long loose body covering garment with veiled holes for the eyes.

Chaharbaiti   Persian word which describes a form of oral poetry that is performed using four verses of matching rhyme and rhythm.

Dobaiti   Persian word which describes a form of oral poetry that is performed using couplets of two rhyming verses.

Farsiwan   Pashtun word for a Persian speaker in Afghanistan.

Ghayrat   Concept of chivalry within the broader Pashtun honour code of Pashtunwali.

Haram   Arabic word which means "forbidden" and refers to any actions taken by a Muslim which would contravene the Qur'ran.

Hawala   Arabic word which literally means "to change or transform" and refers to an Islamic system of money lenders who facilitate the transferral of wealth via their remote associates.

Islah   Islamic Principle that relates to the promotion of peace and maintaining community social cohesion through negotiation and reconciliation.

Izzat   Pashtun woman or man's personal honour.

Jalasa   Persian word which refers to the meeting set up for the mediation of disputes.

Jirga   Pashtun word which refers to the meeting set up for the mediation of disputes.

Jerib Agricultural unit of measurement which is equivalent to one fifth of a hectare.
Jirgamar/Jirgamaran Pashtun words which refer to the men who attend and help to resolve problems in a Jirga.
Joma'a Pashtun word which literally means "the gathering", i.e. society.
Khairat Arabic Islamic term which refers to voluntary alms which can be donated by wealthier families to the poor.
Khan Large landowner and traditional source of authority.
Landay Distinctive form of Pashtun poetry accompanied by music which is performed by Pashtun women among themselves.
Loya Jirga This form of Jirga refers to a grand assembly of tribal chieftains and elders.
Machalga Deposit given or agreed to at the beginning of a *jirga* to guarantee the disputants will accept the final decision.
Maldar Persian word for a nomadic herd-owner.
Malik/Malikan Hebrew/Arabic term which came to be adopted in Afghanistan referring to the representative of a *qawm* or a village leader.
Matluna Pashtun word which refers to "proverbs" or "sayings" of a society.
Mir Persian word for a leader, commander or tribal chief.
Mirab Persian word which means "water master".
Naf/Nafsh Arabic words for desire.
Namus Pashtun word which refers to the way in which a household's honour is bound up in women's chaste and virtuous behaviour.
Nang A Pashtun word relating to honourable and chivalrous conduct which denotes both honourable actions in everyday life and in battle as well as actions taken to restore any slights to one's honour such as revenge (*badal*).
Pashtunwali Pashtun phrase which literally translates as "way of the Pashtuns", i.e. the Pashtun code of honourable conduct.
Pir Sufi religious leader.
Purdah Persian word which literally translates to "curtain" or "barrier" in relationship to the sexual segregation of women from men.
Qawm Word of Arabic origin which refers to a community of people who share a solidarity which could be variously based on family, tribe, descent group, geographical location, etc.
Reesh-safdean/sar-safedan Hazaragi/Dari terms which literally translate as "white-Beards" (senior men) and "white hairs" (senior women).
Sayyed People who trace their lineage back to the prophet Mohammed through his daughter's descent; communities of Sayyed exist among all of Afghanistan's different ethnic groups.
Spin-geree/Spin-saree Pashtun terms which literally translate as "white-beards" (senior men) and "white-hairs" (senior women).
Shura Arabic word which means "consultation" and refers to a council or group of people who meet to discuss issues and conflicts.
Tayefa Hazaragi word for kinship group.

Ulema Arabic term which literally translates as "the learned ones". It refers to the Muslim scholars or authorities in the broader hierarchy of Islamic religious studies.

Ummah Arabic word that denotes the collective community of Islamic peoples.

Wakil Official Community Representative of a District.

Woleswil District Governor.

Woleswil Jirga Afghanistan Legislative Assembly.

Zakat Arab Islamic term which refers to the obligatory alms Muslims must donate to the poor and clergy annually, based on a percentage of their income.

Index

Abirafeh, Lina 3, 9, 72, 83–4, 86, 87, 142
Achin District 101–2
Adorno, Theodor 26
Afghan Development Compact 81, 82
Afghan National Development Strategy (ANDS) 82, 93, 138, 150
Afghanistan: as co-production 72–5; creation of "state" 57; images of 133; map x
Afghanistan Independent Human Rights Commission (AIHRC) 103
Afghanistan Research Evaluation Unit (AREU) 16, 52, 106, 121, 126, 143, 150
African feminisms 34
agriculture: Bamyan Province 113; capitalisation 41; Nangarhar Province 93–4, 100–2
aid industry 42, 137; *see also* international aid
Andersen, Erna 121, 128
Anderson, Jon W. 41, 53–4
Anglo-Afghan War 91
aql 53–4
Aradau, Claudia 27
Aryans 74
autonyms 50–2
Azarbaijani-Moghaddam, Sippi 41, 103–4

baad 11, 106–7, 156, 165
bacha posh 87
Bachi-Yi-Saqoa 74
Bakhtin, Mikhail 85, 134
Bamyan Province: agriculture 113; aid inequity 123–4; Bamyan district 120–2; Buddhism 111; coal mining 123–4; dispute resolution 129; gender relations 117–19; identity 112; international aid 112, 113–15; invasion 111; Kahmard 122–5; kinship breakdown 126; land ownership 113; marriage 115–17, 127; micro-credit 120–1; migration 117, 127–8; National Solidarity Programme (NSP) 121–2; poverty 112, 113, 123–5; Shia marriage law 125; *see also* Hazaras
begging 147
Billaud, Jill 72, 83–4, 85–6, 87, 134–5, 153
Bin Laden, Osama 91
Bonn Process 80–1
Booth, Ken 26, 27, 32
bride price 57–8, 62–3, 97, 100, 102, 106–7, 124, 129, 148
bubble economy: Bamyan district 114, 120; Kabul Province 134–6, 139, 147; Nangarhar Province 92, 95, 101
burqa, in Western imaginary 2
Butt, John, Mohammed 7, 40, 166–7
Buzan, Barry 21–4

Campbell, David 29
Canfield, Robert 66, 115–16
care ethics 35–7
carnivalesque 85–6, 134–5, 153
Chandler, David 32
Chandrasekaran, Rajiv 163–4
Charahi Qambar 146, 147, 148, 154
child labour 124–5, 147–8, 150–1
child prostitution 87, 98, 141
child-rearing 126–7
childbirth 148–9; sex of child 57, 59, 63–4
children: beating 126–7, 143; opportunities for 154–5; pregnancy and childbirth 148–9
coal mining 123–4
Cold War 21
commodification, of women 41, 54–5, 83, 100–1, 102, 124
community bakeries, Kahmard 123, 143

community decision-making 53, 107, 122, 127; *see also* decision-making, role of women
Community Development Councils (CDCs) 13, 104, 121–2, 123
community governance 156; *see also shura*; *jirgas*
community solidarity 149–50; *see also* solidarity groupings
community-based dispute resolution processes (CBDR) 11, 108, 126, 129–30, 154–6, 166
constitution, rhetoric and reality of 135–6
constitutional democracy, rhetoric and reality of 83–4
Convention on the Elimination of all forms of Violence Against Women (CEDAW) 83
Cooke, Miriam 30
Copenhagen School 21–4
cosmopolitanism 33
counter-insurgency (COIN) 93–4, 108, 163, 164–5
counter-narcotics (CN) 13, 42, 82, 93
coup 1978, effects of 76
Cox, Robert 26
credit, access to 95, 108, 121
credit relations 128, 151–2; *see also* micro-credit
critical feminist perspective 2, 4, 35
Critical Security Studies (CSS) 26–7
critical theories 25–30
cross-dressing 87; *see also bacha posh*
Cullather, Nigel 74–5
cultural awareness 161–4
cultural imperialism 2–3, 74, 144–5

Daulatzai, Anila 143–5
Davis, Diana 59
debt 92, 101–2, 121, 128
decision-making, role of women 55, 107, 122, 127, 129, 154
Deh Mazang Square bombing 135
democratic process, women's participation 84
democratisation 136, 153
development 75–6; Bamyan Province 113–5; corporate outsourcing 81; development aid 42, 93; Kabul Province 136–40; neo-liberal approach 42, 82, 85, 93–4; Nangarhar Province 92–6; *see also* international aid; international spending
displaced persons' camps 146

divorce 62, 65–6, 97–8, 107, 116, 129, 155
Dupree, Nancy Hatch 7, 111–12

economy, licit and illicit 81; *see also* bubble economy
egalitarianism: Bamyan Province 128–9; Kabul Province 154; loss of 41; nomadic communities 58–9
Ehsan, Mansoor 7
Emadi, Hafizullah 52, 75
emancipation 27, 153
empowerment, gender programming for 87; Eurocentrism 10
Enlightenment philosophy 3–4, 32
ethical interventions, cultural contexts of 10
ethical theory, dimensions of 38–9; *see also* phenomenology
ethics: articulation of 4; Copenhagen School 24; critical security studies 26–7; ethic of care 35–7
ethnic conflict 73–4, 77–8
ethno-linguistic groupings 49, 50–2
Eurocentrism 3, 10, 32
exchange marriage 107
exonyms 51–2

Feminist Security Studies 27–8, 29–30
feminist theory: gendering HS 33–7; revisioning HS 20
focus group discussions 14–15; child beating 126–7; ethnic conflict 73; gender-based violence 78–9, 97–9, 142–3; gender relations 58, 63–6, 117–19; gender roles 105–6; growing up 57–8; Hazaras 65, 116–19, 126–7, 129; marriage 116–17, 129; on naming 50; "New Home, New Life" 167–8; Pashtuns 57–8, 59–60, 145, 167–8; relevant to Nangarhar Province 96–9; rural vs. city life 63; strategic use of Islam 155; Tajiks 61–2, 73, 77–9, 142–3, 153, 155–6; use of term "Tajik" 61; violence 77–9; Western aims 145; women's resistance 59–61, 66
forced resettlement 73
Frankfurt School 26
freedom from fear (FFF) 33
freedom from want (FFW) 33
Fukuyama, Francis 75

Gang, Rebecca 150, 154, 155, 156
gender, as socially constructed 8, 27–8; *see also* gendering

Index 175

gender and development (GAD) 84–5
gender dynamics: effect of US and NATO intervention 82–7; Hazaras 65–7; Islam 53–4; Pashtuns 56–61; recognition struggles 102–8; Tajiks 62–4; traditional social context 53–6
gender programming 3, 9–10, 83, 87, 134–5
gender relations: Bamyan Province 117–19, 127–9; contestation 87; disjuncture 106; Kabul Province 153–4; Nangarhar Province 100–4, 106–7; "New Home, New Life" 39–40, 166–7; variations in 10–11
gender roles, performance of 40–1
gender-based violence 41, 42, 78–9, 82–3, 97–9, 142–3
gendered hierarchies of power 10–15, 42, 107–8, 127–8, 165–6
gendering 8, 27–8
genealogical process 38–9, 72
Giustozzi, Antonio 74
Gopal, Anand 165
Grace, Jo 122
Gramsci, Antonio 26
Green Zone 137–9
Gregorian, Vartan 57, 133

Haldar, Ankita 7, 116
Hall, Samuel 101
Hansen, Lene 22, 23–4
harassment, of women 84
Hawala system 128
Hazaras 64–7; community solidarity 149–50; divorce 65–6; external influences 117; gender dynamics 117–19; middle class 120, 150; migration 117; slavery 64; societal change 118–19; *see also* Bamyan Province
Hegel, G.W.F. 38
Helvetas 123
Herold, Marc 136, 139
Hirschkind, Charles 2
Hobbes, Thomas 20, 32
homes, destruction of 139–40
Honneth, Axel 20, 38–9, 42, 71, 72
honour 40–2, 53, 54–5, 57–8, 60, 86, 96, 118, 147; *see also Pashtunwali*
honour killings 24, 36, 98
Hoogensen, Gunhild 34
Horkheimer, Max 26
Hudson, Heidi 34
human security (HS): Bamyan Province 115–25, 127–9; critiques 31–2;

emergence of 30–3; engaging with 19–20; feminist critique 8; gender issues within approach 3–4; gendering 8–11, 33–7; institutionalisation 30, 32; Kabul Province 141–51; Nangarhar Province 96–102; normative dimension of 37–43; ontological framing 32; overview 3–4; produced by relationships 35, 39, 96, 115, 141; re-visioning 34; *see also* security debate
human subjects, construction of 32–3
Hunte, Pamela 151
Hussein, Said Reza 7, 65
Hutchings, Kimberly 9, 20, 36–9, 48, 71, 72
hyper-masculine violence 77–9, 98
hyper-masculinity, effects of 41–2

identities, collective 23, 24
identity: ambiguity of 52; Bamyan Province 112; ethnicity and gender 78–9; flexibility 49; and land ownership 53; and language 78–9; politics of 50–3; primary vs primordial 49; reformulation 105–6; security of 33
ideologies, gendered 86, 141–4
illicit economy 81
images: of Afghanistan 72, 133; of agricultural modernisation 93–4; of women 2–3
institutional misogyny 84
international aid: Bamyan Province 112, 113–15, 120, 123–4; and gender ideology 141–5; political aspects 141; *see also* development aid; international spending
International Labour Organisation (ILO) report 101
International Relations (IR): accounts of security 5, 19; feminist responses to 8, 27–8
International Security Assistance Force (ISAF) 81–2, 93
international spending 80, 82; aid targeting 87; gender-focus 84; *see also* development aid; international aid
Islah 156; *see also* peace-building
Islam: alms giving 128; contestation 156; and contestation of gender 11; gender dynamics 53–4; non-compliance 62; politicisation of 41, 76; Shia Islam 54, 61, 64; Sunni Islam 54, 62, strategic use of 155–6

Jackson, Ashley 95

Jalalabad 91, 92, 94, 100
Jalasas 11, 155, 166
Jan, Rafik 86
jirgas 11, 83, 84, 107, 166
Jolyon, Leslie 138, 147
joma'a 54
Jones, Richard Wyn 26–7
Joya, Malali 84
justice systems: Afghanistan 83–4; Nangarhar Province 103

Kabul City 139–40, 146–51; District 5 146–9; District 13 149–51
Kabul Province: as carnivalesque 134–5; credit relations 151–2; democratisation 136; dynamics of change 154; earnings potentials 139; gender egalitarianism 154; Green Zone 137–9; inflation 139; informal settlements 152; infrastructure 136–7, 138–9, 150; land grabbing 136; migration 136–7, 151–2; Persian influence 133; population 134; poverty 134, 141–3, 146–51; terrorism 135; urban development 138; urbanisation 134; water 140, 150; Kahmard 122–5
Kahn, Abdur Rahman 57, 64, 72, 73, 74
Karimi, Ali 114
Keller, Evelyn Fox 28
Keohane, Robert 25
khairat 128
Khan, Emir Habibullah 73
Khan, Genghis 111
Khan, Amanullah 64, 73–4
Khans, transformation of 41; *see also* agriculture, capitalisation
Khatam-al Nabyeen Islamic University 155–6
kinship breakdown 126, 144
kinship groups, relations between 59
Kipling, Rudyard 74
Kothari, Miloon 140
Krause, Keith 26–7

labour: attitudes to women's role 85; sexual division of 55, 57, 117; slavery and economic exploitation 64, 75, 101, 112
land disputes: Bamyan Province 119; Kabul Province 139–40, 150, 152; Nangarhar Province 95–6
land grabbing: Kabul Province 136, 139–40; Nangarhar Province: 95
land ownership: Bamyan Province 113, 115; and identity 53

Landays 60, 67
language: and identity 61, 78–9; loss of 133; of moral debate 9, 20, 39; usage by "New Home, New Life" 167
Lety, David 122
licit economy 81
Lindisfarne (Tapper), Nancy 6–7, 40, 50–1, 53, 54, 55, 57, 60, 73, 96
livestock 128
Locke, John 32
Loya Jirga 83, 84

McKay, Susan 31
Mahmood, Saba 2
Manalan, Shelley 129
Mansfield, David 102
Marchand, Marianne 84–5
Marhia, Natasha 8, 32
marriage: abuse within 97–8, 105–6, 107, 125, 143; *baad* 11; Bamyan Province 115–17, 127, 129; brideprice 57–8, 62–3, 106–7; changing views on 106–7, 165; and commodification 41; financial pressure 151; lack of choice 55, 58, 97–8; rights 58; selling girls into 102; Shia marriage law 125; Tajiks 62, 63
masculinised ontologies 35–6
masculinity: belief systems 54–5; honour codes 40–2, 54–5, 57–8; and labour 117, 142; and male authority 104; Nangarhar Province 96; political man 28; valorisation of 8
matluna 60
Maykuth, Andrew 139
Metcalfe, Victoria 139, 149, 150, 152
methodology: approach taken 9; choice of 7; fieldwork 14–15; *see also* phenomenological process; phenomenology
micro-credit 13, 120, 121, 128
migration 100, 117, 127–8, 136–7, 151–2; *see also* Hazaras
modernisation 73–4; development 75–6; external support 75; resistance to 75; rural areas 81; Surkh-rud 100; Tajiks 63; theory 3, 75, 80; and women 84–5; *see also* security development nexus
Mohammed, Haji Din 94
Mohanty, Chandra 6
Monsutti, Alessandro 52, 117, 127
moral debate 9, 20, 27, 37–9, 166, 168
moral grammars 37–8, 72
moral judgements, authenticity 48

morality, self-other relations 35–6
Morgenthau, Hans 28
Mujahadeen 41, 76–8, 92–3

Nadir Shah 74
nafsh 54
naming 50–2
Nangarhar Province: Achin 101–2; bubble economy 92; development aid 92, 93; elites 95; gender relations 96–9, 101–3; governing institutions 93; infrastructure development 94; justice system 103; land disputes 95–6; modernisation 91–2; NATO 93; opium poppy 94, 100, 101–2, 108; patronage 94–5; resistance campaigns 91; Surkh-rud 100–1; US involvement 92–3; USSR 92
National Risk and Vulnerability Assessment (NRVA) 113
National Solidarity Programme (NSP) 104, 121–2, 123
National Urban Programme (NUP) 138
NATO: Nangarhar Province 93; role of 80–7
neo-liberalism: approach to development 81–2, 93–4; influence of 42, 85; international order 27, 29, 35;
neo-realism 21
"New Home, New Life" 39–40, 166–8
nomadic communities: effects of settlement 59–60; egalitarianism 58–9
non-governmental organisations (NGOs): expectations 104; Kahmard 123; role of 82
Nordland, Rob 148
normative reconstruction 38–9
norms, Copenhagen School 24

Obama, Barack 163–4
Oleson, Asta 61, 86
Operation Enduring Freedom (OEF) 93
opium ban, Nangarhar Province 95, 102, 108
opium poppy cultivation, Nangarhar Province 94; Achin 101–2; Surkh-rud 100
Orientalism 3, 29–30
Osman, Borhan 165
Ottawa Treaty 30
Owen, Taylor 31

Pain, Adam 102
Paris, Roland 31
Pashtunisation, effects of 74

Pashtuns: description 56–7; Durranis 50–1, 57, gender dynamics 56–61; Ghilzai 50–1, 57, 100; Shinwari 94, 101, 106, 108
Pashtunwali 54–5
patronage, Nangarhar Province 94–5
peace: negative 165; positive 165; need for 147, 153
peace-building 156; *also see Islah*
phenomenological process 9, 11, 12, 38–9, 71–2, 168
phenomenology 9, 14, 38, 48
poetry, as resistance 60, 66–7, 86; *see also Landays*
policy-making: engagement with local actors/communities 5, 105, 161; human security 20, 30–1; recommendations for 164–5
political man 28
politics of identity 50–3
post-colonial theory 4, 29–30
poverty: Bamyan Province 112, 113, 123–5; and inequity 119; Kabul Province 134, 141–3, 146–51; Nangarhar Province 101; and vulnerability to external events 119–20
power: exercising 10; and truth 29; structures of 10–11
power dynamics: Bamyan Province 113–15; Kabul Province 135–40; Nangarhar Province 92–6
pregnancy 148–9
prostitution 98–9, 102, 141; *see also* sex work
Provincial Reconstruction Teams (PRTs) 81–2
Pul-e-Charki prison 135

qawm 49, 52, 55–6; Bamyan Province 115–16; erosion of affiliations 152; Kabul Province 152, 154; Nangarhar Province 106–7

RtoP 30
racial theories 74
radio drama, "New Home, New Life" 39–40, 166–8
rape 42, 77, 83–4, 98–9, 103, 136
recognition: societal relations of 38–9, 41; struggles for 39
recognition struggles: Bamyan Province 125–9; gender hierarchies 105–8, 153–6; Kabul Province 151–6; Nangarhar Province 102–8

Index

remittances 117, 128, 151; *see also* Hawala system
research participants 14, 58; *see also* focus group discussions
resistance: Nangarhar Province 91; ongoing 107–8; poetry and song 60, 66–7, 86
Robinson, Fiona 35–7
Rubin, Barnett 72, 73, 74, 76

Said, Edward 3, 29
Sayyeds 53, 64
Schütte, Stefan 139, 143, 146, 147, 152
securitisation 22–3
security debate: advancing ethical ideas 19–20; conventional accounts 20–4; Copenhagen School 21–4; critical accounts 25–30; Critical Security Studies (CSS) 26–7; critical theories 25–30; critiques of HS 31–2; dimensions of ethical theory 38–9; emergence of HS 30–3; engaging with HS 19–20; Feminist Security Studies 27–8, 29–30; gendering HS through feminist theory 33–7; normative reconstruction 38–9; Post-Colonial theories 29–30; Post-Structural Security Studies 29; security-development nexus 93–4
sex work 98–9, 102, 141; *see also* prostitution
sexual abuse: Nangarhar Province 103–4; *see also* rape
Shalinsky, Audrey C. 61
shame 64, 118, 129, 141; *see also* honour
Sharia law 79, 136, 155
Sherzai, Gul Agha 94–5
Shilliam, Robbie 32
shura 104, 156
Shura-i-mahal 156
Smith, Deborah 106–7, 126, 127, 129
Smith, Steve 26
social change 40–3; conservative backlash 86; consolidation 72; context and overview 71–2; and gender dynamics 82–7; Hazaras 118–19; modernisation programme 73–4; rise of Taliban 79–80; role of elites 81; role of NATO 80–7; role of NGOs 82; role of US 80–7; rural areas 81; violent contestation 76–80
social context *see* traditional social context
solidarity groupings 52; *see also qawm*
Spivak, Gayatri 30

state-building 42; external intervention 80–7; militarisation 81–2; spending 81–2
state-formation 72–5
Stockman, Farah 137
Stuvøy, Kirsti 34
Surkh-rud 100–1

Tajiks 61–4; Bamyan Province 123–4; diversity 62–3; Kabul Province 142–3; modernisation 63; revolt 74; use of term 61
Taliban: Bamyan Province 113, 123–4; Kabul Province 133; pragmatism 165; rise of 79–80
Tapper, Richard 49, 50–1
terrorism, Kabul Province 135
Thomas, Caroline 33
Tickner, Ann 6, 28
traditional social context: breakdown of 77; change from 106–7; context and overview 48–50; gender dynamics 53–6; Hazaras 64–6; Pashtuns 56–61; politics of identity 50–3; Tajiks 61–4
Truong, Thanh-Dam 35

United Nations Development Project Report 1994 30
United Nations High Commission for Refugees 148
United Nations Office on Drugs and Crime 94
United Nations Security Council Resolution (UNSCR) 1325 83
United States: Agency for International Development (USAID) 88, 93; Kabul Province 133–4; priorities 83; role of 80–7; support for Mujahadeen 92–3; Surkh-rud 100
Universal Declaration of Human Rights 83

violence: as discipline 126; ethno-sectarian 77–8; towards children 126; and under/ unemployment 142; against women 41, 42

Wæver, Ole 21–4
Wahdat party 113, 114
Wakefield, Shawna 52–3, 122
Waldman, Matt 82
Waltz, Kenneth 20
Walwar 63
warlords 80–1, 83–4, 94, 134, 136, 137

water, Kabul 140, 150
Western Intervention: attitudes to women 42; cultural awareness 160–4; effects of 160–1; Kabul Province 135–6, 137, 147; research reconstruction 42; underlying beliefs 160–1; underlying perspective 165; views on 145
Wibben, Annick T.R. 32
widows 141, 143–5
Williams, Michael 26–7
winter 148
Wolesi Jirga 84
women: arrest for non-crimes 103; as battleground 141; commodification 41, 100–1, 102, 124; control of 54–5, 129; decision-making 107; in democratic process 84; dispute resolution 129, 166; effects of honour codes 147; experience of Taliban rule 79–80; imprisonment 136; mobility 41; necessity of work outside home 141–3; neo-liberal view of 85; preservation of tradition 67; as targets of aid 87
Wood, Geoff 146
Woodward, Bob 163–4
World Food Program (WFP) 143
Wright, Joanne 85

Zahak, Jawad 114
Zahir Shah 75
zakat 128

 Taylor & Francis eBooks

Helping you to choose the right eBooks for your Library

Add Routledge titles to your library's digital collection today. Taylor and Francis ebooks contains over 50,000 titles in the Humanities, Social Sciences, Behavioural Sciences, Built Environment and Law.

Choose from a range of subject packages or create your own!

Benefits for you
- Free MARC records
- COUNTER-compliant usage statistics
- Flexible purchase and pricing options
- All titles DRM-free.

Benefits for your user
- Off-site, anytime access via Athens or referring URL
- Print or copy pages or chapters
- Full content search
- Bookmark, highlight and annotate text
- Access to thousands of pages of quality research at the click of a button.

REQUEST YOUR FREE INSTITUTIONAL TRIAL TODAY

Free Trials Available
We offer free trials to qualifying academic, corporate and government customers.

eCollections – Choose from over 30 subject eCollections, including:

Archaeology	Language Learning
Architecture	Law
Asian Studies	Literature
Business & Management	Media & Communication
Classical Studies	Middle East Studies
Construction	Music
Creative & Media Arts	Philosophy
Criminology & Criminal Justice	Planning
Economics	Politics
Education	Psychology & Mental Health
Energy	Religion
Engineering	Security
English Language & Linguistics	Social Work
Environment & Sustainability	Sociology
Geography	Sport
Health Studies	Theatre & Performance
History	Tourism, Hospitality & Events

For more information, pricing enquiries or to order a free trial, please contact your local sales team:
www.tandfebooks.com/page/sales

 Routledge Taylor & Francis Group | The home of Routledge books

www.tandfebooks.com